ALSO BY JAMES D. TABOR

The Jesus Dynasty: The Hidden History of Jesus,
His Royal Family, and the Birth of Christianity

Why Waco? Cults and the Battle for Religious
Freedom in America (with Eugene V. Gallagher)

A Noble Death: Suicide and Martyrdom
Among Christians and Jews in Antiquity
(with Arthur J. Droge)

Things Unutterable: Paul's Ascent to Paradise
in Its Greco-Roman, Judaic, and Early Christian Contexts

ALSO BY SIMCHA JACOBOVICI

The Jesus Family Tomb: The Evidence Behind
the Discovery No One Wanted to Find
(with Charles Pellegrino)

THE JESUS DISCOVERY

The New Archaeological Find

That Reveals the Birth of Christianity

JAMES D. TABOR *and*
SIMCHA JACOBOVICI

Simon & Schuster

New York   London   Toronto   Sydney   New Delhi

Simon & Schuster
1230 Avenue of the Americas
New York, NY 10020

First Simon & Schuster hardcover edition April 2012

SIMON & SCHUSTER and colophon are registered trademarks of Simon & Schuster, Inc.

For information about special discounts for bulk purchases, please contact Simon & Schuster Special Sales at 1-866-506-1949 or business@simonandschuster.com.

The Simon & Schuster Speakers Bureau can bring authors to your live event. For more information or to book an event, contact the Simon & Schuster Speakers Bureau at 1-866-248-3049 or visit our website at www.simonspeakers.com.

Designed by Nancy Singer

Map by Paul Pugliese

Manufactured in the United States of America

10   9   8   7   6   5   4   3   2   1

Library of Congress Cataloging-in-Publication Data

Tabor, James D., date.
  The Jesus discovery : the new archaeological find that reveals the birth of Christianity /
James D. Tabor and Simcha Jacobovici—1st Simon & Schuster hardcover ed.
      p.   cm.
  includes bibliographical references (p.   ) and index
    1. Jesus Christ—Burial.   2. Jesus Christ—Family.   3. Tombs—Jerusalem.
4. Jerusalem—Antiquities.   5. Jesus Christ—Resurrection—History of doctrines—
Early Church, ca. 30–600.   I. Jacobovici, Simcha.   II. Title.
BT460.J248 2011
232.96'4—dc23   2011025449
ISBN 978-1-4516-5040-2
ISBN 978-1-4516-5052-5 (ebook)

Illustration Credits: Associated Producers, Ltd.: 1, 4, 5, 15, 17, 18, 19, 20, 21, 24, 25, 26, 27, 30, 34, 35, 41; Shimon Gibson: 2, 9, 11, 38; Oded Golan: 39; Israel Antiquities Authority: 6, 8, 14, 28, 29, 40, 42; James D. Tabor: 3, 7, 10, 16, 22, 23, 31, 32, 33, 36, 37, 43; Lori L. Woodall: 12, 13.

To the incomparable Morton Smith (1915–1991)

who pioneered the way . . .

CONTENTS

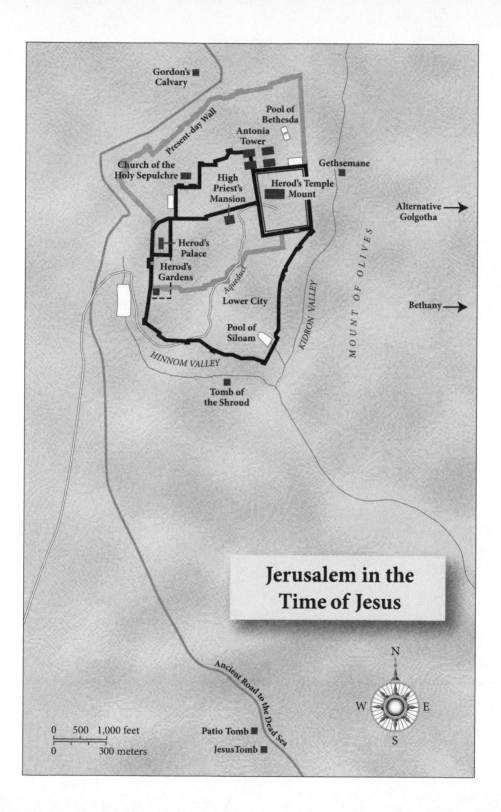

Gordon's
Calvary

Pool of
Bethesda

Antonia
Tower

Present-day Wall

Church of the
Holy Sepulchre

High
Priest's
Mansion

Herod's Temple
Mount

Gethsemane

Alternative
Golgotha →

Herod's
Palace

Herod's
Gardens

Aqueduct

Lower City

Pool of
Siloam

MOUNT OF OLIVES

KIDRON VALLEY

Bethany →

HINNOM VALLEY

Tomb of
the Shroud

Jerusalem in the
Time of Jesus

Ancient Road to the Dead Sea

N

W   E

S

0   500   1,000 feet

0   300 meters

Patio Tomb

Jesus Tomb

THE JESUS DISCOVERY

PREFACE

On the morning of Tuesday, June 29, 2010, outside the Old City of Jerusalem, we made an unprecedented archaeological discovery related to Jesus and early Christianity. This discovery adds significantly to our understanding of Jesus, his earliest followers, and the birth of Christianity. In this book we reveal reliable archaeological evidence that is directly connected to Jesus' first followers—those who knew him personally—and to Jesus himself. The discovery provides the earliest archaeological evidence of faith in Jesus' resurrection from the dead, the first witness to a saying of Jesus that predates even the writing of our New Testament gospels, and the earliest example of Christian art—all found in a sealed tomb dated to the 1st century CE.[1]

We refer to this tomb as the *Patio tomb*, since it is now located beneath an apartment patio, eight feet under the basement of a condominium complex. Such juxtapositions of modernity and antiquity are not unusual in Jerusalem, where construction must often be halted to rescue and excavate tombs from ancient times. The Patio tomb was first uncovered by construction work in 1981 in East Talpiot, a suburb of Jerusalem less than two miles south of the Old City.

Our discoveries also provide precious new evidence for evaluating the "Jesus son of Joseph" tomb, discovered a year earlier, which made international headlines in 2007.[2] We refer to this 1980 tomb as the *Garden tomb*, since it is now situated beneath a garden area in the same condominium complex. These two tombs, both dating to around the time of Jesus, are less than two hundred feet apart. Together with a third tomb nearby that was unfortunately destroyed by the construction blasts, these tombs formed a cluster and most likely belonged to the same clan or extended family. Any interpretation of one tomb has to be made in the light of the other. As a result we believe a compelling argument can be made that the Garden tomb is that of Jesus of Nazareth and his family. We argue in this book that both tombs are most likely located on the rural estate of Joseph of Arimathea, the wealthy member of the Sanhedrin who according to all four New Testament gospels took official charge of Jesus' burial.

Who was Joseph of Arimathea and how did he enter the historical picture? *The Jesus Discovery* explores the answers to this and a series of related questions. The recent discoveries in the Patio tomb put the controversy about the Jesus family tomb in new light. We now have new archaeological evidence, literally written in stone, that can guide us in properly understanding what Jesus' earliest followers meant by their faith in Jesus' resurrection from the dead—with his earthly remains, and those of his family, peacefully interred just yards away. This might sound like a contradiction, but only because certain theological traditions regarding the meaning of resurrection of the dead have clouded our understanding of what Jesus and his first followers truly believed. When we put together the texts of the gospels with this archaeological evidence, the results are strikingly consistent and stand up to rigorous standards of historical evidence.

Accessing the sealed Patio tomb was a tremendous challenge. The technological challenge alone was daunting. Our only access to this tomb was through a series of eight-inch drill holes in the basement floor of the condominium. We were not even positive these probes would open into the tomb. We literally had only inches to spare.

Investigating the tomb required getting agreements from the owners of the building over the tomb; the Israel Antiquities Authority,
which controls permission to carry out any archaeological work in
Israel; the Jerusalem police, whose task is to keep the peace and avoid
incitements to riot; and the Heredim, the ultra-Orthodox authorities whose mission is to protect all Jewish tombs, ancient or modern,
from any kind of disturbance. None of these parties had any particular motivation to assist us and for various reasons they disagreed
with one another about their own interests. Any one of them could
have stopped us at any point along the way, and there were many
anxious times when we thought the exploration would never happen. Ultimately we were able to persuade each group to support the
excavation. That we succeeded at all is more than a minor miracle. At
the same time we had no evidence that our exploration of this tomb,
if it were possible, would yield anything of importance. But we both
agreed it was a gamble worth taking.

At many points the entire operation seemed likely to collapse. We
pushed on, however, not because we knew what was inside the tomb,
but because we could not bear the thought of never knowing. Since
that time we have begun to put the entire story together and a coher-
ent picture is emerging that offers a new understanding of Jesus and
his earliest followers in the first decades of the movement.

Archaeologists who work on the history of ancient Judaism and
early Christianity disagree over whether there is any reliable archaeological evidence directly related to Jesus or his early followers.[3] Most
are convinced that nothing of this sort has survived—not a single site,
inscription, artifact, drawing, or text mentioning Jesus or his followers, or witnessing to the beliefs of the earliest Jewish Christians either
in Jerusalem or in Galilee.

Jesus was born, lived, and died in the land of Israel. Most scholars agree he was born around 5 BCE and died around 30 CE. We
have abundant archaeological evidence from this period related to
Galilee, where he began his preaching and healing campaigns, and

Jerusalem, where he was crucified. There is evidence related to Herod Antipas, the high priest Caiaphas, and even Pontius Pilate, who had him crucified, but nothing that would connect us to Jesus himself, or even to his earliest followers—until now. Our hope is that these exciting new discoveries can become the catalyst for reconsidering other archaeological evidence that might well be related to the first Jewish-Christian believers.

The oldest copies of the New Testament gospels date to the early 4th century CE—well over two hundred years after Jesus' lifetime. There are a few papyri fragments of New Testament writings that scholars have dated to the 2nd century CE, but nothing so far in the 1st century. The earliest Christian art is found in the catacomb tombs in Rome, dating to the late 2nd or early 3rd centuries CE. Our discovery effectively pushes back the date on early Christian archaeological evidence by two hundred years. More significantly, it takes us back into the lifetime of Jesus himself.

This has been the most extraordinary adventure of our careers, and we are pleased to be able to share with readers the surprising and profound story of *The Jesus Discovery*.

James D. Tabor
Simcha Jacobovici
Mishkenot Sha'ananim, Jerusalem
June 15, 2011

CHAPTER ONE

THE DISCOVERY

It was a bright summer day in Jerusalem. We were crowded together with our film crew in a narrow corridor around a group of camera monitors in the basement of the condominium building in East Talpiot. The building had been built over the tomb shortly after its discovery in 1981. The tomb itself had been left sealed and the archaeologists who briefly examined it at the time had apparently missed its precious contents. We never set foot in the tomb. We were able to get an archaeological license to explore it remotely using a set of state-of-the-art cameras at the end of a sophisticated robotic arm that we had lowered into its dark interior through holes drilled into the floor of the basement.

We had been filming inside the tomb for two days, painstakingly moving our camera probe from one area to another. We had stuffed our equipment, cables, and high-resolution monitors into a small corridor leading to a storage area in the basement. What we had observed so far was fascinating enough. Just the experience of being able to "enter" this ancient tomb and see its contents kept us on the edge of our seats with our eyes focused on the camera monitors for hour after hour. The robotic arm slowly made its way around the tomb. Suddenly some-

1. Camera shot of the interior of the Patio tomb showing an ossuary in place.

thing unusual came into focus. Carved into the side of a limestone ossuary, or "bone box," was a startling image that we recognized, one never before seen on an ossuary or on any other ancient artifact from the 1st century CE. Right next to this ossuary was a second one with a four-line Greek inscription. We stared at the monitor as the image and the Greek letters came into sharper focus, and adjusted the light to get a better look. A shout went up in the cramped corridor when we read the inscription. What we saw was clear evidence of faith in Jesus' resurrection from the dead from this sealed tomb securely dated to the time of Jesus. The implications struck us immediately. We were gazing at the carved imagery and writing of some of Jesus' earliest followers. It was very likely that some of those people buried in this tomb had actually seen and known Jesus, maybe even witnessed his death, and were hereby proclaiming their faith in his resurrection as well.

Reeling from this discovery, we flew to Rome to investigate similar, but much later, images in the catacombs in Rome. The catacombs consist of hundreds of miles of many-leveled tunnels and passageways filled with burial chambers deep beneath the ancient city of Rome. It was here that the ancient Romans, and later the Jews and early Christians, buried their dead. The catacombs belonging to the Christians date to the late 3rd and early 4th centuries CE. On the walls of these family burial chambers one finds what was until now the earliest examples of Christian art—painted frescos, carvings, and inscriptions, many having to do with faith in Jesus' resurrection from the dead as offering hope of eternal life to his followers. In order to provide a wider context for what we had discovered in the Jerusalem Patio tomb we invited Professor Robin Jensen of Vanderbilt University to join us as a guide in the catacombs. She is one of the most distinguished historians of early Christian art in the world.[1] We spent hours walking in the deep underground passageways where the pungent odor of damp earth fills the stale air. Jensen took us from chamber to chamber, through the tangled maze of tunnels and levels, offering us a tour of some of the main images and inscriptions in the catacombs of Priscilla and San Sebastiano.

In the evening at our hotel after our first long day of exploration we showed Robin a photograph of the image carved on the ossuary that we had discovered in Jerusalem. She was completely taken back by what she saw. She instantly recognized the image. She kept saying, you mean this was found in a 1st century tomb in Jerusalem? How is that possible? Nothing like this has ever been found dating earlier than the 3rd century CE—and only in Rome, never in Jerusalem. The date and the location connected this discovery to Jesus' earliest followers. This discovery left us all a bit stunned. It seemed impossible, but a photograph of the evidence was lying on the table before our eyes.

JERUSALEM BURIAL CAVES IN THE TIME OF JESUS

It is against Israeli law to willfully excavate, violate, disturb, or destroy a tomb, whether ancient or modern. Nonetheless, 18th and 19th century explorers, modern tomb robbers, and construction crews have all taken their toll—particularly on ancient Jewish cave burials in Jerusalem. Yet there has been an unexpected positive benefit to these disturbances. Jewish cave tombs in this period contain little of obvious value. Typically Jews did not bury their dead with jewelry, coins, or other items of value. A tomb might contain clay oil lamps and ceramic vessels used for ritual purposes, such as perfume vials and even cooking pots, but little more—except for ossuaries. It is these ossuaries that the thieves want. Carved from soft limestone, these "bone boxes" became the repositories for the bones of loved ones. When a Jew died the corpse was washed and prepared for burial and then laid out in a niche or, in some tombs, on a shelf carved into the walls of the tomb, until the flesh decayed. These burial niches are called *kokhim* in Hebrew and they served for the initial placement of bodies as well as for the storage of ossuaries. The shelves within the niches are called *arcosolia*. This initial laying out of the body is referred to as a "primary burial" and was usually followed by a "secondary burial" a year or more later when the flesh had decayed and the bones of the deceased were gathered and placed in an ossuary.

Typically these ossuaries were wide enough to hold the skull of the deceased and long enough for the femur bone, the largest bone in the human body, to fit diagonally. For an adult that would be an average of 25 inches in length, 12 inches high, and 10 inches wide. In some cases the bones of more than one family member were put in a single ossuary—whether a husband and wife, two sisters, or even children with their parents. Other times wives and children had their own separate ossuaries, depending on the wishes and custom of a given Jewish family. We have an ancient rabbinic text that describes the process quite poignantly:

Rabbi Eleazar bar Zadok said, "Thus spoke my father at the time of his death, 'My son, bury me first in a niche [Hebrew *kokh*]. In the course of time collect my bones and put them in an ossuary; but do not gather them with your own hands.' And thus I did attend him: Jonathan entered, collected the bones, and spread a sheet over them. I then came in, rent my clothes for them, and sprinkled dried herbs over them. Just as he attended his father so I attended him." (*Semahot* 12.9)[2]

Jesus once told a would-be follower "Let the dead bury the dead," when the man protested that he needed to wait until he had buried his father to join Jesus. The cryptic reference most likely reflects this practice of secondary burial—not that the man was waiting for his father to die, but that his father had recently died and he needed to pass the obligatory first year following his father's death, when the family would gather his bones and put them in an ossuary. Only then could he leave his family and follow Jesus (Luke 9:59).[3]

Tomb robbers usually dump the bones and take the ossuaries, oil lamps, and other pottery vessels. The ossuaries can be sold through

2. A group of broken and restored ossuaries from a looted Jerusalem tomb.

the illegal antiquities market for a few hundred dollars—but they are worth much more if they are inscribed with the names of the deceased. Think of these tombs, with their inscribed ossuaries, as time capsules, preserving a tiny slice of history. Rather than a pile of bones of an unnamed and forgotten family, we have the names and relationships of the family that used a particular tomb—and in rare cases, as we will see, much more. These tombs provide a way for us to peer back into the past and recapture a moment in antiquity.

Jerusalem has experienced a huge building boom since 1967, when the Israelis unified the city and took down the dividing barriers between east and west. The population, both Jewish and Arab, has skyrocketed. But whenever you dig below a half meter or so in this ancient city or its environs you are more than likely to uncover archaeological antiquities, whether mosaics, ruins of ancient walls and buildings, or, often as not, ancient Jewish tombs. Antiquities are defined as any human-made material remains that can be dated earlier than the year 1700 CE and any zoological or biological remains older than 1300 CE.[4] As a result, with the construction of practically every road, highway, bridge, park, housing unit, or building, the Israeli Antiquities Authority (IAA), responsible for excavating, preserving, and safeguarding historic ancient sites, is called in. This work is called "rescue" or "salvage" archaeology, and it is usually done as quickly as possible so as not to unduly delay the construction project that has been halted.[5] It is against Israeli law for anyone to willfully ignore or destroy a site that contains antiquities. One simply never knows what might turn up with the next construction blast or sweep of the bulldozer.

Jerusalem is ringed with ancient tombs. These burial caves are carved into the limestone bedrock and hidden from modern eyes. The city was destroyed in 70 CE by the Romans and nineteen centuries of subsequent building and periodic destruction have obscured the landscape. Most of these tombs date back to the 1st century BCE through the 1st century CE, when the Roman destruction brought a halt to normal Jewish life. Scholars label this time period the Late Second Temple period, and often refer in particular to Herodian Jerusalem, named after Herod the Great, the Roman client king who ruled the country from 37 to 4 BCE. Christians loosely refer to this period as "Jerusalem in the time of Jesus."[6]

The use of ossuaries is a practice that is almost exclusive to Jerusalem and its environs in this period. Only a handful of ossuaries have been found in other parts of the country from this time. Scholars debate the reasons for this custom but the archaeological evidence is clear—this localized use of ossuaries flourished from the end of the 1st century BCE to the destruction of Jerusalem by Roman armies in 70 CE and then largely ceased.[7]

Approximately 1,000 cave tombs have been opened in the Jerusalem area in the past 150 years with over 2,000 documented ossuaries.[8] Thousands more have been lost or sold and scattered into private hands. The latest catalogue of inscriptions from Jerusalem lists nearly 600 inscribed ossuaries, or approximately 30 percent of the total.[9] Typically these ossuary inscriptions, written mostly in Hebrew and Aramaic or Greek, preserve the names of the dead.[10] For historians and archaeologists these ossuaries represent a different kind of treasure, much more valuable than jewelry or coins. In a very few cases these inscriptions include warnings against opening or violating the tomb, or even more rarely, something about the deceased—perhaps where one was from if outside the land of Israel, how one might have been related to others in the tomb, or what one's occupation might have been. Many ossuaries are plain, but others are decorated, most often with rosettes, various geometric patterns, architectural façades, and occasionally images of plants such as vines or palms. Images of humans and animals were forbidden as violations of the biblical commandment not to make "graven images"—so when there are exceptions, as is the case with our Patio tomb find, they stand out. Epigrams, in which something is said about the beliefs of the deceased about death and the afterlife, so common on Greek tombs in this period, are virtually nonexistent on Jewish ossuaries. As a result, the newly discovered Greek inscription on a *Jewish* 1st century CE ossuary is unprecedented in the archaeological record from this period.[11]

THE TALES TOMBS TELL

Construction blasts and bulldozers build the future but sometimes also unearth the past. These Old City tombs represent a valuable cross section of Jewish life—and death—in this period. The inscribed ossuaries, with names of individuals who lived and died before, during, and after the time of Jesus, lie at the crux of our investigation and indeed are what led us to the new discoveries that this book documents. We have spent many hours working side by side, studying and photographing scores of ossuaries all over Jerusalem—in the basement of the Rockefeller Museum, at the Israel Antiquities Authority warehouse in Beth Shemesh, in the storerooms of the Israel Museum, and elsewhere. The experience of walking through row after row of tall shelves of ossuaries, literally surrounded by these silent witnesses to the people who lived and died in Jerusalem in the 1st century CE, is for us a moving one. Most of the names are of long-forgotten individuals who lived and died without leaving behind any other record. But from time to time a tomb or ossuary can be identified with an individual we know from history—in a few cases even someone mentioned in the New Testament gospels. When that happens this hazardous process of tomb violation, whether by explorers, robbers, or modern construction, offers an amazing connection to the past—and the possibility of learning something entirely new, and connecting in a more tangible way with a person whom we had known only from a written text. It is as if the two-dimensional text suddenly becomes a three-dimensional life.

A dramatic example of such a discovery occurred on November 10, 1941. A single-chamber burial cave was found in the Kidron Valley, just southeast of the Old City of Jerusalem, by archaeologists Eleazar Sukenik and Nahman Avigad. The entrance was sealed and the cave had not been looted. Of the eleven ossuaries inside nine were in-scribed, one in Hebrew/Aramaic, another bilingual, and the rest in Greek. Archaeologists were able to determine this was a tomb for a family of Jews from Cyrene, in present-day Libya. It was dated to the 1st century CE. One of the eleven ossuaries had two names inscribed: *Alexandros* as well as *Simon* with "the Cyrenian" included.[12] Those names will ring a bell with many readers. Simon of Cyrene is famous for helping Jesus carry his cross to the place of execution. Many Christians commemorate his act as the fifth station of the cross. But the gospel of Mark significantly adds that this Simon was the father of "Alexander and Rufus," naming his two sons, as if ancient readers might know them (Mark 15:21).

Is it possible that archaeologists have stumbled upon the family tomb of Simon of Cyrene and his son Alexander, the very ones men-tioned in the New Testament gospels? One might think this very pos-sibility would be an occasion for excitement and celebration. Surely this ossuary would be on display in the Israel Museum, visited by mil-lions of Christian tourists each year who come to see the Dead Sea Scrolls and other wonders of archaeology. But such is not the case.

We went looking for the ossuary in 2005 and finally located it with some difficulty, in a back storage room at Hebrew University on Mount Scopus in Jerusalem, under a table. It did not appear to be of any particular interest to the curator who brought it out for us to ex-amine. He even seemed a bit curious as to why we would have shown up with an interest in seeing it. We brought with us biblical scholar Tom Powers, who had written several articles about this intriguing ossuary but had never seen it firsthand. He had done all his work from published photos.[13] We studied the bone box in great detail, photographed it, measured it, and examined it for any possible ad-ditional markings. We all felt awe in the little storage room where we were gathered that day. We had to ask ourselves, Is it possible we are standing around the ossuary that once held the bones of Alexander, Simon of Cyrene's son, and perhaps Simon himself as well?

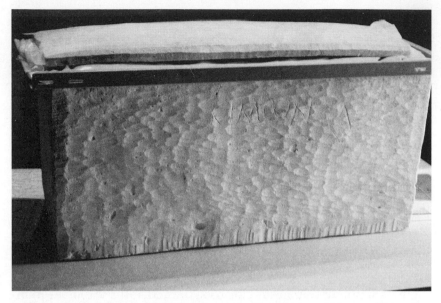

3. The ossuary of Simon of Cyrene, who carried the cross, and his son, Alexander.

Archaeology connects us to our ancient past, but there is something about a tomb and a burial that is particularly moving. It is easy to imagine Alexander the son being present that day with his father, as Jesus passed by carrying the cross. The gospels say Simon was a passerby who was coming in from the countryside for Passover. Since the festival of Passover is a family event, his sons Rufus and Alexander would have undoubtedly been with him (Mark 15:21).[14] Might Alexander have been present when the Roman soldiers impressed Simon to carry the cross? Would he then have followed his father to the place of execution and have even witnessed the crucifixion of Jesus? The name Simon is fairly common among Jews of this period but the name Alexander much less so—and this Alexander, like his father, is from Cyrene. That day, standing in the storeroom at Hebrew University, we were all contemplating that spine-tingling probability and experiencing firsthand the remarkable ways ancient archaeological finds can connect us to the past.

We have the bulldozers to thank for an even more astounding ac-

cidental discovery in November 1990. Builders working on a park in
the Peace Forest, just south of the Old City, uncovered a 1st century
CE burial cave with twelve ossuaries, five inscribed. Unfortunately
the tomb had been looted so its contents were in disarray, but two
inscribed ossuaries caught the archaeologists' special attention—one
was inscribed *Yehosef bar Qafa*—Joseph son of Caiaphas; the other
simply *Qafa*—the family name Caiaphas. The archaeologists were
convinced that most likely they had uncovered the ossuary of the
very man before whom Jesus stood condemned in the early morning hours of the last day of his life—Joseph Caiaphas, the Jewish high
priest in the time of Jesus (Matthew 26:57–67).[15]

Although the ossuaries were elaborately decorated, it is important
to note that the inscriptions themselves were scratched on the plain
sides of the ossuaries in a very informal cursive script and that the tomb
was quite modest for a person of such wealth and importance. Also,
one of the other ossuaries, inscribed *Miriam daughter of Shimon*, had a
coin in the skull—presumably reflecting the pagan custom of putting a
coin in the mouth to pay Charon, the ferryman over the Hadean river
Styx in Greek mythology. Recently Simcha has tracked down two nails
likely from the Caiaphas tomb that had gone missing. One expert has

4. Simcha and Felix examining the Caiaphas ossuary in the Israel Museum.

identified them as crucifixion nails.[16] In Greek and Jewish tradition nails used for a crucifixion carried special magical powers, so one has to wonder if two such nails, connected to the Caiaphas family, might also be connected to the execution of Jesus. Regardless of that possibility, from this tomb we learn that a person of influence and means might have a modest tomb, with very informal, even sloppily executed inscriptions on their ossuaries, and that even the family of the high priest of Israel was not immune to pagan or Greek customs.

The discovery of these two tombs, containing the remains of these individuals mentioned specifically in the gospels, is truly extraordinary— and to think that these men were directly involved with Jesus during the last day of his life, witnessing his trial and his crucifixion. Archaeology is very much a "surprise" science, as one simply never knows what will turn up next. What one most hopes to find might never come about, but we have all learned that what one least expects can appear at any time.

And that's exactly what happened in the spring of 1980 and again in 1981. Two tombs—the Garden tomb and the Patio tomb—were exposed by construction blasts in East Talpiot, a neighborhood just a mile and a half south of the Old City of Jerusalem. The tombs are less than two hundred feet apart. One was blown open from the front, with its courtyard destroyed, exposing its main entrance. The roof of the other was blasted open, allowing one to drop down from the top inside the still-sealed tomb. An Israeli construction company that was building a series of condominiums in the new neighborhood exposed both tombs. Easter and Passover do not always fall together in the same week, though they did in 1980 and again in 1981, when the two tombs were uncovered.[17] We believe these tombs relate directly to Jesus, his family, and to his first followers. It seems more than ironic that both were uncovered around Easter and Passover, nineteen and a half centuries after his death.[18]

The Garden tomb, excavated by archaeologists in 1980, is located in a garden area today, between two condominium buildings. The tomb was left open, as are many ancient tombs in Jerusalem that have been excavated, but it was later covered over by the condominium owners with a concrete slab to keep children from falling in. The second tomb was examined by archaeologists in April 1981 but never excavated. This is the tomb in which we made our discoveries in June 2010. The Patio tomb has two ritual vent pipes, required by Jewish religious custom, that run up through a patio of one of the condo units built above it. According to Jewish law, tombs convey ritual impurity, so a space is maintained between the floor of any building and the ground surface above a tomb so that technically the building is not touching the tomb itself. The vents, commonly called "soul pipes," allow the spirits of the dead to leave the tomb. Locating these two tombs again after twenty-five years was not an easy task, especially with streets, parking lots, and buildings now covering the area, but the concrete slab and the vent pipes turned out to be key indicators.

THE 1981 DISCOVERY OF THE PATIO TOMB

In April 1981, the Patio tomb, the site of our recent discoveries, was first uncovered. The tomb was exposed by a dynamite blast by the Solel Boneh construction company, which was preparing the area for a condominium building on what is today Dov Gruner Street in East Talpiot.[19] Amos Kloner, Jerusalem district archaeologist and a Ph.D. student, went immediately to investigate the tomb on behalf of the IAA as soon as construction workers reported its discovery. Kloner was able to enter the tomb through the break in the ceiling. The tomb was twelve feet under the modern ground surface and its original entrance was closed, blocked by an ancient sealing stone. The tomb had a single central square chamber measuring 11.5 by 11.5 feet. It contained nine nicely carved gabled burial niches, three on each of three sides, each sealed with a heavy blocking stone. Four of the niches held a total of eight ossuaries. There were skeletal remains in the others.

Kloner reports that he was only in the tomb a very short time, just a few minutes, on his initial visit when a group of ultra-Orthodox Jews arrived, determined to protect the sanctity of the tomb and especially its bones from being disturbed by the archaeologists. He only had time to quickly examine the cave before being forced to leave by their protests. He was able to carry off one smaller ossuary, decorated but not inscribed, probably that of a child, which he turned over to the authorities at the IAA's Rockefeller Museum headquarters.[20]

The tomb was assigned permit 1050 and Kloner left his assistants, the late Joseph Gath and Shlomo Gudovitch, to continue the investigation since he had to leave the country on a previously scheduled trip abroad.[21] They were able to remove the heavy blocking stones from the various niches, briefly examine the ossuaries, and take photographs before the Orthodox returned and forced them to leave. In a subsequent publication Kloner mentions cooking pots in three different locations in the tomb.[22] Only one pot made it to the IAA ware-

5. Simcha and Felix examining the child's ossuary in the IAA storage warehouse.

house, where all artifacts are required to be stored as property of the state of Israel. We recently held it in our hands. It is still in perfect condition and properly tagged with the date and license number, at the IAA storage facility in Beth Shemesh.[23] No one knows what happened to the other cooking pots or whether anything else might have been removed from the tomb. We can say that there are no such pots or other artifacts, other than the seven ossuaries, in the tomb today, based on our recent reinvestigation of its contents.

Kloner further reports that all the ossuaries but one were decorated and two had Greek names inscribed. The eyewitnesses we have interviewed confirm that IAA archaeologists worked at the tomb for several days, finally removing all the ossuaries from their niches,

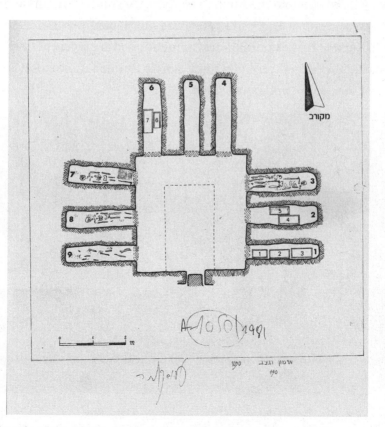

6. Kloner's original 1981 drawing of the Patio tomb and its contents.

opening their heavy stone lids, and numbering the ossuaries with chalk marks. They were preparing to hoist them up with ropes through the opening in the ceiling for transport to the Rockefeller when they were stopped at the last moment by an irate group of ultra-Orthodox Jewish protesters who had returned. The positions the ossuaries occupy today in the niches are different from what is shown in the 1981 photos and on the map Kloner subsequently published, indicating that they were put back in the niches randomly, either by the archaeologists or the Orthodox religious authorities that halted the work.

The Patio tomb was sealed on April 16 with the seven ossuaries inside, and not seen again until twenty-nine years later by our remote cameras. In mid-July 1981 the builders poured a thick concrete support pillar down into the tomb to support the condominium building they were constructing.[24] The tomb was subsequently sealed off under the basement of the building, and as mentioned the construction crew installed the "ritual" vent pipes that ran up through the concrete pillar to exit on a patio on the first floor.

7. The condominium building built over the Patio tomb, with exploration equipment in place.

Apparently, in their haste, and under pressure from the Orthodox, the archaeologists failed to notice what we discovered in June 2010. We found the two Greek names the archaeologists mentioned but we also discovered a Greek inscription with four lines of text, plus a mysterious image. The image offers a key to interpreting both of the Talpiot tombs and their probable relationship to Jesus. Together the inscription and the image constitute one of the most significant finds in recent archaeological history.

THE 1980 DISCOVERY OF THE GARDEN TOMB

Every small detail matters to an archaeologist. Getting the facts straight is critical in interpreting both these tombs. We know much less about the details of the discovery of the Patio tomb since it was never excavated and was only briefly examined when it was exposed in 1981. Even the IAA records are sparse. In the case of the Garden tomb we have a lot more information with more pieces to the puzzle, but just as many questions as we have answers. Here are the facts as we understand them.

The Garden tomb was uncovered one year earlier by the same construction company preparing the area for a series of terraced condominium units. It is less than two hundred feet from the Patio tomb. It was exposed by a dynamite blast on Thursday morning, March 27, 1980.[25] Engineer Ephraim Shohat and his supervisor immediately notified the IAA, who dispatched archaeologist Eliot Braun, who happened to live in the area, to investigate.[26] The outside covered courtyard of the tomb had been completely blasted away, exposing an unusual façade with a chevron and a circle, carved on the face of the small inner entrance to the tomb itself. This entrance, measuring eighteen by eighteen inches, would have normally been covered with a sealing stone but it was missing, perhaps indicating the tomb had been left open or was disturbed at some time in the past. Braun crawled inside the tomb and found that it was filled knee deep with the local terra rossa soil that had apparently washed in over the centuries, even covering the tops of the ten ossuaries, yet unseen, that were stored inside. The inside of the square tomb measured only nine by nine feet and the ceiling was about four feet above the floor, so Braun could not stand inside. It is a much more modest tomb than the Patio tomb, both in terms of size and the architecture of the niches, which are more roughly cut. The Garden tomb's interesting façade is its most distinguishing feature.

There were six burial niches, or *kokhim,* measuring six feet deep, twenty-one inches wide, and thirty-four inches high, carved into the east, north, and west sides of the tomb, two per side, with ossuaries stored in five of them.[27] The tomb had two arched shelves, or *arcosolia,* six feet in length, carved into the north and west sides of its walls. It was on these shelves, as we have said, that corpses would be initially laid out for decomposition before the bones were collected into ossuaries a year or so following death. Archaeologists later noted

8. The exposed façade of the Garden tomb shortly after it was revealed.

that there were bone fragments on the shelves and when the two feet of terra rossa soil fill was removed, exposing the ancient floor of the tomb, they found skeletal remains, including skulls, just below the two shelves.

District archaeologist Amos Kloner supervised the operation and he assigned IAA archaeologist Joseph Gath to carry out the excavation. Gath invited Shimon Gibson, a young archaeology student with a talent for drawing, to prepare a survey or map of the tomb. Kloner applied for the necessary license to excavate on Friday, March 28, with Gath as the license holder. The "Permit for a Salvage Dig 938" was issued on Monday, March 31, the day before Passover, but apparently, according to IAA files, Gath had begun his work with the aid of Braun and three or four construction workers on the 28th, the Friday morning after the discovery. The excavation continued, with short breaks for the Passover holiday, until Friday, April 11, two weeks later.

Around noon on Friday the 28th, the day after the tomb was exposed, an eleven-year-old schoolboy, Ouriel Maoz, whose Orthodox Jewish family lived near the site, passed by and saw the distinctive façade of the exposed tomb, clearly visible from the street below. He ran home excitedly to tell his mother, Rivka Maoz, who immediately called the Department of Antiquities to report the newly visible tomb; she was concerned that if it were left unguarded its contents might be plundered. She could not get through to anyone since businesses close early on Friday afternoon for the Jewish Sabbath. The mother and son then went together to the tomb as the light was fading and they remember that they could see some skulls and bones inside. They saw no signs of any archaeologists or workers on the scene.

The next day, Saturday, was the Sabbath. Ouriel remembers running home from synagogue to tell his mother that some local kids had entered the tomb, found the skulls and other bones, and were *playing soccer* with them, kicking them about the area. The tomb had been left unguarded over the Sabbath. Rivka and her husband ran the children off and gathered all the bones they could locate, going door to door asking parents to be sure they made their children return all the bones. They gathered all they could collect, putting them in plastic bags for safekeeping until the next morning. On Sunday morning, when the archaeologists arrived to continue their work, she delivered the bags of bones to Gath.[28]

Gibson arrived about noon on Sunday to do the map survey of the tomb. In 2003, when we first interviewed him about his arrival at the scene, he distinctly recalled seeing the ossuaries that had been removed from the tomb lined up outside, waiting for a truck from the IAA that would transport them to the Rockefeller Museum headquarters of the IAA. Gibson recalled how Gath took him inside the tomb, where the workers were removing the soil that had accumulated, and he could still see the impressions left by the ossuaries. Gath indicated to him where each had been located so he could include the original locations of all ten on his map. If Gibson's initial memory was correct, that would mean the ossuaries were not removed until midday Sunday and had been left in the tomb Friday and Saturday. This would explain how the neighborhood kids were able to pull skulls out of the ossuaries in the tomb for their makeshift soccer game since the ossuaries were buried under a foot and a half of soil and not visible when the archaeologists first began their work.

Getting these chronological facts straight is critical. If the tomb was indeed left open and unattended with ossuaries inside from its opening on Thursday through Sunday morning, there is a real possibility that the tomb could have been looted and ossuaries removed. The construction workers who exposed the tomb were aware of it and by Saturday those living in the neighborhood were aware as well. We are convinced that one or more ossuaries did go missing and in chapter 6 we will offer the results of our own investigation of what most likely happened.

The matter of the scattering of the bones is also troubling. How many bones were scattered and lost? Were the rest left in the ossuaries that were then taken to the IAA for analysis by an anthropologist? This would have been the normal procedure. What did Gath do with the bag of bones that the Maoz family gave to him Sunday morning? We don't know the answers to any of these questions. It is quite disconcerting to think the bones from this ancient Jewish family, including the skulls from inside the ossuaries, were scattered and kicked about when the tomb was left unguarded over that fateful weekend.

Joe Zias, the anthropologist at the Rockefeller Museum who routinely received bones from tomb excavations, says he does not remember receiving bones from this particular tomb, but he notes that construction crews were uncovering many dozens of tombs in the 1980s and there was no reason for any particular set of bones to receive special treatment. Zias was the main "bone man" or anthropologist there at the time, but there is no record that he ever examined them or prepared a report. This is very unfortunate, since a full study of all the bones in all ten ossuaries might have contributed immeasurably to our knowledge of this tomb and those buried therein.

At that time, ossuaries with the bones inside were usually transported intact to the laboratory, where the bones could be separated for analysis and study. Depending on their state of deterioration they could be typed for age, sex, and any other distinguishing forensic information. This examination would also allow any potential correlation between the ossuary contents and any ossuary inscriptions.

Since Joseph Gath never published a full report of the contents of the Garden tomb, and the bones were never examined, our information regarding the excavation is extremely limited. The first publication in 1996 by Amos Kloner resulted from media attention to this tomb by the BBC, but by that time, fourteen years later, no bone reports could be done and much information was lost. One must assume that these and all other skeletal materials in various Israeli labs were turned over to the Orthodox religious authorities in 1994 when the Israeli government agreed to return such remains for reburial.[29] These bones were presumably buried in unmarked common graves by the Orthodox authorities.

Fortunately, when the bones of ossuaries are removed significant bone fragments often remain, sticking to the sides of these limestone coffins. The ossuaries are rarely cleaned or brushed out unless they are going on display in the Israel Museum. In the case of the Garden tomb, enough bone fragments were left, even in 2005 when we first examined the ossuaries, to allow for DNA tests of some of the remains from two of the ossuaries. It is only recently that DNA tests have been done on skeletal remains from tombs of the period in an effort to determine familial relationships in a given tomb.[30] What we have managed to recover fills in a few missing pieces of the overall story. The fascinating results of those tests will be presented in the final chapter of this book.

Amos Kloner reports that he visited the tomb when it was first reported to the antiquities authorities on Thursday, March 28, took photos, applied for the permit, and *by noon Friday* Gath and his workers had extracted all ten ossuaries from the niches, after digging them out of the soil that filled the tomb. Kloner insists that all ten ossuaries, with their bones, were transported to the Rockefeller Museum by midday, hours before the Sabbath arrived on Friday night.[31] Kloner's photos, now part of the official IAA files, do indeed show the niches in the tomb filled with soil to a level that made the ossuaries resting on the floor invisible. The IAA records show that Gath, Braun, and some workers had begun at least to clear the soil over the ossuaries on Friday morning. Various eyewitnesses, including Gibson in his original testimony, dispute whether Gath and his workers removed all ten ossuaries by noon that Friday for transport to the Rockefeller. It seems unlikely, since several of the ossuaries were broken and extracting them all from their encasement in two feet of soil would have required considerable effort.

The Maoz family says they never saw any archaeologists working at the tomb on Friday afternoon when they first visited. That they saw skulls and bones exposed might indicate the archaeologists had reached the tops of the ossuaries that morning before suspending their work and leaving the scene. Apparently the tomb was left *unguarded,* as it had been the previous Thursday afternoon and evening. An open tomb, with its striking façade, visible from a distance up on the ridge, was an invitation to local children or other intruders to enter the tomb and ransack things Friday night. The presence of skulls is particularly note-worthy, since these skulls would have come from inside the ossuaries—indicating that at least the soil covering the tops of the ossuaries had been removed on Friday morning by the archaeologists. Rivka Maoz gave us several color photos from the family album, two taken inside the tomb, showing that the ossuaries had been removed when the photos were taken. But *when* were these photos made by the Maoz family? Kloner and Gibson insist they were made on March 29, on the Sabbath, but the Maoz family are observant Jews and are not permitted to take photographs on the Sabbath. The photos were most likely made late on Sunday since there are no workers in the photos and the ossuaries had already been removed. Shimon Gibson is now convinced that his initial memory was faulty and that when he arrived Sunday morning he must not have seen the ossuaries outside after all, since they would have already been taken away by the archaeologists by noon on Friday, according to Amos Kloner. Everyone has the right to revise their recol-lections and change their mind, but Gibson does have a photographic memory and in his initial interviews with us he was quite explicit about seeing them all outside. The exact timing of the removal of the ossuar-ies, either on Friday or Sunday, is critical since one of the ossuaries, a potentially very significant one, may have gone missing.

INSIDE THE GARDEN TOMB

According to all the records the Garden tomb contained a total of ten ossuaries, and they were catalogued as numbers 80.500 through

80.509 in the IAA collection. The current card catalogue at the IAA warehouse in Beth Shemesh only lists nine; the tenth, numbered 80.509, is not included, nor are there any photographs or measurements of it in the IAA excavation files. In chapter 6 we discuss this tenth and missing ossuary and what might have happened to it.

Gibson's drawing shows all ten ossuaries in place in five of the six niches, marked with a number and a letter. Unfortunately, Kloner reports that he can find no record that would match up the ossuaries and their catalogue numbers with their original locations in the tomb on Gibson's map. That sort of information, correlating finds with their location at an excavation site, is basic to any archaeological fieldwork. Recording precisely where things were found is perhaps the most important aspect of any excavation, as every beginning student of archaeology knows. It is impossible to imagine that Gath failed to tag the ossuaries with locus numbers. No one would send a group of ten ossuaries—or any artifact for that matter—to the Rockefeller without filling out a proper identification tag. Six of the nine ossuaries were inscribed with names and if we had their original locations we would know how the names were grouped in the tomb, giving possible hints as to the relationship of the individuals buried there to one another.

The six inscriptions, one in Greek and the rest in Aramaic are, in English: Jesus son of Joseph, Mariam called Mara, Joses, Judah son of Jesus, Matthew, and Maria. Since we clearly have a father named Jesus and his son Judah in this tomb, one wonders if one of the named women, Mariam called Mara or Maria, might have been the mother, and if so, which one. One might expect that the ossuaries of the father, mother, and son would be grouped together in the same niche. There is one niche, just on the right as you enter the tomb, that, according to Gibson's drawing, held three ossuaries, clustered together. It is tempting to imagine that the Jesus of this tomb, his son Judah, and the mother might have been clustered together in this place of honor—first on the right as you enter the tomb. Unfortunately, given the lack of proper records we now have no way of knowing. At the time the os-

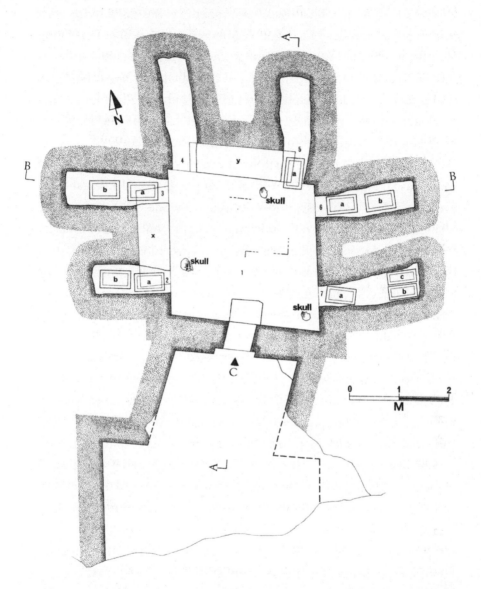

9. Shimon Gibson's original map of the Garden tomb from 1980.

suaries were removed and taken to IAA storage the archaeologists noticed that some of the ossuaries were inscribed in Greek and Aramaic but the name "Jesus son of Joseph," which might have at least raised an eyebrow or two, is quite difficult to read as it is written in an informal cursive style.[32] In due time Israeli epigrapher Levi Rahmani, along with Joseph Naveh and Leah Di Segni, deciphered the names, but how long after the tomb's discovery we do not know. The nine ossuaries with descriptions and photos were included in the official *Catalogue of Jewish Ossuaries* in 1994, authored by Rahmani. The publication of Rahmani's catalogue was the first time these six names from the Garden tomb were publicly revealed—fourteen years after their discovery.

Remarkably no one in any official capacity noticed or considered this unusual cluster of six names as having any special interest—not even the Jesus son of Joseph inscription. Only one other ossuary inscribed "Jesus son of Joseph" has ever been found, out of approximately two thousand ossuaries that have been uncovered over the past two hundred years. The famous Israeli Dead Sea Scrolls scholar Eleazar Sukenik brought it to light in 1931. He had stumbled across it in the basement warehouse of the Rockefeller Museum. It seems no one had ever noticed it before, and no one knows where it came from. As one might expect, the news of its existence caused a minor stir in the world press. Could this ossuary have possibly been that of Jesus of Nazareth?[33] The scholars who commented on the discovery when Sukenik made his announcement emphasized that these names were sufficiently common to make any such identification irresponsibly speculative. Besides, no one knew where this ossuary had been found, when it was discovered, or who had found it. No such attention was given to the Jesus son of Joseph ossuary from the Garden tomb, even with these five other names all associated with Jesus of Nazareth and his family.

Joseph Gath died in June 1993, a year before the Rahmani catalogue was published. Gath never published a full report on the tomb, but we know he must have talked with Rahmani once the names were deciphered since Rahmani thanks him, as the excavator of the tomb, for giving permission for the ossuaries to be published.[34] His widow, Ruth Gath, has told us that when her husband learned of the names of the inscriptions, he told her privately that he believed that the tra-

10. The Garden tomb entrance between the apartments—it is covered by the cement slab at bottom center.

ditional burial site of Jesus, in the Church of the Holy Sepulchre, was the "wrong tomb." He explained that as a Jew he planned to remain silent about this opinion since any claim that the Garden tomb was that of Jesus of Nazareth and his family might result in an anti-Semitic backlash from the Christian church.[35]

In 1995 a British film crew working on an Easter special on the resurrection of Jesus had noticed the two "Jesus son of Joseph" ossuaries listed in Rahmani's catalogue and asked to film one or both of them. When the director discovered that the 1980 Garden tomb had contained ossuaries with a clustered set of names like Joseph, Mary, Jesus, Judah, and Matthew, all names associated with Jesus and his family in the New Testament, the film crew's interest was considerably piqued. The subsequent 1996 BBC Easter television special, coupled with a front-page story in the London *Sunday Times* titled "The Tomb That Dare Not Speak Its Name," sparked a worldwide flurry of news coverage.[36] Archaeologists, officials from the IAA, and biblical scholars quickly weighed in, assuring the public that "the names were common" and the tomb could have belonged to any man named Jesus, not necessarily the one we know as Jesus of Nazareth. There were even calls from the Vatican to the IAA seeking clarification about the veracity of the stories that were circulating in the media. The story lasted about a week and then was largely dropped. Most academics chalked the whole subject up to an unfortunate case of media frenzy. One positive result of the news coverage was that the late Amir Drori, director of the IAA, embarrassed that he had never heard of this "Jesus" tomb, demanded that a full report of the tomb and its contents be assigned at once. The task fell to Amos Kloner to write up an official report on the tomb so as to dispel irresponsible media speculation. Kloner's article appeared a few months later that same year, surely record time for an academic publication.[37] Had the 1996 publicity bubble never occurred it seems unlikely that anything about the tomb would have ever been published, and the tomb with its contents would have been forgotten.

Both Kloner and Gibson have expressed their view that the

Garden tomb merits no further scholarly attention and that it has become undeservedly famous due to media sensationalism.[38] In their view the names in the tomb are common and have no connection to Jesus of Nazareth. The other major objection to identifying this tomb as the family tomb of Jesus of Nazareth is the assertion that there is no historical evidence that Jesus had a son at all, much less one named Judah. When James was writing his book *The Jesus Dynasty* in 2005, he reacted to the post–Dan Brown, *Da Vinci Code* sensationalism and stated bluntly that the idea that Jesus was married and had children made good fiction but was "long on speculation and short on evidence."[39] However, based on all the evidence as well as the new discoveries in the Patio tomb, James has had reason to change his mind.

The media hysteria to which Kloner and Gibson refer is not so much the 1996 BBC story, which was quickly forgotten, but the aftermath of the investigation that we began in 2004. The preliminary results were made public in March 2007 through a Discovery Channel television documentary, *The Lost Tomb of Jesus*, the bestselling book *The Jesus Family Tomb*, and a number of scholarly articles.[40] We will chronicle that investigation and its results in the following chapter.

THE STRATEGIC LOCATION OF TALPIOT

Few outside of Jerusalem had ever heard of the district of East Talpiot, just south of the Old City of Jerusalem, until the news stories regarding the "Jesus" tomb made headline news around the world in March 2007. According to the gospel of John, the tomb in which Jesus was initially placed in haste, until full burial rites could be performed after Passover, happened to be near the place of his crucifixion (John 19:41). Millions of Christians visit Jerusalem each year and are invariably taken either to the Church of the Holy Sepulchre in the Christian quarter of the Old City, or an alternative site, just north of the city, more popular with evangelical Protestants, called "Gordon's Calvary."

They come to either spot to view the place where they believe Jesus was crucified, buried, and raised from the dead on that first Easter morning. The crowded rows of condos and apartments that make up the various neighborhoods of East Talpiot are understandably not on the Christian tour agenda.

In the time of Jesus things were of course quite different. The hills south of Jerusalem, down toward Bethlehem, were relatively sparsely populated with private lands devoted to agriculture and livestock. The neighborhood where the Garden and Patio tombs are located is called Armon Hanatziv. It is just off a high ridge, called the Promenade, that provides a spectacular view of Jerusalem to the north and Bethlehem to the south, and it still attracts busloads of tourists today. In ancient times there was a main road crisscrossing the area, running southeast, that passed the famous Mar Saba monastery and went down to the Dead Sea, near Qumran, where the Dead Sea Scrolls were found. To the west of the two tombs, just a few hundred yards away, was a spectacular aqueduct that transported water from Tekoa, south of Bethlehem, north to Jerusalem. The area is thick with ancient biblical history. Abraham traveled this route on his way to Mount Moriah, as recorded in Genesis 22:1–4. Rachel, wife of Jacob and mother of Joseph and Benjamin, is buried on the road running south to Bethlehem (Genesis 35:16). Just to the south and east of Bethlehem, clearly visible from the Talpiot tombs, is the magnificent Herodium, the tomb of Herod the Great, the Roman-appointed "King of the Jews."

In the 1980s, when the construction companies were tearing up the area to build residential dwellings, mostly apartments and condominiums, the Garden and Patio tombs were not the only tombs uncovered. Just to the north of the Garden or "Jesus" tomb, less than sixty feet away, was another tomb that had been almost entirely blasted away. All that was left was one of its inside walls, with the partial remains of the niches still visible. None of its contents could be studied or evaluated but it likely belonged to the same farm or agricultural estate. In the immediate vicinity there was also an ancient olive press, various water cisterns, and the remains of a plastered ritual bath called a *mikveh*. Joseph Gath, who surveyed the entire area around the tombs, concluded that these installations belonged to a large farm or wealthy estate and were most likely the family tombs of the owner, clustered closely together.[41]

Ancient historians work with evidence, archaeological and textual, seeking to discern if there is any fit between what we read in our texts, in this case the gospel accounts of Jesus' death, and what is found in excavations. They often construct working hypotheses to test whether the various types of evidence fit together and what the alternative interpretations might be.

As we consider whether the Garden tomb might indeed be the tomb of Jesus of Nazareth and his immediate family a key historical question arises. According to the New Testament gospels Joseph of Arimathea, who had enough wealth and influence to go directly to Pontius Pilate, the Roman prefect of Judea, to request the burial rights for Jesus' body, was responsible for Jesus' burial. Such a task would normally fall to the immediate family, or to the closest disciples of a teacher such as Jesus. For example, we learn in the gospel of Mark that when Herod Antipas beheaded John the Baptizer, his disciples were allowed to come and take his body and bury it in a tomb (Mark 6:29). In all four of our gospels, Joseph of Arimathea appears just after the crucifixion to remove Jesus' corpse from the cross and carry out the Jewish burial rites for Jesus (Mark 15:43–47).[42] We never hear of him again. He is said to be a member of the "council," or Sanhedrin, the indigenous Jewish judicial body responsible for Jewish affairs, as well as a sympathizer with Jesus and his movement. If one wants to understand what happened to Jesus' body after the crucifixion, one has to pay careful attention to Joseph of Arimathea.

What most readers of the New Testament have missed is that Joseph of Arimathea initially placed the body of Jesus in a temporary unfinished tomb that just happened to be near the place of crucifixion. It was an emergency measure so that the corpse would not be left exposed overnight, which was forbidden by Jewish law (Deuteronomy 21:23). It was late afternoon when Jesus died and the Jewish Passover was beginning at sundown that very evening. Although Jewish tradition required that a body be buried as quickly as possible, the full rites could not be carried out before the Passover meal began. The gospel of John explains it best:

> Now in the place where he was crucified there was a garden, and in the garden a new tomb where no one had ever been laid. So because of the Jewish day of Preparation, since the tomb was close at hand, they laid Jesus there. (John 19:41–42)[43]

Jesus was *temporarily* placed in this new tomb, with the entrance blocked with a stone, to protect his body from exposure and from predators. According to Mark all Joseph of Arimathea had time to do was to quickly wrap the bloodied body in a linen shroud—no washing, no anointing, no traditional Jewish rites of mourning—nothing (Mark 15:46). The women, including Jesus' mother, his sister, his companion Mary Magdalene, and others, who followed at a distance, had every intention of completing the Jewish rites of burial, which involved washing the corpse and anointing it with oil and spices, as soon as the Sabbath was over (Mark 16:1). Joseph of Arimathea, in asking to take charge of the proper burial of Jesus, clearly had a more permanent arrangement in mind. The most likely scenario is that he planned to provide Jesus, and subsequently his family, with a cave tomb at his own expense, likely on his own estate outside Jerusalem. That he was a local resident seems likely based on his membership in the Sanhedrin, and he is the one who would have had the means to provide the family of Jesus, who were from Galilee, with a family cave tomb.

The Patio tomb, in particular, shows evidence in both architecture and content of having belonged to a rich family. Our new evidence from the tomb further points in this direction. Once we put things into this biblical context, noting carefully what the earliest gospel traditions actually say, the faith of Jesus' followers that he was raised from the dead can finally be understood in proper historical context. Rather than denying that Jesus was raised from the dead, the Talpiot tombs and their contents give witness to the resurrection faith of these first believers. In an uncanny way, Easter 1980 and Easter 1981 have provided us with a revolutionary new understanding of the implications of that first Easter weekend and all that transpired. In the following chapter we will relate our "rediscovery" of the two Talpiot tombs, their freshly uncovered contents, and how our understanding of Jesus and his first followers has been dramatically reshaped by what we have found.

CHAPTER TWO

TWO TALPIOT TOMBS

When we first went looking for the Talpiot "Jesus tomb" in March 2004 we were not even sure it had survived the building project in the 1980s. At that time we had no idea there was a second tomb located just a couple of hundred feet away. We knew that locating the Garden tomb after twenty-four years, somewhere within or under a complex of condominium buildings, would not be easy. We ended up consulting with the initial archaeologists, the original builders, and local residents, and checking city maps and old photographs. Surprisingly, our search began by simply knocking on doors and it ended with a blind woman leading us to the correct location.

James had been working with Jerusalem archaeologist Shimon Gibson excavating an ancient site in Suba, west of Jerusalem, now known as the "John the Baptist" cave.[1] Shimon has lived in Jerusalem since his family moved there from London when he was a young boy. He knows the history and archaeology of Jerusalem intimately. He also has a remarkable memory for details. As a beginning, James asked Gibson what he knew about a "Jesus tomb" discovered in 1980 in East Talpiot, on the off chance that he would be able to supply some information or know whom to ask about its subsequent fate. Was the tomb destroyed, covered over, or otherwise inaccessible due to the subsequent building boom in Talpiot?

James was stunned when Shimon informed him that not only did he know about the tomb, but that he had assisted Joseph Gath and supervisor Amos Kloner in its excavation twenty-four years ago. He had served as the surveyor, had drawn the official map of the tomb and its contents, and was even listed on the excavation license. Shimon immediately gave Kloner a call to see if he remembered the precise location since Gibson had never been back to the tomb after construction in the area had been completed. Kloner identified the approximate location and added that he did not think the tomb had been destroyed, that it might be preserved under a building. The next day, Shimon and James set off for East Talpiot and began walking around the various condominium complexes in the area around the gas station, talking to residents, and looking for any kind of concrete cover or vent pipes between the buildings that might indicate the presence of a tomb below ground.

It is hard to imagine that scene today, considering how little we knew at the time and how much we have learned since. The two scholars must have appeared a bit strange to the residents on that Sunday afternoon—James, the American academic, and Shimon, the British-Israeli archaeologist, going door to door and stopping people along the walkways between the buildings asking if anyone had a tomb under their apartment or had heard of one in the areas between the building units. After about two hours of ringing doorbells and asking residents they hit pay dirt. A resident who had lived there since the building was first constructed in 1980 remembered talk of a tomb. He directed them to a nearby neighbor's apartment. They rang the doorbell and the owner confirmed that his condominium had been built over an ancient tomb. Both James and Shimon assumed this had to be the Jesus tomb they were look-

11. James standing over one of the ritual vent pipes running down into the Patio tomb.

ing for. They had no idea at the time that there were two tombs in proximity to one another. The owner had lived there since 1980, and he and his wife were able to buy the place at a reduced price because other potential buyers did not want a condo unit built over a tomb.

That evening James called Simcha, who lived in Toronto at that time. He excitedly reported the news: "We have found the Jesus tomb and we think it is intact." James gave Simcha the name and address of the family they had met. That telephone call set everything in motion. We agreed that a first step in any reinvestigation of the Jesus tomb would be to examine the tomb itself firsthand. Empty or not, it might still hold some important clues about the 1st century Jewish family that was buried there. Given the hasty "rescue" excavation in April 1980, perhaps something had been overlooked.

THE INVESTIGATION BEGINS

At that time, in March 2004, we had never met face-to-face. In an initial phone conversation in October 2003 we discovered that we had a lot of common interests—especially involving ancient tombs and ossuaries from the time of Jesus. James was doing research for his book on the historical Jesus called *The Jesus Dynasty*, which involved his own work on the Jesus family and the four brothers of Jesus—James, Joseph, Judas, and Simon, listed two places in the New Testament (Matthew 13:55 and Mark 6:3). James had heard of the Talpiot Jesus tomb when it received a brief bit of publicity in 1996 in the BBC Easter documentary but he had not paid it much attention. He had gotten interested in ancient Jerusalem tombs and their ossuaries in 2000 when he and Shimon had accidentally stumbled upon a freshly robbed burial cave in the Hinnom Valley, just south of the Old City, now known as the "tomb of the Shroud."[2]

Simcha had produced a documentary for Discovery television in 2003 titled *James Brother of Jesus*, which focused on an ossuary that had surfaced in 2001 in the hands of an Israeli antiquities collector. Inscribed "James son of Joseph brother of Jesus," it had caused a sensation. For Simcha, who had won Emmy Awards for a variety of documentaries on diverse subjects, this represented a foray into new territory—biblical archaeology. Hershel Shanks, editor of the *Biblical Archaeology Review*, had published the news of the find in November 2002.[3] The ossuary was put on display in Toronto at the Royal Ontario Museum, where tens of thousands of visitors had viewed it and scholars caught their first glimpse of the actual artifact. Academic experts were divided over whether it might have been the burial box of James, the brother of Jesus of Nazareth. Some were quite excited about the discovery, while others suspected that the owner, in order to connect it to Jesus and make it more valuable, might have forged the portion of the inscription reading "brother of Jesus."[4] If authentically linked to Jesus of Nazareth the ossuary inscription would represent the first ar-

12. The James ossuary on display in Toronto with the academic experts gathered.

chaeological evidence ever found that mentions Jesus and his brother by name. As such it would be priceless. When Simcha began work on that project, invited by Shanks to produce a documentary on the find, Simcha did not even know what an ossuary was, or, like so many others, that Jesus even had a brother named James.

In the course of his work on the James ossuary film, Simcha learned about the existence of the 1980 "Jesus tomb" from the excavator Amos Kloner himself. He was interviewing Kloner at the IAA warehouse when Kloner asked him facetiously, "Why are you so interested in an ossuary that might belong to Jesus' brother when there is one inscribed 'Jesus son of Joseph' found in a tomb in 1980 along with five other names associated with Jesus and his family? Wouldn't you be more interested in the real thing?" Simcha could hardly believe his ears. Kloner quickly assured him he was only teasing him a bit and that these names, Jesus, Joseph, and Mary, are so common in tombs of this period that it would be foolish for anyone to conclude this particular one had any association with Jesus of Nazareth. Simcha was intrigued and wanted to know more. He was not so sure that the tomb's contents should have been so easily dismissed.

Simcha arranged to examine and film the ossuaries from the Jesus tomb, along with their tantalizing set of inscribed names. Of the six ossuaries from the Jesus tomb, all but two had been cleaned and put on display at one time or another. Fortunately, two of them, the ones inscribed "Jesus son of Joseph" and "Miriam Mara," had never undergone any cleaning. Simcha and his team were amazed to see fragmentary bone samples left inside both of them—more than enough for DNA testing.

In that initial telephone conversation in October 2003, Simcha told James about the bone samples. James stopped him in mid-sentence. Even the possibility that skeletal remains of this particular "Jesus" could be DNA tested, whether he could be identified decisively with Jesus of Nazareth or not, was an amazing turn of events since it was assumed that all the bones from that tomb had long ago been lost or reburied by the Orthodox religious authorities. James and Shimon Gibson had already done DNA samples on the bones found in their "Shroud tomb" so James was familiar with the procedures. He offered to send these two samples from the Jesus tomb to Professor Carney Matheson at the Paleo-DNA Laboratory at Lakehead University in Ontario. Matheson was the same researcher that James and Shimon had used back in 2000.[5] Simcha shipped the bone samples to James, who had them tested. The results of those DNA tests are revealed in our final chapter.

By late 2004 Simcha had begun to assemble his team for an investigative documentary on the "Jesus tomb" that would thoroughly reevaluate the tomb and its contents. How common were the names—particularly as a six-name cluster from a single tomb? Was there a solid statistical answer to the probability these particular names would be found in a single tomb? Could the DNA tests tell us anything? What historical evidence was there for Jesus being married with a child? What about the provenance of the James ossuary—might it have been looted from the Jesus tomb? The owner of the James ossuary, Oded Golan, had claimed that he had acquired it sometime around 1980— the same time the Talpiot "Jesus tomb" had been discovered.[6] Finally, could the tomb be reentered—if not physically then perhaps through some kind of remote camera probe inserted through the ritual vent pipes? These avenues of investigation had never been pursued by any- one.

Simcha's initial "tomb team" consisted of Felix Golubev, Simcha's right-hand man on many of his film projects, and Charles Pellegrino, an author and scientist with a fascination with ancient archaeology who was coauthoring a book with Simcha on the Jesus tomb investi- gation.[7] Pellegrino subsequently interested his friend James Cameron, the filmmaker of *Titanic* and *Avatar* fame, in joining the group as ex- ecutive producer on the film.[8]

James and Simcha met face-to-face for the first time in April 2005 in Toronto. On that visit Simcha invited James to officially join the "tomb team" as an academic consultant. After hearing Simcha explain his plans to carry out a thorough scientific investigation of the tomb, James could not resist.[9]

At that initial Toronto meeting Simcha dropped what he called his "bombshell" on James, and James in turn let Simcha in on his most recent investigation involving the rareness of the names on the six ossuaries in the Jesus tomb.

One of Simcha's researchers had discovered that according to Harvard professor François Bovon, the unusual form of the name Mariam, which in Greek is written *Mariamene* is the *precise* form of the name used to refer to Mary Magdalene in a 4th century CE Greek copy of the *Acts of Philip*, where she is also called an apostle.[10] The more common form of this name in Greek is *Mariam* or *Mariame*, or even *Maria*—whereas the form *Mariamene*, spelled with the letter "n" or *nu* in Greek, is rare. This was indeed new information to James and its stunning implications began to dawn on him. If it could be shown that the "Jesus son of Joseph" buried in this tomb *was* Jesus of

Nazareth, it would follow that buried with him was his child named Judah and most likely the child's mother—Mariamene. The second part of her inscription—*Mara*—seemed to support this possibility since it is the feminine form of *Mar,* which in Aramaic means "Lord" or "Master."[11] This would mean that the Mariamene in this tomb was being given an honorific title as Jesus' consort, just as Jesus himself was called *Mar,* "Lord," the masculine form of the title. *Mara* is impossible to translate into English since we don't commonly use the term "Lordess." Perhaps the English title "Lady" is a rough equivalent.

James's instinct was to resist the sensational. After all, Dan Brown's novel *The Da Vinci Code,* published the year before, postulated that Jesus and Mary Magdalene were married and had a child. Like most scholars in his field James held the view that there was no historical evidence to support this idea and he was cautious about participating in any kind of sensationalism of this sort. Surely if Jesus had been married or had children, James had thought, some evidence would have survived in our early sources. The gospels and the rest of the New Testament are silent on this subject—or at least that was James's assumption at the time. As we will see, that particular silence is ironically quite deafening. Sometimes new evidence causes one to see things that were there all the time but were unnoticed.

James then revealed his surprise to Simcha. He had been doing extensive research on the brothers of Jesus for his book *The Jesus Dynasty.* He had noticed that Mark had used a rare nickname *Joses* for the second brother, Joseph (compare Mark 6:3 with Matthew 13:55). That form of the name in Greek is the equivalent to the nickname *Yoseh* in Hebrew. James had noticed that this precise nickname was on one of the six inscribed ossuaries in the Jesus tomb. As far as James had determined, this particular form of the common name Joseph was so rare that of the dozens of ossuaries inscribed with the various forms of the name Joseph, either in Hebrew or in Greek, this was the only one with the Hebrew form *Yoseh.* Of course the fact that Mark uses this form of the name does not prove that the Yoseh in the tomb was Jesus' brother, but along with *Mariamene Mara*, such rare forms of these otherwise common names (Mary and Joseph) affect the odds of their occurring in a cluster with the name Jesus son of Joseph.

FINDING THE JESUS TOMB—ALMOST

Later in 2005, when Simcha was able to meet the family that lived over the tomb and to have his team survey the physical situation, it seemed clear that a first step would be to drop a camera down one of the ritual vent pipes that run up from the tomb to the patio above—assuming the pipes would be clear and accommodate such an operation. That would allow them to film inside the tomb without the need to tunnel in from the basement below, a possibility that was fraught with difficulties—not the least of which would be the physical stability of the foundation of the building. Even such a simple plan was not so easily done. The owners of the condo unit had to agree but there was a further problem. Apparently the patio with the vent pipes off the condo unit was considered common property, so the condo association for the whole building might have to get involved. Also, the Jewish family that owned the condo was Orthodox and they insisted that once the initial camera probe was done, should anything further be attempted Simcha must get official rabbinic approval from the ultra-Orthodox authorities that claimed the right to safeguard the sanctity of any Jewish tomb. Simcha agreed and the plan for the remote camera was set in motion.

Getting the hundred-thousand-dollar camera down a six-inch pipe turned out to be quite a challenge. One pipe led nowhere, stopping far short of the tomb. The second pipe looked more promising but had some blockage about thirteen feet down. Simcha's team had to call a plumber, who was able to clear it after much effort.

On Friday, September 16, 2005, the camera was dropped down the pipe and into the tomb eighteen feet below. Simcha remembers it as a surreal experience, as if one were passing from one reality to another, separated by two thousand years. Suddenly Simcha and his team received a shock. Peering at the small camera monitors they realized they were not inside an excavated empty tomb but quite the opposite. They could hardly believe their eyes. The tomb was *intact*— with ossuaries still inside the lovely carved gabled burial niches on three sides! This tomb did not match the map of the Jesus tomb that Gibson had made in 1980. What's more, the entrance to the tomb was completely sealed, whereas the Jesus tomb had been left open. They could clearly see the tightly fitted stone blocking the ancient entrance from inside the tomb. Since they knew that the Jesus tomb had been excavated and left empty and open in 1980 by the archaeologists, the conclusion was obvious: The tomb under the patio could not be the Jesus tomb, even though it seemed to be the right location in East Talpiot.

When it comes to discoveries and investigations there seems to be a mysterious truism at work. What one most expects to find seldom turns up and what is least expected or even overlooked often turns out to be highly significant. Even before the Patio tomb camera probe, Felix Golubev, Simcha's associate, had noted in the IAA files a reference to *two* tombs in the Dov Gruner Street area: the Jesus tomb that we thought we had located and a second tomb about two hundred feet to the north. We were so certain that we had located the Jesus tomb below the patio marked by the ritual vent pipes that we had not focused on the second tomb. We subsequently learned that the Patio tomb had been exposed in 1981 and briefly examined, but left unexcavated—so we knew this was the tomb we were looking at. Now we knew that there were two Talpiot tombs. Our investigation had widened considerably.

Amos Kloner, who had supervised the discovery of both tombs for the IAA, had noted that two of the ossuaries in the Patio tomb had Greek names inscribed.[12] As Simcha reviewed the film footage from inside the Patio tomb he began to realize the awesome implications of our mistake. We were filming inside a sealed 1st century tomb from the time of Jesus—something that had never been done before. Moreover, it was not just any tomb but one located yards away from the so-called Jesus tomb. What if the two tombs were related and this second tomb could eventually be explored? Imagine the possibilities of reading the two inscriptions and perhaps finding others, not to mention anything else that might still be sealed inside. But for now the business at hand was to find the Jesus tomb and determine if it was still intact and accessible after twenty-five years.

Simcha located the engineer who had supervised the construction of the condominium in the 1980s, Ephraim Shohat, and brought him to the site. He clearly remembered both tombs. Shohat confirmed that the first tomb, the one that had the Jesus family inscriptions, was free and clear of buildings and was left intact in one of the terraces constructed between the buildings, while the other, the Patio tomb, was indeed under one of the condo buildings with ritual vent pipes running down to the tomb below. As Shohat and Simcha's team wandered the areas between the buildings, curious neighbors began to gather offering various opinions as to the location of the tomb. After getting his bearings, Simcha pointed to a five-by-five-foot cement slab covering a raised rectangular area alongside the sidewalk in one of the terraced gardens. At that moment a local resident, a blind woman, walked by, asked what they were looking for, and put her hand on that very cement slab, declaring, "The tomb is here." She had lived there since the 1980s and remembered that the tomb had been initially left open but was later covered by residents to prevent kids from climbing in and out and possibly getting hurt.

ENTERING THE JESUS TOMB

Simcha's team wasted no time. On Sunday, September 18, 2005, they broke the seal on the concrete cover over the Garden tomb and slid it aside, exposing a cavity about twelve feet deep directly in front of the open entrance to the tomb. There was no doubt they were at the right spot. The distinctively carved chevron façade on the face of the tomb was clearly visible. In seconds they were inside. To their amazement the tomb was not empty. There were no ossuaries but the entire tomb was filled to a depth of several feet with decaying books, pamphlets, and loose manuscript pages. The tomb had become a *genizah,* a depository for old and worn-out holy texts that Jewish law requires not be thrown away but be properly "buried," in keeping with their holiness. Apparently the local rabbinic authorities had used the tomb for this purpose before it was finally sealed with the concrete slab.

Simcha got Shimon Gibson on the phone, explained to him that the Patio tomb was the wrong location, and invited him to come take a look. Simcha wanted to film Shimon and get his thoughts and recollections right at the scene, inside the tomb, since he had been involved in the 1980 excavation. In the meantime all hell broke loose outside the tomb above. Some tenants had called the police saying the film crew had no permission to remove the slab cover and were trespass-

13. The Garden tomb close-up, covered with a concrete slab.

ing on private property, while others, including the blind woman and some of her fellow residents, insisted it was common property and had been left open for years after the excavation by the IAA. A shouting match ensued. The police arrived but refused to take sides and insisted on order. By the time Shimon arrived there was a semblance of a truce. Simcha had promised to donate some funds for a swing set for the kids in the garden and to seal up the tomb again once the filming was complete. Shimon was hesitant to go inside the tomb since he was not clear who had sealed it up—the IAA or the residents. He called someone at the IAA, described the situation, and was told it was all right to enter a tomb that had already been excavated. There are hundreds of such ancient tombs all around Jerusalem, left open once their contents have been removed. For Shimon it was a trip back to his past. He was only twenty-one years old when the tomb was discovered and was just beginning his career in archaeology. He crawled into the tomb with Simcha and revisited on camera his memories of the tomb after twenty-five years. While they were inside filming another ruckus broke out. A local resident who happened to work for the IAA and lived across from the tomb showed up. She had heard the commotion and shouting. She made a call to the IAA and apparently got someone else who did not understand the situation. She told the official that a film crew was violating an ancient tomb without permission. He told her to tell them they were violating the law and would be arrested unless they ceased their activities immediately, exited the tomb, and resealed it. Simcha decided to comply, even though he was quite certain that an excavated tomb, left open by the IAA and subsequently covered over by the condo residents for safety reasons, could not be illegal to enter. That would be a battle for another day. The team had succeeded beyond anything they could have imagined for a weekend's activity. Not only had they entered the Jesus tomb but also they had peered into the nearby sealed tomb through a camera. They had confirmed there were two tombs, in very close proximity to one another, the second still intact. This was by any measure a successful first step.

THE WORLD REACTS

Simcha's film, *The Lost Tomb of Jesus*, aired on the Discovery Channel on March 4, 2007.[13] It was preceded by a press conference in the New York Public Library with over 350 journalists from all over the world in attendance. The ossuaries inscribed "Jesus son of Joseph" and "Mariamene Mara" had been flown in from Israel for the occasion. Although the two-hour documentary included the brief camera probe of the Patio tomb nearby, its focus was on the Jesus tomb and its thesis was the likelihood that the family tomb of Jesus of Nazareth had been discovered in 1980. The film covered all the evidence our investigation had generated at that time. This included a peer-reviewed statistical study by Dr. Andrey Feuerverger on the probabilities of the names on the ossuaries occurring in a cluster, the results of our DNA tests on the bones from the Jesus and Mariamene ossuaries, the historical evidence for Jesus and Mary Magdalene being husband and wife and bearing a child, and a scientific analysis of the patina surfaces of the ossuaries in the Jesus tomb with that of the James ossuary, which indicated that the James ossuary most likely was looted from the Jesus or Garden tomb.[14]

The evangelical Christian community mobilized a protest directed at the Discovery Channel demanding that the film not be shown again. Discovery received more than one and a half million e-mails from this irate constituency within twenty-four hours. Its switchboard was jammed with protesting phone calls for several days after the film aired. An orchestrated campaign directed toward the main advertisers supporting Discovery Channel programming quickly followed. As a result of this onslaught several major advertisers threatened not to advertise on Discovery if the show were ever aired again.

These Christians believed that it was impossible that Jesus' tomb could have been found, certainly not with his bones intact in an ossuary, since he had been raised physically from the dead and ascended to heaven. This is the standard interpretation among the evangelical Christian community: the resurrection of Jesus from the dead means his physical remains, flesh and bones, were taken to heaven. As we will see, Jesus' earliest followers had a different view. They understood Jesus' resurrection as a spiritual not a physical phenomenon. Since the airing of the controversial documentary there have been a half-dozen or more books and DVDs published by evangelical Christians seeking to refute the thesis of the film.[15]

At the same time, but for entirely different reasons, a cadre of historians and archaeologists weighed in through interviews, e-mails, and blog posts on the Internet, largely critical of the film and its thesis. They offered two main responses. First, that the names in the Garden tomb were so common in Jerusalem at that time that it was baseless speculation to identify this particular "Jesus son of Joseph" with Jesus of Nazareth. Second, that there was no reliable historical evidence supporting the thesis that Jesus had been married and had a child—so this particular Jesus could not be the one in the gospels.[16]

A CONFERENCE IN JERUSALEM

In January 2008, James Charlesworth of Princeton Theological Seminary convened a conference in Jerusalem attended by over fifty academics from around the world. The theme was "Jewish Views of the Afterlife and Burial Practices in Second Temple Judaism: Evaluating the Talpiot Tomb in Context." The gathering drew a who's who of experts from all relevant fields—archaeologists, historians, epigraphers, paleographers, DNA specialists, statisticians, and theologians. For four days the scholars listened to papers, participated in panels, and discussed, argued, and debated between sessions and after hours. Charlesworth's intent was to provide a proper academic forum for a thorough discussion of all the relevant issues that had been raised about the Garden tomb in Talpiot and its possible connection to Jesus of Nazareth and to publish an edited volume of papers based on the conference.[17] A final concluding panel summed things up. There was no consensus on many of the major issues but most participants were unconvinced a persuasive case for identity had yet been made.[18] Everyone did agree that there was a need for more evidence. At the end of the conference there was a unanimous vote calling for further investigation of the Garden tomb itself, and most important, if possible, an examination of the contents of the nearby Patio tomb. Simcha had shown the film footage from the Patio tomb that he had taken with the camera probe through the vent pipe. The audience was fascinated.

ACHIEVING THE NEAR IMPOSSIBLE

It might be possible to get permission to reexamine the Jesus tomb in the garden area since it had been cleared and left open in 1980 but the Patio tomb was a different matter. The IAA does not issue permits to excavate intact ancient tombs. Amos Kloner had tried to excavate the Patio tomb in 1981 with a valid permit, but the ultra-Orthodox showed up in protest and halted his efforts. Since 1981 Israeli laws had, if anything, become more stringent. The Israeli government had made agreements with the Orthodox that no intact tomb would be disturbed, out of reverence for the dead. Although Simcha had been able to drop a small camera into the tomb through the patio vent pipe and do some limited filming, he had no ability to maneuver the camera and get close to the ossuaries that were stored in the niches to examine them for inscriptions. The patio was located eighteen feet above the tomb and the condo building was covering the tomb itself. The tomb was thirty feet below the street level outside the building. The idea of tunneling under the building and breaking into a tomb carved out of bedrock was not only impractical but it would never be allowed by the municipal building authorities even in the unlikely event that the IAA gave permission. Besides, the ultra-Orthodox would muster thousands of protesters to stop any such effort and the condo association would surely step in and refuse to give permission for such a risky endeavor. The costs of such an effort would be enormous and there was no guarantee that the inscriptions or any other evidence inside the Patio tomb would have any relevance to the Jesus tomb nearby or have any significance themselves to justify such herculean efforts. It appeared that any further examination of the Patio tomb was a fool's dream.

Felix Golubev, Simcha's associate producer, thought otherwise. He had been mulling over the situation since 2005, when the first camera probe had been inserted in the vent pipe. He and his local Israeli associate, Meyer Bensimon, had gotten hold of the building plans for the condo and spent hours measuring floors and walls trying to determine just where the parameters of the tomb were in reference to the building and what would be the closest way to get in. Their only reference point was the vent pipe, which ran into the tomb. The camera footage showed approximately where in the tomb the vent entered. Felix and Meyer reported their results to Simcha. They came up with a brilliant but risky plan. They had figured out that the end of a narrow corridor in the basement storage area of the building was possibly just over the inside bedrock wall of the tomb. According to their calculations the tiled basement floor was just seven feet above the roof of the tomb itself. Felix's idea was to drill a series of eight-inch-diameter probe holes through the basement floor, down through the bedrock, and into the tomb. That would allow some kind of robotic arm to be inserted into the tomb, equipped with a camera on the end that could then perhaps be maneuvered around to reach all the ossuaries and examine them remotely.

It was a long shot. If their measurements were off by even a few inches, the drill might miss the tomb and hit the bedrock. But assuming they could get in, could anyone build a robotic arm that was sophisticated enough to be maneuvered remotely from above into a tomb barely four feet high and with the leverage to reach deep into the niches and film all around the ossuaries? They knew from the vent camera footage that several of the niches had two or more ossuaries pushed tightly together. There was no guarantee any kind of camera could get close enough and maneuver accurately enough to film all sides of the ossuaries, any of which might contain inscriptions.

Simcha and his team went to work on three fronts at once—commissioning the creation of a special robotic arm, getting the permission of the ultra-Orthodox, and convincing the condo owners' association to allow drilling in the narrow corridor of their basement storage area. Everything had to happen together or the whole operation could not take place. But prior to any of these efforts the IAA had to give some kind of permission: if not an excavation license, then perhaps permission to survey the site of the tomb in a noninvasive way. Simcha, who had moved to Israel from Canada in 2008, had already made some initial inquiries of Shuka Dorfman, head of the IAA, as to what would be required.[19] James would need the sponsorship of his university, the University of North Carolina at Charlotte, and since he is a historian and not an archaeologist, he would have to invite a qualified archaeologist to join him as well as have the endorsement of the anthropology department at his university. UNC Charlotte would also have to certify that proper funding was in place and that timely academic publication of the results would follow.

James invited Rami Arav, an Israeli archaeologist at the University of Nebraska at Omaha who has years of experience excavating at the ancient city of Bethsaida on the Sea of Galilee as well as experience with ancient tombs of this period. Rami enthusiastically agreed. James and Rami put together all their documentation for the license and submitted it to the IAA in July 2009. They asked for permission to "survey" both the Patio and the Garden tombs. To our surprise we were told that any license given would be an "excavation" license, even though we planned only to enter the Patio tomb via remote camera. Apparently it was the position of the IAA that both tombs had been exposed by construction work in the 1980s, so technically they had been previously authorized for excavation. Even though the excavation of the Patio tomb had not been completed, it was technically not a new or intact tomb—so its proper excavation could theoretically be completed. The license would also allow us to excavate further in the Jesus tomb if we saw the need, since it had been investigated in 1980 rather hastily, as a "rescue" dig. One additional caveat that the IAA stressed: any dealings with the ultra-Orthodox were our problem not the IAA's. We were of course elated that so far as the IAA was concerned, the extent of our exploration of either tomb was open to whatever circumstances we could work out.

In early August we heard that the internal IAA license committee had forwarded our license application to the Archaeological Council because of its unusual nature. The Archaeological Council is the highest advisory board to the director of the IAA. Its decision could make or break any request to excavate in Israel. Unfortunately, the council was not meeting until November. Time was ticking away.

The Archaeological Council approved the license on November 15, 2009. There was one catch. IAA licenses are issued annually, no matter what time of year one applies. Ours would expire on December 31, 2009—just six weeks from the date it was issued. It would of course be impossible to have everything ready by the end of the year; on top of that, James and Rami would not be free to come over to Israel until after December 15, when their university semesters ended. That would leave us only two weeks to work. We decided to go ahead with some preliminary work regardless and reapply for a renewal of the license for the entire year 2010.

In the meantime, Simcha had received permission from the condo association allowing us access to the property to do our measurements, and most important, to bring in a company that could run ground penetrating radar (GPR) along the corridor of the basement where we planned to drill the probe holes to access the tomb with the robotic arm and cameras. This amazing technology can produce

ISRAEL
ANTIQUITIES
AUTHORITY

רשות
העתיקות

License No. G-73/2009 to Conduct an Archaeological Excavation
In accordance with the Antiquities Law – 1978

Issued to
Arav Ram on behalf of University of North Carolina at Charlotte
Tabor James on behalf of University of North Carolina at Charlotte

And to:

University of North Carolina at Charlotte

To conduct an archaeological excavation at:

South West   North East
Long.   Lat.   Long. Lat.
222250-628800 222260-628900

These Areas are within the Site of
Jerusalem, Talpiot Mizrach (2917/0)
Jerusalem, Armon ha-Naziv (2918/0)

Maps :
102 : Jerusalem; 106 : Talpiot
This License is subject to the conditions and provisions detailed in the attached document, in
accordance with the Antiquities Law-1978 and the rules specified therein.

"The bearer of an excavation license shall, both during the excavation and thereafter, until the
expiration of the license, take all measures required –

(1) to ensure the well-being of the workers and visitors at the excavation site, including fencing
potentially dangerous areas.
(2) to protect and insure the preservation of the excavation site and the antiquities discovered therein.
(3) to prevent all damage or nuisance to neighbouring property".

This license is valid until
31/12/2009

Shuka Dorfman
Director,
Israel Antiquities Authority

14. Israel Antiquities Authority license to excavate both tombs.

images "underground" and detect voids. The GPR indicated there was a void just at the point we had identified by our measurements as our only option for drilling. It was an area less than three feet long and a foot wide. If we were correct the drill would drop into the tomb just inside its outer wall—but we would be inside!

The drilling itself would have to wait until 2010 and a renewal of our IAA license. In the meantime Simcha was working hard to come to an agreement with the ultra-Orthodox and the condo owners to allow for the actual penetration of the basement floor. Even though we had every expectation of receiving a renewal license for 2010, until we had it in hand we had no assurance that our project could move forward. Rami and James turned in a report to the IAA on our activities at the end of 2009 and on February 23, 2010, we had our new license in hand. This meant we had the rest of 2010 to complete our work.

THE DRILLING BEGINS

Our plan was to begin the drilling in early May. Meanwhile, in Toronto, Simcha and Felix had approached Walter Klassen, one of the best engineers in the business of constructing complex props and mechanical devices for movies.[20] When he heard what we needed, he was clearly intrigued but also recognized the incredibly difficult challenges inherent in the task. He was willing to try. He would have to custom-build a robotic probe that could drop down through an eight-inch drill hole into the tomb, then expand with a controllable arm that had enough leverage to mount a high-resolution camera on the end. It would have to reach anywhere inside the 11.5 by 11.5 foot tomb that was just under four feet deep from ceiling to floor. The real challenge, assuming that could be done, was to construct a secondary extension arm that could reach at least six more feet into the niches with a snake camera in order to examine all sides of the ossuaries. Walter was fairly certain he could have at least a prototype of the ro-

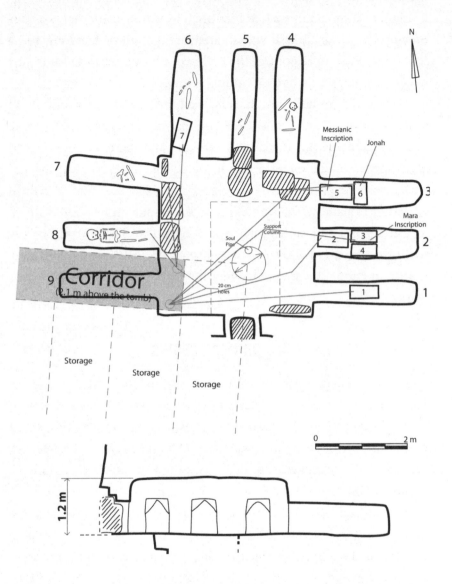

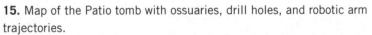

15. Map of the Patio tomb with ossuaries, drill holes, and robotic arm trajectories.

botic arm done by May to test its main capabilities in the tomb itself, as well as obtain further measurements from inside.

As May arrived things were coming together. Simcha had worked out a formal legal agreement with the condo owners. He had met with Rabbi David Schmidl, whose permission we would need to enter the tomb without objection from the Orthodox. Then we met a snag.

Rabbi Schmidl was willing to agree to the camera probe so long as it did not touch or move anything, but he was adamant that nothing be taken out or disturbed. Klassen was planning to equip his robotic arm not only to hook and grab any small artifacts, coins, or other items we might discover and want to remove, but to give it the ability, using an inflatable bladder, to slightly move the ossuaries that were jammed up against one another. This might be the only way they could be examined for inscriptions. Rabbi Schmidl was unbending. Unless we agreed, the whole thing was off. He also insisted that his representatives be on site at all times observing our actions. We decided to go along with his restrictions even though our license allowed us much more, including physical entry into the tomb if need be. We intended to play by the rules. This was a first step, to explore and take a look—if we could even get in—and that was still a big if. Based on Kloner's original report we knew there were at least two Greek inscriptions in the tomb. If we could shed further light on the Jesus family tomb nearby then any effort we made was more than justified.

The drilling began the first week of May 2010. The drill crew used specially constructed diamond drill bits that Felix had had made for our specific purposes. Bill Tarant, who worked for General Electric, joined the expedition, bringing a much better camera than we had had in 2005. The drilling went on for a few days with stops and starts. On Thursday, May 6, Simcha called James to report the exciting news—they had gotten into the tomb and dropped a small camera inside. The view was spectacular, with much more clarity and maneu-

16. The initial drilling of the probe holes in the corridor basement floor.

verability than in 2005. All the measurements and calculations had proven accurate. James booked a flight that evening and was on his way to Israel the next morning.

The team spent the week surveying and measuring the tomb with a preliminary look at the seven ossuaries inside. All but two were elaborately decorated and painted with lovely carved rosette designs and borders. The nine niches were skillfully carved with gabled tops and the stones that once blocked them were still intact. The seven ossuaries were distributed in four of the niches; the other five held human bones that were never gathered for secondary burial. Those bones suggested that the tomb had been used up to the Roman siege of Jerusalem in 68 CE. Most likely the family that owned the tomb never returned to gather the bones of their dead and put them in ossuaries before the

17. First view of a previously unseen ossuary in niche one, blocking stone at the side.

Romans destroyed the city and killed or exiled them with the rest of the population.

As we peered through our monitors, watching the camera on the end of the prototype robotic arm sweep flawlessly around the tomb, our excitement mounted. The laser feature of the camera had gathered the precise data that Walter needed in order to complete the full version of the robotic probe. As we packed up that day we felt a sense of awe about where we were and what we were now poised to do. We were unseen visitors of the present remotely entering the past—to 68 CE when the tomb had been left sealed and the generation who knew Jesus had scattered. We agreed that the last week in June we would return to the tomb with Walter and his fully constructed robotic arm. Then the real search for ossuary inscriptions could begin.

A BREAKTHROUGH DISCOVERY

On Sunday, June 27, 2010, our entire team gathered in Jerusalem—
Rami Arav, our archaeologist and codirector of the "excavation";
Bill Tarant, with a set of sophisticated cameras donated by GE; Felix
Goluber and Meyer Bensimon, who had worked out all the measurements; the film crew; security police; a representative from the IAA;
a couple of Rabbi Schmidl's assistants; and most important, Walter
Klassen with his final version of the robotic arm. The feeling of an-
ticipation was intense. Our team bonded together as our work pro-
gressed and Rabbi Schmidl's representatives were genuinely drawn to
our project and its fascinating scientific value.

We decided to explore the tomb systematically, niche by niche,
working counterclockwise from the sealed entrance. Once inserted,
the robotic arm worked beautifully. There were a few bugs to work
out but Walter had the equipment with him to make necessary altera-
tions as we went along. Several times in the days to follow he pulled

18. The entire team gathered outside the basement area of the condominium.

his robotic arm completely out of the tomb and made adjustments. Other times he had to clean the lens of the camera when it hit the walls of the tomb or picked up soil from the floor. The whole apparatus broke down once after one of the pulley cords had gotten tangled. Our hearts sank, contemplating the possibility the entire operation would have to be given up. For a tense couple of hours Walter was not sure he could retract the robotic arm. He was finally successful and we were back in business. We breathed a collective sigh of relief.

Walter was hoping that the extension he had installed on the end of the robotic arm with its snake camera and light would be able to reach all the ossuaries for close examination, including several that were the farthest from the drill holes and pushed deep into the niches. Every minute was filmed in real time for the record. Inscriptions can show up on any surface of a four-sided ossuary, even on the lid, so every inch had to be carefully examined. The inscriptions are easy to miss. Some are deeply chiseled and obvious but they are more often informal and sometimes faint.

19. Walter preparing the robotic arm for insertion into the tomb.

The first niche contained ossuary 1, one of the most beautiful and elaborately decorated ossuaries we had ever seen, but there were no inscriptions. We had a moment of passing excitement when it appeared that there might be some defaced letters on its lower front, but closer examination showed them to be random scratches. Our first surprise came in the second niche, which held three ossuaries. Ossuary 2 had a strange symbol on its front that looked at first glance like a four-legged, stick-figure animal of some sort. Since Jews in this period were forbidden to put animal or human images on their ossuaries, based on the commandment to avoid graven images, James suggested the symbol might be the name Yahweh written in stylized Hebrew—the letters Yod, Heh, Vav, Heh. That possibility would be quite significant since writing the sacred name of God—the Tetragrammaton—was forbidden. Was it possible the family that buried their dead in this tomb would dare such a heretical action? There is surely no other

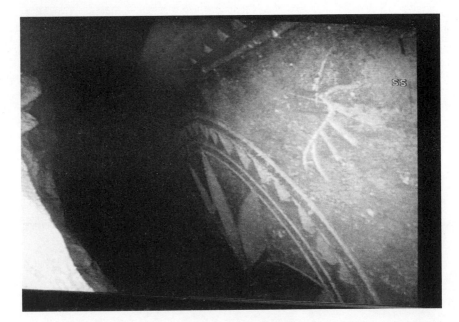

20. The mysterious symbol on the front of ossuary 2.

21. The faint MARA inscription in Greek on ossuary no. 3, inked in for clarity.

such example of something like this mysterious symbol, whatever it was, on any of the 600 inscribed ossuaries that are known.

As we moved along to ossuary 3, a gasp went up in the cramped corridor. As we stared into the monitors, we began to see the faded Greek letters *MARA* etched faintly into the end facing us, just above an incomplete rosette marking. *Mara* is the feminine form of *Mar* in Aramaic, which means "Lord" or "Master," as explained in the previous chapter. It occurs on only four other ossuaries from the period, one of them just two-hundred feet away—in the Jesus tomb—where we have *Mariamene Mara*. We were amazed. To find a *Mara* at all would be extraordinary, but that it was just a stone's throw from the ossuary in the Jesus tomb seemed to us beyond chance or coincidence. This was our first indication that maybe the two tombs were related in content, not just in proximity.

On Monday, June 28, we continued our camera exploration of the second niche with its three ossuaries, including number 4, jammed close up against number 3 with the *Mara* inscription. Our snakelike camera moved slowly all around each ossuary. On the back of ossuary 4 we thought we could barely see the outlines of some faint Greek lettering—it looked like a name, maybe the letters *ION* or *IOM* but we could not get close enough or get the right light and angle to see more. Kloner had mentioned seeing two Greek words or names in his quick 1981 foray into the tomb. We had found one—*Mara.* This seemed to be the second. We are still not sure what the name might be on the far end of ossuary 4—maybe *IONAS* (Jonah), *IONES* (John), or maybe even *IOULIA* (Julia). We later found a faint black-and-white photo in the IAA archives of this ossuary that Kloner had taken in the dim light in 1981, when he hastily photographed the seven ossuaries in their original positions. You can clearly see that there are Greek letters on the end that we were trying to reach, but they are impossible to make out—even with attempts to enhance the old photograph. We also began to realize, in comparing Kloner's 1981 photos of the four niches that contained the ossuaries with their present placement, that they had been moved. This fits with the narrative we had reconstructed of the discovery of the tomb in April 1981. Kloner's IAA assistants had moved all the ossuaries out of the niches, and even chalk-marked them inside in numerical order, 1 through 7. Although we were not allowed to move anything in the tomb, not even a hair's breadth, one of the lids of Kloner's ossuary 5 was ajar and we could actually peer inside with our cameras and see bones. The circled chalk mark "5" was still visible inside the bone box.

Our third day, Wednesday, June 29, was devoted to niche 3, which held two ossuaries (nos. 5 and 6) perpendicular to one another but jammed very closely together. About midmorning the big surprise came. Suddenly we all shouted in unison to Walter, who was maneuvering the robotic arm, "Wait, wait, stop there!" "Back, back, back!" "Hold it, right there!" We were staring at the strangest thing we had ever seen on any ossuary. We began to examine it from every angle. It was definitely an image—but of what? At first Rami thought it might be the prow of a boat, as we did not yet have the complete image in view. He then suggested a vase or amphora with handles, examples of which are known on other decorated ossuaries.[21] Rami began quickly sketching what he saw, trying to make sense of it as we all hovered close to the camera monitors. Finally Rami suggested it was some kind of tower. Jewish ossuaries sometimes have images of pillar-shaped funerary monuments carved on them, called *nephesh* in Hebrew.[22]

As Walter brought the whole image into focus it suddenly dawned on us what we were seeing. It was not a vase, or a boat, or a tower. It was a big fish. There was no doubt about it. But it was not just a large fish. There was also a small, stick figure coming out of its mouth. Everyone was shouting, "It's a fish!" and someone pointed to the two little flippers on each side. It took us about thirty seconds to process what we were seeing but it was unmistakable. "It's Jonah and the big fish!" We were certain of it. The fish was spitting out the human figure onto the carved border at the bottom of the ossuary, which seemed to represent land. But what would an image of Jonah and the fish be doing on an ossuary? First, Jews do not normally put such pictorial representations on their ossuaries in this period—whether animals or humans. Jews of course know the story of Jonah, since a book of the Hebrew Bible or Old Testament bearing his name relates his strange tale of being swallowed and vomited out alive by a large fish (not a whale) in the Mediterranean Sea. But to draw such an image was to risk breaking one of the Ten Commandments—that one make no "graven image," including anything "that is in the water" (Exodus 20:4). Yet for one special group, this particular image took on enormous significance, so much so that they permitted its use. For the earliest followers of Jesus, who were for the most part Jewish, Jonah came to symbolize something central to their faith, based on the mysterious saying of Jesus about the "sign of Jonah."

We had not yet examined ossuary 5, which was blocking the Jonah ossuary, but we turned to it next. It had two highly decorated rosettes with elaborate borders, similar to several others we had already examined in the tomb. As our camera passed along its façade another shout went up. "Stop! Hold it there!" we shouted to Walter and Bill. We could see clearly a four-line Greek inscription coming into focus. Names may occur with some frequency on ossuaries, but something like this, an epigram carrying some kind of message, was extremely rare. James began to sketch the letters. For the most part they were clearly written. The inscription seemed to say something like "*The Divine Jehovah raises up . . .*" We could not immediately make out the final word but we knew the verb "to raise up" was often used for resurrection of the dead or exaltation to heaven. Was this some kind of ancient affirmation of resurrection of the dead? Or a reference to someone being raised up to heaven? The possibility was intriguing. Next to the Jonah image it seemed not only possible, but even likely. We kept telling ourselves none of this should exist, not in a 1st century Jewish tomb, on the side of an ossuary, where neither images nor epigrams of this type ever occur.

The following day we called in Professor James Charlesworth, an expert in Greek and early Christianity, who was in Jerusalem doing research on the Dead Sea Scrolls. After reinserting the robotic arm and swinging the camera once again over to the third niche, we showed him what we had discovered: first the inscription, then the image. He immediately and independently offered the same interpretation we had come to the day before. He excitedly sight-read the inscription. "*The Divine Jehovah raises up from* [the dead]." He also offered without hesitation the same interpretation of the fish. What we are looking at, he said, appears to be the earliest representation from Jesus' followers of their faith in his resurrection of the dead. A quiet shudder went through the room as the implications of his conclusion sunk in. It was not only what we were seeing, but *where* we were seeing it—peering into a sealed 1st century tomb not two hundred feet from one that could arguably be that of Jesus and his family.

In the next chapter we will explore what the gospels call the mysterious "sign of Jonah" and its implications alongside an inscription affirming one being raised from the grave. As we packed up that evening, it was hard to fully absorb what we had seen. Was it possible that these tombs in East Talpiot offered us the first archaeological evidence of Jesus, his family, and the faith of his followers in his resurrection?

CHAPTER THREE

DECODING THE MYSTERIOUS SIGN OF JONAH

According to our earliest gospel sources, Jesus often spoke in code. Everyone has heard of the "parables" of Jesus but the word *parabole* in Greek literally means to "lay alongside." The idea is that one uses a symbolic term or story, *laying alongside* the real meaning—both obscuring it and revealing it at the same time. In other words, the "sign" is not the thing itself, but a kind of code or riddle for the concealed or secret meaning.

Our earliest New Testament gospel is Mark. Although it follows Matthew in the New Testament we use today, scholars are convinced it was our first written gospel, dated before Matthew, Luke, or John.[1] It represents our earliest version of the "story" of Jesus, a narrative account of his preaching and healing that culminates in his execution by crucifixion. Early in Mark's narrative Jesus explains his use of parables, shocking his listeners with his forthright declaration that he is *purposely* obscuring his meaning so that people would not understand:

And when he was alone, those who were about him with the twelve asked him concerning the parables. And he said to them, "To you has been given the secret of the kingdom of God, but for those outside everything is in parables; so that they may indeed see but not perceive, and may indeed hear but not understand; lest they should turn again, and be forgiven." (Mark 4:10–12)[2]

This is surely a contrast to the normal Sunday school approach to the parables of Jesus, which asserts that Jesus told his parables in order to help people understand. Here Jesus says just the opposite. The parables are riddles that only those whom God chooses can understand. To the rest, called "outsiders," the parable, sign, or symbol is intended to obscure, not reveal, the true meaning.

Often when Jesus would offer one of his riddles he would end with the admonition, "Let the one who has ears to hear, hear!"[3] The idea is that some who hear will understand the secret meaning, while others will "hear" the words but not comprehend their message.

Over one hundred and fifty years ago scholars in Germany identified a lost gospel.[4] Its discovery results from an amazing bit of textual sleuthing. In terms of biblical studies it is one of the greatest discoveries of modern times, but few outside academic circles have heard of it. Scholars refer to this "gospel" as Q, short for the German word *Quelle,* meaning "source." It was not found in a cave or buried in a clay jar, as were the Dead Sea Scrolls and the lost Gospel of Thomas. It is embedded in the New Testament gospels of Matthew and Luke. In other words it had been there all along, hidden away for centuries, but no one had noticed it.

Mark wrote first and Matthew and Luke drew upon Mark as their basic narrative source. In other words, Mark provides the storyline and structure for both these subsequent works. Some scholars even call Matthew and Luke "rewritten Mark," much the way one might publish a subsequent edition of a work with revisions, changes, and additions. Besides using Mark, Matthew and Luke had access to this older source we call Q. By extracting from Matthew and Luke the material that they have in common, that is not in Mark, we are able to reconstruct this lost gospel source with a reasonable degree of certainty.[5] Q turns out to be an early collection of the sayings and deeds of Jesus that predates even Mark. It is not a narrative or story but primarily a collection of Jesus' teachings and deeds. Many scholars consider it to be a lost gospel of Jewish Christianity, uninfluenced by later Gentile Christian developments.[6] It is usually thought to date to about 50 CE—just twenty years after Jesus' death.

Recovering Q has allowed us to go behind the gospels as they now stand and see an earlier time when the Jesus movement was young and first developing in Galilee and Jerusalem. Q predates Paul and all the theological changes that developed as a result of his mission work to non-Jews in Asia Minor, Greece, and Rome. Q is about 350 lines and contains approximately fifty separate "teachings" of Jesus. It would have fit on a roll of papyri or parchment much like some of the Dead Sea Scrolls that come from the same period. For our recent discovery in the Talpiot Patio tomb the lost gospel source of Q turns out to be critical, for it is in Q that we learn one of the earliest interpretations of the mysterious "sign of Jonah," attributed directly to Jesus.

In both Mark and Q we have accounts of the enemies of Jesus asking him to give them a "sign" in order to test him—was he the "son of David" or not (Matthew 12:23)? The phrase "son of David" is code for the expected king or Messiah, who was to be a descendant of the ancient king David and would appear in the last days to establish the kingdom of God.[7] These enemies had seen Jesus' healings and exorcisms but were not convinced, charging that he performed these wondrous deeds through magical powers from Beelzebul—the prince of demons (Mark 3:22; Matthew 12:23–24; Luke 11:15).

In Mark's gospel, when these enemies demand a sign, Jesus' reply is stark and abrupt: "Truly I say to you, no sign shall be given to this generation" (Mark 8:12). As outsiders they are simply dismissed. Matthew knows this tradition about no sign and repeats it when he is following Mark as his narrative source (Matthew 16:4). However, he, like Luke, has the second source—Q. It is in this older source that we can glimpse the traditions that circulated among Jesus' earliest followers who still lived in the land of Israel, some of whom would have heard him preach and teach.

The Q source records a similar scene in which Jesus' enemies taunt him for a sign, but his response is quite different from Mark's tradition. Rather than say "no sign will be given," as he does in Mark, Jesus in Q speaks in a riddle. It is clear that Mark, writing many decades later, probably from Rome, has no access to this tradition. In Q Jesus tells the crowds that were flocking around him: "This generation is an evil generation: it seeks a sign; but no sign shall be given to it except the sign of Jonah" (Luke 11:29). This is our earliest reference to the mysterious "sign of Jonah." The Greek word for "sign" used here is *semeion.* It is related to our English term *semantics,* which refers to the ways in which words *signify* ("sign") meaning. Here in Luke's version of Q the "sign" is not explained, but in Matthew's parallel version we read its interpretation: ". . . but no sign shall be given to it except the sign of the prophet Jonah, for as Jonah was three days and three nights in the belly of the great fish, so will the Son of man be three days and three nights in the heart of the earth" (Matthew 12:40).

This is quite extraordinary, since it is the *only* sign Jesus says he will give to his generation, preserved for us in this earliest gospel source Q. Matthew is, of course, writing long after Jesus had died, been buried, and—according to the faith of his followers—been raised from the dead. What he offers his readers here is a clear interpretation of the sign of Jonah—namely that Jesus would be three days and three nights in the tomb. The sign of Jonah has to do with faith in

Jesus' resurrection and this is how it has been interpreted throughout Christian tradition.

It is rare to find contemporary archaeological evidence related to a saying of any ancient figure, much less Jesus. Most of what we know of the teachings of Socrates or Plato or the ancient rabbis comes to us from copies of manuscripts dating as late as the Middle Ages. Even in the case of Jesus, our first complete copies of the New Testament gospels date to the time of Constantine in the 4th century CE. Our discovery in the Patio tomb is unprecedented in that it reflects one of the earliest sayings of Jesus, preserved in Q, contemporary to the generation that saw him and heard him teach.

WHY JONAH AS A SIGN?

The biblical story of Jonah and the great fish, often a favorite in children's Bible storybooks, is preserved in the Hebrew Bible or Old Testament in the book of Jonah—one of the Hebrew prophets. God tells Jonah to go to the great city of Nineveh, the capital of ancient Assyria, and call upon the people to repent of their sins or face destruction. Jonah refuses to obey God. He flees on a ship from Israel's Mediterranean coastline, headed for Tarshish, a coastal city in Spain—as far west as one could go. A mighty storm erupts, threatening to break up the ship and take it under. Everyone is praying to their gods and Jonah finally confesses his sin to the crew. He tells them that he is a Hebrew, fleeing from Jehovah his God, refusing to do his bidding. At his request they throw him overboard as a scapegoat, hoping the Hebrew God would turn his wrath away. Immediately the sea becomes calm. Then we read: "And the LORD appointed a great fish to swallow up Jonah; and Jonah was in the belly of the fish three days and three nights" (Jonah 1:17).

Jonah prays fervently from the belly of the fish that threatens to become his living tomb. God hears his prayer and causes the fish to vomit Jonah out onto dry land. The words of Jonah's prayer of thanksgiving show that the belly of the fish represents entering Sheol, the underworld of death in Hebrew:

> I called to the LORD, out of my distress, and he answered me; out of the belly of Sheol. I cried, and thou didst hear my voice . . . The waters closed in over me, the deep was round about me, weeds were wrapped about my head . . . I went down to the land whose bars closed upon me forever; yet thou didst bring up my life from the Pit, O LORD my God (Jonah 2:2, 5–6).

Jonah's language here about going down through the gates of death and then being lifted back to life becomes a perfect model for the notion of resurrection from the dead. The story is all the more fitting as appropriated by the Q source since Jesus, according to this tradition, spent three days and three nights in the tomb and then was raised from the dead.[8]

One might assume that Jews in the time of Jesus would have seized upon the Jonah story to illustrate the more general notion of resurrection of the dead, but such is not the case. In Jewish writings of this period Jonah is not a major, or even much of a positive, figure at all.[9] There is not a single reference to him in the entire collection of Dead Sea Scrolls and the book of Jonah is never mentioned. In other Jewish texts, such as the collection known as the *Pseudepigrapha*—Jewish writings that are later than the Hebrew Bible and were written between 200 BCE and 200 CE—he is only mentioned twice, once in passing as an example of one who repents of sinning against God's command, the other as an illustration of how God hears the prayers of those sinners who cry out to him.[10]

There is an obscure Armenian translation of a Greek text of unknown date and origin called *De Jona* that recounts the Jonah story in full. Although some scholars date the original text to the 2nd or 3rd century CE, this is uncertain since the original Greek text is lost and the Armenian translation comes from the 6th century CE or later. It does seem to be Jewish and, significantly, it describes the rescue of Jonah from the belly of the fish as a "sign of rebirth," as if he is being delivered from the "womb" of the fish. Jonah declares, in this text: "You have to regard me; I was taken out of the sleep to be a sign of rebirth, and I shall be a warrant to everyone of his own life" (*De Jona* 95).[11] Although this is not properly an image of resurrection of the dead, it does seem to form our closest Jewish parallel to the kind of interpretation of Jonah's rescue that became so widespread in early Christianity. One question that must be asked is whether this text, coming so late, might have been influenced by Christian traditions or beliefs about Jonah.

The Mishnah (circa 200 CE), the first major collection of rabbinic materials that later became the core of the Talmud, has one passing reference: "He who answered Jonah in the belly of the fish will answer you and hear the sound of your cry this day. Blessed are you, O Lord, who answers prayer in a time of trouble." (*m. Taan* 2:4).[12] Apparently, the reason for the dearth of Jonah traditions in rabbinic literature is that during the 4th and 5th centuries CE, when much of that material was being edited, the rabbis had little interest in praising or empha- sizing Jonah because the Christians had claimed and co-opted him as foreshadowing the resurrection of Christ.[13]

JONAH IN EARLY CHRISTIAN TRADITION

In ancient Jewish art there are no attested representations of Jonah and the fish. That fact alone puts our Patio tomb discovery in a new light. By the 3rd and 4th centuries CE, when Jews did begin to cre- ate iconographic art, depictions such as Abraham's sacrifice of Isaac, Noah and the ark, Moses and the burning bush, the Exodus, Elijah and the widow's son, Daniel in the lion's den, the Ark of the Covenant, and Menorahs abound. Jonah never appears.[14] These images are preserved on mosaic floors of synagogues, in murals and frescos, and in funerary art.[15]

In sharp contrast, Jonah and the fish is the most common motif in early Christian art from the 2nd and 3rd centuries CE. Graydon Snyder tabulates a total of 108 examples of the "Jonah cycle" (Jonah cast into the sea, Jonah spat out of the fish, and Jonah at rest) on murals, frescos, and sculptures in catacombs, churches, and other Christian sites.[16] This compares with eight representations of Noah and the ark, six of Daniel in the lion's den, six of Jesus' baptism, five of the sacrifice of Isaac, and five of the resurrection of Lazarus—all in Christian contexts. The difference in these numbers is truly remarkable. The explanation seems to lie in the dominant influence of Jesus' saying about the "sign of Jonah."[17] Christians saw the Jonah story not only as a powerful image of Jesus' resurrection from the dead, but also as a way of affirming their own faith in the resurrection of the faithful at the end of days. The Jonah image was both a proclamation and an affirmation of personal faith. That is why the Jonah cycle is predominantly found in tombs—particularly in the catacombs of Rome. *Jonah and the fish is the quintessential early Christian biblical image*—more so even than the baptism of Jesus, the cross, or any other depiction of Jesus.

After discovering the image of Jonah and the great fish on the ossuary in the Patio tomb we decided to visit two of these Christian catacombs in Rome—San Sebastiano and Priscilla—to see firsthand what we had been reading in dozens of books on early Christian art. We were astounded at the number of Jonah representations we saw in these two locations. We arranged to visit after hours and the guides showed us several burial chambers with Jonah images that are not open to tourists. The motif was unmistakable.

One particular chamber, clearly of an extended family, had a complete set of murals depicting Jesus as the Good Shepherd, the sailors throwing Jonah into the sea, Jonah being spat out of the fish's mouth, and Noah in the ark. Noah, second only to Jonah, had also become a symbol of salvation based on a passage in the New Testament book 1 Peter about Christian baptism putting one into an "ark" of safety, protecting and saving from sins: "Baptism, which corresponds to this [i.e., Noah in the ark] now saves you, not as a removal of dirt from the body but as an appeal to God for a clear conscience, through the resurrection of Jesus Christ" (1 Peter 3:21). What the early Christians did, beginning with Jesus' appropriation of Jonah, was to draw upon a series of images from the Hebrew Bible—Adam and Eve in paradise, Noah and the ark, Abraham and the sacrifice of Isaac, and Jonah and the fish—to illustrate their new understanding of salvation in Jesus through his resurrection. Baptism itself, according to Paul, was like a new "Exodus" from Egypt, a crossing of the Red Sea, into the Promised Land (1 Corinthians 10:2). Baptism also pictured the death and burial of the old self—in a watery grave—

22. Jonah vomited out of the sea monster, as depicted in the San Sebastiano catacombs.

23. Jonah cast into the sea, depicted in a tomb in the catacombs of Priscilla.

and the resurrection or rebirth of the new person free from sins (Romans 6:4).

Jonah functioned in a similar way, being cast into the sea and swallowed by the fish or sea monster, which represented death. The belly of the fish was likened to the grave, or alternatively, the womb. Being spat out onto dry ground represented resurrection from the dead or rebirth. It is common for Jonah to emerge from the mouth of the fish with his hands raised, reflecting what is called the orant pose, indicating prayer and spiritual devotion, as shown in these murals.

This iconographic use of Jonah to represent the resurrection of Jesus is echoed in early Christian writings of the 2nd and 3rd centuries as well.[18] Justin Martyr, who wrote around 150 CE, argues with pagan opponents that Jesus fulfilled the one sign he gave—the "sign of Jonah," since he rose from the dead after three days.[19] The Acts of Paul, written in the late 3rd century CE, condemns those who doubt the resurrection of the body, citing the example of Jonah and applying it to Jesus and his resurrection.[20]

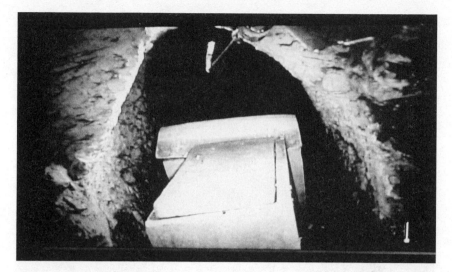

24. Looking into the third niche with the two ossuaries—5 blocking the face of 6.

THE SIGN OF JONAH ON THE TALPIOT TOMB OSSUARY

To understand the significance of the Jonah image to the early Christians, we turn to the sign of Jonah found in the Patio Tomb. The ossuary with the image of Jonah and the fish is in the third niche, ossuary 6 on our map. It is turned perpendicularly in the niche and ossuary 5 is jammed up against it so closely we were unable to see its full decorated façade. Fortunately the Jonah image is on the left side of the ossuary's decorated front panel if you are looking into the niche from outside, which allowed us to see it with our camera probe.

The fish is clear, with fins and scales, an eye, and a huge etched-in tail with a human stick figure being expelled from its mouth. All the other decorated ossuaries in the tomb have formally executed façades with typical rosettes and border designs similar to hundreds of other examples from the period. Families could have ordered them from a shop that specialized in ossuary manufacture. Certain patterned styles and motifs were common and probably carried meanings now lost to us.

25. First camera shot of the Jonah figure on the left panel of the ossuary.

The Jonah ossuary is completely different. Its patterns and markings look much more crude and homemade, which indicates that the family took a plain ossuary and created a unique design to express something that was no doubt deeply meaningful. In other words, the Jonah ossuary carries a specific message. Nothing like it has ever been seen on any of the two thousand ossuaries that have been documented.

The tail of the fish is oriented to the top of the ossuary and the mouth is turned to the bottom, as if the fish is spitting the figure onto land. There is a border to the side with what appears to be representations of mountains. The clear area the fish occupies within the borders of the panel represents water. The human stick figure's head looks like it is wrapped in the style of a mummy. We suggest that the artist is trying to represent the seaweed that was wrapped around Jonah's head when he emerged, based on the biblical text in which Jonah says "weeds were wrapped about my head" (Jonah 2:5). There are also fins and scales on this fish. Even though in popular imagination the story of Jonah and the "whale" is widespread, the text of the book of Jonah never identifies the creature as a whale—but as a "great fish." In Jewish mythology the great fish that swallowed Jonah is associated with Leviathan, one of two great sea monsters that God created on the fifth day of creation. Leviathan, along with Behemoth, represents evil, chaos, and death. Leviathan lives in the Mediterranean Sea. He is prominent in rabbinic literature in connection with the coming of the Messiah. Leviathan is a kosher fish with fins and scales, not a mammal like a whale. The Torah forbids consumption of any kind of sea creature lacking fins and scales (Leviticus 11:9–12). According to these traditions, in the messianic age, at the time of the resurrection of the dead, Leviathan will be killed and eaten by the righteous in a great celebratory banquet. His skin will then be used to make shelters for the righteous.[21] It is significant that we see evidence in our ossuary representation of the fish reflecting these details of the biblical story and Jewish tradition. When art historians interpret images, especially funerary art, they base their analysis on antecedents and precedents. A given image is then compared with other similar images, since various cultures develop and reuse certain stylistic motifs. It is common to find patterns and motifs used on furniture and frescos transferred to funerary art. That is why many of the images of Jonah and the fish in the catacombs of Rome are quite similar. A basic style of portraying the story had developed by the 3rd and 4th centuries CE among the Christians and it was then repeated hundreds of times.

In the case of this newly discovered Jonah image there is nothing to compare it to. We know of not a single example of anything similar in the entire world of early Jewish art. The person who drew this image is turning an *idea* into an *image*. He or she had a concept in mind, but no example or model to imitate or adapt. The design is most likely based on the text of the book of Jonah, but more important, the oral tradition reflected in Q that Jesus had likened his resurrection from the dead to the story of Jonah and the fish. It makes no sense to think that someone would arbitrarily decide to put a Jonah fish image on his or her ossuary, violating the biblical prohibition of making images. It is all the more unlikely since we have no other such images on ossuaries in this period and Jonah and the fish is not even developed as a motif in Jewish texts of this period. The artist is clearly trying to express a concept. It is an affirmation of faith. But it is also a daring and heretical move. That it is in a tomb on an ossuary holding the bones of the deceased is all the more telling.

As we examined the rest of the ossuary this interpretation was further reinforced. On the left end of the ossuary was another design, also done in a simple lined style. There was a bell-shaped object with

26. A composite representation of the ossuary image of Jonah and the big fish.

27. The "cross" image on the left end of the ossuary.

a crosslike design in the middle. It looked as though it might represent an entrance into the ossuary—and thus an entrance into death. Whether the cross was there to represent an entrance, or whether it might have a more symbolic meaning, is open to interpretation.

On the opposite right end of the ossuary was another fish, very similar to the Jonah image, but only one-third of it was drawn. You can see the tail and part of the body of the fish with its scales, but then the rest is drawn so close to the bottom of the ossuary that the image could not be completed. We were not able to get a clear or wide shot of this end of the ossuary due to its tight fit against the wall of the niche. All we could see was some kind of grid pattern that looked like the scales. Later, in looking at the archive photos that Amos Kloner took of the ossuaries back in 1981, the image jumped out at us—it is definitely a partial fish, drawn in the same style as the one on the front.

Next we examined the right side of the front panel of the ossuary. It had a design similar to the left side, with the mountain-like borders running along its edge and something that looked like rivers or canals with several smaller fish in them. Taken together, the images on the front and the two side panels seem to represent a kind of narrative. It is as if the ossuary itself presents death, and the various scenes on its panels portray stages of entering the grave and emerging alive again—just

28. An enhanced close-up of the partial fish from the 1981 IAA archive photo.

as Jonah does in the biblical story. Our biggest disappointment was that we could not see the middle of the front of the Jonah ossuary, where there might have been some kind of inscription. Ossuary 5, in front of the Jonah ossuary, was pushed so closely against its face, less than a half-inch, that we could not get a clear shot between the two. Walter had equipped the robotic arm so it could have easily and gently moved the ossuary in front just an inch or two, using an inflatable balloon, but we felt bound to honor our agreement with the ultra-Orthodox stipulating that nothing be moved even a fraction of an inch. The day we made our discovery one of Rabbi Schmidl's representatives who had stuck close to us the whole time was present. Over the course of our investigation he had become a part of our team and seemed to share our excitement at each new discovery. We had formed a bond with the Orthodox and gained their respect based on keeping our word and demonstrating that our interest was to gather information about the deceased in the tomb as a way of honoring and remembering them.

Later in assessing our Jonah ossuary findings we made yet another important discovery. In carefully studying the original photos that Kloner had taken of the ossuaries in 1981 we realized that the Jonah ossuary had originally been the first one, in the first niche, on the right as one enters the tomb. By carefully comparing these archive photos with our camera probe footage we have been able to recover the original positions of all the ossuaries in the tomb the day it was first entered. Rather than being tucked away deep in one of the other niches, as it is today, the Jonah ossuary occupied the place of honor reserved for the patriarch of the family—first on the right.

What's more, the photo clearly shows that this particular ossuary was filled to capacity with bones, indicating it held the remains of more than one individual. Jewish ossuary burials of this time often have the bones of several family members in a single ossuary.[22] In contrast to the other elaborately carved and painted ossuaries, including the one Kloner had removed from the tomb in 1981, the Jonah ossuary seemed uncharacteristically simple, even crude, compared with the standard ornamentation found on ossuaries. We were convinced that it was an ossuary with a message and therefore its proclamation took precedence over its formal beauty. We could not help but wonder— could this be the humble ossuary of Joseph of Arimathea and his family? Was there something about his faith or piety as part of the Jesus movement that would lead him to prefer such a modest bone box?

29. The Jonah ossuary, full of bones, in its original position in the 1981 photo.

From what little we know of him in the gospels, Joseph of Arimathea seems to have been a person who was bold and daring enough to depict his faith in Jesus' resurrection in such a unique and even heretical manner. He was willing to use his influence to go to the Roman governor Pontius Pilate and get charge of Jesus' proper burial at a time when sympathy with Jesus or his movement was not an easy thing to choose. Even the disciples of Jesus had gone into hiding after his death. The plainness of this ossuary reminds one of the ossuaries of Jesus, Maria, Matthew, and Joses in the Jesus tomb nearby. Might Joseph of Arimathea have chosen a similarly modest ossuary for himself and his most immediate family—but one that boldly proclaimed their faith even in the midst of opposition and conflict?

THE GREEK INSCRIPTION

The Greek inscription, right next to the Jonah ossuary, seemed to silently interpret the entire context of the tomb in a new light. Epigrams on ossuaries in this period are extremely rare. Of the 650 inscribed ossuaries on record there are only a dozen or so with any kind of message written on them. Typically these messages are emphatic protective formulae—unequivocal warnings against disturbing the bones of the deceased, such as:

> Bones of our father, do not open them!
> Our parents: Do not ever open!
> Our father Dositheos—not to be opened!
> Miriam, wife of Mathia: whoever moves these, blindness
>   strike![23]

There is one possible exception, on an ossuary found on Mount Scopus in Jerusalem. It is written in Aramaic and scholars have debated its proper translation. Some say it reads, "No man can go up [from the grave]," while others translate it "his entering [the grave] nobody has abolished."[24] In either case the idea is that it is impossible to reverse death. Although such expressions are abundant in Greek culture at this time, and even on later Jewish burials from the 3rd and 4th centuries CE, such an epigrammatic statement on a 1st century Jerusalem ossuary was unique until our discovery.[25]

The four-line inscription, written in uncial (uppercase) Greek letters, reads as follows:

ΔΙΟΣ (Divine or Wondrous)
ΙΑΙΟ (Jehovah)
ΥΨΩ (Lift up)
ΑΓΒ (Lift up)

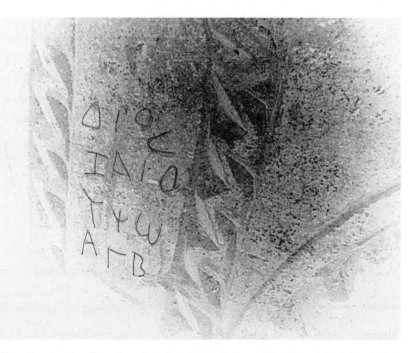

30. Negative image of the four-line Greek inscription with letters inked for clarity.

When James returned home from Israel he began to consult with several expert epigraphers to get their evaluations of the text. All were duly impressed with the extraordinary nature of the find, realizing that an epigram of this sort was a "first" so far as Jerusalem ossuary inscriptions from this period. Based on their input James considered several alternative translations, including the possibility that this was a dedicatory inscription: "To God Jehovah [most] high holy," but that would require the verb "to raise up" to be a contracted form of the adjective "most high." This is problematic since the inscription seems to represent the word as a verb.[26]

The final line of the inscription consisting of three Greek letters— A G B—is most intriguing. This is not a standard Greek word; it seems to be some kind of coded abbreviation. Perhaps it represents the initials of the name of the deceased. Such cryptic sets of letters occur on a half-dozen other ossuaries and so far no one has been able to figure out their meaning, though it is clear they are purposeful.[27] It is possible that these three Greek letters represent the Hebrew verb *hagbah*, which means "lift up." If that were the case we would have a repetition of the verb—*lift up, lift up*—once in Greek, the other in Hebrew written in Greek. This would parallel the first two lines, which refer to God in both Greek and Hebrew.

The first word, *DIOS,* can be taken as an adjective, modifying the divine name of God—Yahweh or Jehovah—transliterated into Greek as *IAO* or here *IAIO*—thus the "divine" or "wondrous" Jehovah. We know this form in various literary sources, especially on magical papyri and amulets.[28]

The core of the inscription is the contract verb *hupsoo*—"to lift, to raise up." As is common in inscriptions it is written in an abbreviated form. It could be translated "he raised up" or even "he will raise up"—one can't tell from this contracted form of the verb.[29] In nonbiblical Greek this verb is rare and comes only in later sources.[30] In contrast it occurs 260 times in the Greek Old Testament. It is used for exaltation in general, and understood as deliverance and redemption from danger and enemies. More specifically, in several passages it is used to express a developing view in resurrection of the dead: "Be gracious to me, O LORD! Behold what I suffer from those who hate me, O thou who *lifts me up* [*hupson*] from the gates of death" (Greek text of Psalm 9:14). In the *Apocalypse of Abraham* this verb is used for Abraham, who like Enoch and Elijah, is taken up to heaven by angels, so it comes to mean heavenly exaltation as well as being brought up from the grave (10:1). In the Dead Sea Scrolls it is used specifically for "raising up" from death as well as awakening or resurrection.[31]

There are three passages in the New Testament that use this precise Greek verb—*hupsoo*—to refer to the crucifixion and resurrection of Jesus from the dead as well as his exaltation to heaven:

> And I, when I am *lifted up* from the earth, will draw all men to myself. (John 12:32)

> This Jesus God raised up . . . being therefore *lifted up* to the right hand of God. (Acts 2:32–33)

> The God of our fathers raised Jesus whom you killed by hanging him on a tree. God *lifted him up* at his right hand as Leader and Savior . . . (Acts 5:31)

The verb comes to do double duty, referring both to Jesus' resurrection from the dead as well as to his being lifted up to heaven. Paul uses a compound form of the verb that intensifies it: "Therefore God has lifted him to the highest . . ." (Philippians 2:9).

We can't say with certainty whether this four-line inscription refers to Jesus' resurrection from the dead or the hope of the deceased in the ossuary who believed he or she would be "lifted up."

Given the context provided by the image of the "sign of Jonah," it seems more likely to us that it refers both to Jesus as a celebratory declaration of faith in his resurrection as well as to the resurrection of those in the tomb who have faith in him. This would clearly be the intention of putting Jonah and the fish images on one's tomb in the catacombs at Rome. We must take into account that both the Jonah image and the inscription are on ossuaries—in a tomb—not on a wall, a pillar, an amulet, or other artifact. It is that funerary context that seems to most strongly point to Jesus. It could be a more general expression of faith in resurrection, but since we have no such general expressions on any of 650 inscribed ossuaries, it seems more likely that its connection is to faith in Jesus' resurrection. It further seems that this family, buried not two hundred feet from the Jesus family tomb, is calling upon God to raise their messiah or proclaiming and celebrating that he has already been exalted to heaven.

THE IMPLICATIONS OF THE DISCOVERIES

These discoveries in the Patio tomb provide a new context for our discoveries in the Jesus tomb, but they also open the way for a re-evaluation of ossuaries and their inscriptions and ornamentations in general. There has been a sharp debate among scholars as to whether we have any evidence that the Jewish followers of Jesus in 1st century Jerusalem left any distinctive evidence of their faith by the way in which they inscribed and marked the ossuaries in which they were buried.

In the 1970s Pau Figueras came across a small fragment of an ossuary in the IAA warehouse of unknown provenance that had the name *Yeshua*—Hebrew for Jesus—inside a circle that he identified as a fish. He was convinced that he had discovered the first archaeological evidence that could be tied to Jewish followers of Jesus.[32] Most scholars disagreed, taking the so-called fish as a carelessly drawn circle simply calling attention to the name of the person buried in the ossuary. Levi Rahmani wrote, "The similarity of the circle to a fish is coincidental and the inferences drawn by Figueras excessive."[33]

Jonathan Price recently concurred, labeling Figueras's suggestion "an over-interpretation."[34] These editors of the two most prestigious catalogues of ossuary inscriptions from this period represent a general consensus. They maintain that not only is there no distinctive archaeological evidence left behind by Jesus' first followers, but also that ossuary ornamentations in general are nonsymbolic and have nothing to do with expressions of hope for resurrection or the afterlife.[35] However, images that fall out of the ordinary pattern and seem to have some individual stamp of expression such as the Jonah image in our Patio tomb challenge this standard opinion. We are convinced that a new examination of the evidence might reveal much that has previously been overlooked.

We recently examined the Figueras ossuary fragment in the warehouse of the Israel Museum and discussed it with the collections curator David Mevorach. Although he supported the minimalist position that the artifact was simply a crudely drawn circle, he admitted that

31. The Yeshua "fish" ossuary fragment.

with further evidence—perhaps more examples of fish with a clearly symbolic meaning—he might change his mind. We suggest here, in light of our recent discoveries, that the Figueras fragment is a representation of the "sign of Jonah"—Jesus inside a fish. It appears to be a fairly well-drawn fish, not a careless circle, and the inscription inside the fish—the name of Jesus—might not refer to a person named Jesus who was buried in the ossuary, but rather to that deceased person's faith *in* Jesus and his resurrection. In other words it would be a symbol of faith, not a careless marking.

Price mentions that there are only two other examples of names within "circles" on ossuaries, and one of them is from the Jesus tomb: the name Mariamene Mara—the name associated with Mary Magdalene. We had never paid attention to it before but from the photo one can clearly see the sweeping flourish of a bulging circular shape enclosing her name. We recently examined the inscription in the IAA warehouse at Beth Shemesh. The "circle" is in the shape of a fish—maybe even a great fish. Was this just a thoughtless flourish or was it purposely and carefully executed to convey some kind of symbolic meaning? If the custom of drawing circles around names occurs only three times out of 650 ossuary inscriptions, and two of them are connected to a "Jesus" name, we think these inscriptions might be quite important.

We began to investigate further and made a rather startling discovery. The only other example of the name *Mariamene,* which in the Jesus tomb we have interpreted as the ossuary of Mary Magdalene, is now stored in the basement storage area of the Rockefeller Museum.[36] This unusual spelling of the name, written with the *n* rather than the more common name *Mariame,* is engraved *under* the lid of the ossuary—which is not visible from the outside. It is extremely faint and difficult to see. When we examined the ossuary itself we were quite surprised to see that it had three little fish, very similar in style to the Figueras find, carved along the front of its façade. The distin-

32. The Mariamene Mara ossuary inscription with the oval shape around it.

guishing mark seemed to be the little crossed tails and a mouth. One of them had what looked like a Greek letter scrawled inside but it was too crudely drawn to decipher.

The name Jesus itself is a case in point. One of the most frequent observations made by theologians and academics alike regarding the Talpiot Garden or Jesus tomb was that the name Jesus was very common in 1st century Jerusalem. As a result, the discovery of a tomb with the name "Jesus son of Joseph" says nothing—or so the argument goes—since there were many males named Jesus with a father named Joseph in 1st century Jerusalem.

The name Jesus is known but hardly common. The definitive *Lexicon of Jewish Names in Late Antiquity* includes *all* named references to Jewish males in Hebrew or Greek from 330 BCE to 200 CE in the land of Israel.[37] Based on that hard data we can say that approximately 3.9 percent were named Jesus. This is a valid statistical sampling that compares the name Jesus with other known male names and their frequencies in all our sources—literary as well as epigraphic. In a sampling of one hundred Jewish males of the time only four would have the name Jesus. One would hardly call this common.

If we take all known inscribed ossuaries there are only 21 out of approximately 600 that have any form of the name Jesus, whether *Yeshua* in Hebrew or *Iesous* in Greek. Two of these are in the Talpiot Jesus tomb—"Jesus son of Joseph" and "Jude son of Jesus," and a third, the controversial "James son of Joseph brother of Jesus," we argue might well be from the Jesus tomb as well. If that were the case, we are left with eighteen others to consider. We recently examined all of these Jesus inscriptions that are available firsthand. Four of the twenty-one have disappeared and are known only through drawings or reports. We have spent countless hours in basement storage areas, warehouses, and museums, filming and closely studying each ossuary using special cameras and lights. We have visited the Rockefeller Museum, the IAA collection at Beth Shemesh, the Israel Museum, the Franciscan Museum, and a half-dozen other scattered locations where we have diligently tabulated all the evidence.

We have a working hypothesis that a number of the eighteen Jesus inscriptions on ossuaries refer not to the skeletal remains of a person in the ossuary named Jesus, but to Jesus of Nazareth. In other words, we think there are cases where families wrote "Jesus" on their ossuaries as a devotional tribute to their faith in him.

The ossuary fragment with the Yeshua inscription inside the fish discussed above is our first case in point. Since we don't have the entire ossuary we cannot be sure, but if the "circle" is not a careless circle but a fish, we think it is most likely an example of someone with faith in Jesus representing the "sign of Jonah" on his ossuary.

In 1945, Eleazar Sukenik, who was the first to identify the Dead Sea Scrolls as being authentically from the Second Temple period, discovered a tomb off Hebron Road in southern Jerusalem. The tomb contained fourteen ossuaries; five were inscribed. Sukenik was convinced that this tomb contained the earliest records of Jewish follow-ers of Jesus ever discovered.[38]

One of the ossuaries in this tomb had the inscription "Jesus Woe" (*Iesous Iou*), written faintly in charcoal, which Sukenik took to be a plaintive cry, either to Jesus or in memory of Jesus, perhaps referring to his suffering on the cross. A majority of scholars today dispute Sukenik's reading and have argued that the word *Iou* is an abbrevi-ated form of the name *Ioudas* or Jude/Judas—so the ossuary would read "Jesus [son of] Jude." Many other interpretations have been sug-gested, some of them agreeing with Sukenik that this is some kind of a cry of woe.[39] The ossuary is now stored in the basement of the Rockefeller Museum. We looked at it closely, using special lights and cameras that can enhance invisible or faded letters, and are satisfied there are no letters after the word *Iou*, faint or otherwise. There is a faint slanting diagonal stroke far to the right of the inscription, but it is certainly not a letter. It seems to us highly unlikely that anyone wanting to write the name Judas would have written it *Iou* leaving off the last letters.

The argument that the inscription represents the two names of son and father—Jesus (son of) Judas—is based upon an assumption that we think should be questioned, namely, that ossuaries invariably have the names of the dead inscribed rather than epigrams or icono-graphic expressions of faith.

But there was more in the Sukenik tomb. In addition to this first ossuary was another, this time with the strange formula *Iesous Aloth*. The first word is the name "Jesus" in Greek but what is the meaning of *Aloth*? Is it just another name, or perhaps a nickname, for the de-ceased person named Jesus? Or is it, as Sukenik argued, another cry of faith? He translated it as "Jesus Alas!" parallel to "Jesus Woe!" He connected it to the Hebrew word *'alah*, "to lament." Others have since argued that it might come from a similar Hebrew word, *'alah*, which means "to rise," that looks almost the same in English but in Hebrew is spelled one letter differently. In that case it would read "Let Jesus

arise" or "Jesus has gone up." There is an amazing parallel in the Dead
Sea Scrolls that says, "You brought me up out of the grave," using this
same Hebrew verb, *aloth* (4Q437.2.11). In the light of our new inscription, in which there is either hope for, or celebration of, Jehovah "raising up" someone from the dead, we think it is time to revisit Sukenik's
interpretation. But the story of the Sukenik tomb doesn't end there.

On the "Jesus Aloth" ossuary were four charcoal crosses—on the
two sides and two ends. Sukenik, rightly in our view, believed these
crosses could not be random markings because they were too carefully executed. He believed that they had to refer to Jesus and early
Christianity. Usually such marks are dismissed as meaningless "mason's marks," but in this case these four crosses are so symmetrical
and carefully placed, one on each surface side of the ossuary, that they
can hardly be accidental. They are also written with the same charcoal style as the inscription itself—so they were definitely done by the
same hand.

So far we have mentioned three possible "Jesus" inscriptions, the
fish and the two in the Sukenik tomb, counted among the eighteen
total but which could well refer to Jesus of Nazareth and faith in him,
not to the names of the deceased. This possibility should be reconsidered. We have read all the literature pro and con and we don't find the
skeptics' arguments convincing.

There is another inscription, discovered on the Mount of Offense,
just south of the Mount of Olives, two miles north of Talpiot, which
was inscribed twice in Greek: "Jesus Jesus." It is of course possible
that the bones in the ossuary belonged to a Jesus and that the family simply wrote his name twice. However, since the two names are
written together on a single line, one should at least consider the
possibility that someone is writing "Jesus" on their ossuary, as in the
case of the Sukenik tomb, to invoke or express some kind of faith in
Jesus of Nazareth. In front of the first name Jesus there is also a cross
or X mark. Scholars have dismissed this as a mason's mark that was
scratched on the body of an ossuary to match a similar X on the lid,

33. The "Jesus Aloth" ossuary with the crosses drawn on four sides.

showing how the lid should be turned to fit the ossuary properly.[40] Unfortunately the ossuary has disappeared and the mason's mark argument cannot be further examined. We have examined dozens of other such X's on ossuaries, and although some of them have a matching X on their lids, the great majority do not.[41]

Another name on one of the inscribed ossuaries in this same tomb was "Judah," with a cross mark below the name almost identical in style to the four on the ossuary from the Sukenik tomb. Again, scholars have interpreted it as another mason's mark, without symbolic value. Unfortunately the lid is missing, which might have a corresponding mark to show its orientation on the ossuary, so we cannot be sure. The style of the cross is identical to the four cross marks on the Sukenik "Jesus Aloth" ossuary, and its placement under the name seems to serve no function as a mason's mark. As it happens the "Jesus son of Joseph" inscription in the Talpiot Garden tomb also has an X or cross marking just in front of the name Jesus. It, like the others, has been dismissed as a random scratch, or mason's mark. This Mount of

Offense tomb contained other strange markings, including one very clear Christian cross, but it is assumed that it must have been carved onto the ossuary centuries later by a Byzantine Christian visiting the tomb, since crosses simply don't exist in the 1st century according to the standard interpretation.[42]

In considering our eighteen instances of the name "Jesus" on ossuaries, apart from the three we are associating with the Talpiot Garden tomb, over half a dozen might well refer *not* to a deceased person named Jesus whose bones are in the ossuary but to Jesus of Nazareth. In several cases there are symbols on these ossuaries that we take to be expressions of Jewish-Christian faith. We are not arguing that every "Jesus" refers to Jesus of Nazareth but that many do.

We also are convinced that the locations in which these "Jesus"-inscribed ossuaries were found might be relevant to this discussion. They are not, as one might expect, evenly distributed throughout the Jerusalem area wherever ancient burial caves have been found. Five of the total are of unknown provenance—so we have no idea where they were found. Among these is the fragment of Jesus in the fish.[43] The Sukenik tomb is near Talpiot, about a mile from the Jesus Garden tomb. Eight others are within a mile and a half from Talpiot, mostly fanning out to the north, toward the Mount of Olives.[44] Only three are far removed from Talpiot, north or southeast of the Old City, but each of those three ossuaries names a Jesus who is the son of someone other than a Joseph—disqualifying them as a reference to Jesus of Nazareth.[45] What this means is that we have a cluster of Jesus inscriptions, some of which refer to Jesus of Nazareth, in close proximity to these two Talpiot tombs.

The entire scholarly discussion of whether the early Jewish followers of Jesus left any symbols on their ossuaries suffers, in our view, from a predisposition to dismiss any evidence that might argue to the contrary. On the face of it, this assumption that *none* of the Jewish followers of Jesus who lived and died in Jerusalem from 30 CE to

70 CE ever left behind any testimony to their resurrection faith is unwarranted. The recent discoveries in the Talpiot Patio tomb have put the entire discussion of the archaeological evidence for Jewish-Christianity in 1st century Jerusalem in a new light so that previous assumptions should now be questioned.

CHAPTER FOUR

RETURNING TO THE JESUS FAMILY TOMB

The new finds from the Patio tomb offer a dramatic new context for the Talpiot Garden tomb and increase the likelihood that this latter tomb may be the burial tomb of Jesus of Nazareth and his family.

That a tomb contains an ossuary inscribed in Aramaic *Yeshua bar Yehosef*—"Jesus son of Joseph"—is not in dispute. The question is whether this particular Jesus can be reliably identified with Jesus of Nazareth—or was an otherwise unknown Jesus who lived in the 1st century.

HOW COMMON ARE THE NAMES?

The major objection of those who have disputed connecting this tomb to Jesus of Nazareth is that the six names inscribed on the ossuaries from the Garden tomb are extremely common among Jews in this period. Shimon Gibson and Amos Kloner, the excavators of the tomb, in their recent comprehensive article on the subject, conclude: "We are simply left with a group of ossuaries bearing common Jewish names of the first century CE . . . As a result, there is nothing to commend the Talpiot tomb as the family tomb of Jesus."[1] This objection has been repeated so often—spread over the Internet, in the media, and in books on the subject of the Talpiot tomb—that many who have not had the opportunity to review the evidence take it as a truism.

We strongly disagree that such is the case. Let's imagine a future archaeologist finding a burial plot from our own generation with a John, a Paul, and a George—common names in the English language, far too common to attempt any specific identification even though a certain British musical group comes to mind. Then we find out that the John was the son of an Alfred. With a bit of research we learn that John Lennon's father was named Alfred. Could this possibly be the burial plot of the famed musical quartet known as the Beatles? It seems possible but there is still not enough evidence. Then a fourth grave turns up with the name Ringo. Finally, not two hundred feet away we find a burial monument dedicated to the memory of the Beatles and all they contributed to pop music in their long career together. We believe that this is essentially what we have in the case of the two Talpiot tombs. We in fact have our "Ringo" in the Jesus tomb, as we will see—and what's more, we believe that we have a "Yoko" as well—and the Patio tomb now provides us with a new context in which we can better understand the resurrection faith of Jesus' first followers.

Far from being extremely common, several of the names in the Jesus tomb exhibit unique markers that tie them specifically to Jesus and his family. The six names, five in Aramaic and one in Greek, are the following.[2]

1. *Yeshua bar Yehosef* (Aramaic)—Jesus son of Joseph
2. *Yoseh* (Aramaic)—Joses
3. *Mariamene Mara* (Greek)—Miriam [also known as the] Lady
4. *Yehuda bar Yeshua* (Aramaic)—Judah son of Jesus

5. *Maria* (Aramaic)—Maria

6. *Matya* (Aramaic)—Matthew

Maria or its variant *Mariam*—the English name Mary—was the second most common women's name of this era after Salome.[3] It makes up about 21.9 percent of known female names from the period. Judah and its variations (Jude, Judas) account for approximately 6.5 percent of known male names. Matthew, in its various forms, is less common and accounts for only 2.4 percent of the total. There is no disagreement that Mary is common and so is Judah. The addition of Matthew is still not distinctive enough to strengthen the odds that this is the tomb of Jesus. Although we have no record of anyone named Matthew being part of Jesus' immediate family, the name occurs five times in Jesus' mother's genealogy so it seems to have a strong link to his family (Luke 3:23, 24, 26, 29, 31). He might be a son of one of Jesus' brothers. We just can't know.

It is the other three names—Jesus son of Joseph, Joses, and Mariamene Mara—that make the cluster of six names far from common.

"Jesus son of Joseph" is precisely the ossuary inscription we would expect for Jesus. Individuals are usually identified by their names alone, but sometimes one's parents or, in the case of a wife, the name of one's husband, is included, or more rarely, one's brother.[4] Jesus is legally known as the "son of Joseph" in our New Testament gospels (Luke 3:23; 4:22; Matthew 13:55; John 1:46; 6:42). Based on the Jewish tradition, ancient and modern, of designating the father to identify an individual, this is the name we would expect to see for him.[5]

Some have argued that for this to be the New Testament Jesus we would more likely have an ossuary inscription reading "Jesus of Nazareth," or perhaps "Jesus the Messiah" or at least "Jesus our Lord." This is not the case. Names on ossuaries are not intended as public proclamations, but rather as private, intimate identification "tags" to

34. The "Jesus son of Joseph" ossuary with inscription.

help the family who is burying their dead over several generations keep straight which loved one's bones were put in which ossuary. This point is further reinforced by the informal cursive style of this inscription. It was not formally carved by a stonemason but instead was scratched on the end of the ossuary by a family member. This custom is well illustrated by the inscription on the ossuary of Caiaphas, the high priest in the time of Jesus who delivered him to Pontius Pilate to be crucified. As we noted in chapter 1, Caiaphas's name is written in a similar informal cursive script without any title indicating that he was the high priest of the nation.

In the New Testament gospels Jesus is referred to as "Jesus of Nazareth" only ten times, out of six hundred references. He is called Jesus Christ (that is, Messiah) just four times, and only in Matthew and John, who want to make a theological, not a historical statement. So far as expecting the town Nazareth to be named, a survey of ossu-

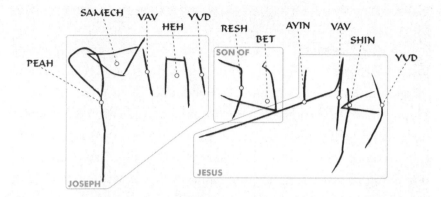

35. The "Jesus son of Joseph" inscription with a transcription in English.

ary inscriptions indicates that towns of origin are rarely given at all unless one is from outside the land of Israel, and titles or other such designations are exceptionally rare.[6] So "Jesus son of Joseph" is just what we would expect to find if an ossuary had been prepared for Jesus of Nazareth.

We can confidently say that 3.9 percent of males had the name Yeshua (Jesus) and that it occurs, as we saw in the last chapter, on 18 other inscribed ossuaries out of approximately 600 that have been discovered. So far as males named Jesus with a father named Joseph, however, we have evidence of only two—the one in the Talpiot tomb and another on the ossuary that Sukenik discovered in 1931.[7] We have already seen in chapter 3 that even if we consider all nineteen of the "Jesus" inscriptions ever found on ossuaries, excluding the two in the Talpiot tomb, up to half a dozen might, ironically, refer to Jesus of Nazareth—rather than to some other male named Jesus. As we pointed out in the previous chapter, these factors have to be considered when one evaluates the assertion that Jesus is a common name that could be expected in many tombs.

What about the remaining two inscriptions, *Yoseh* and *Mariamene Mara*? Understanding these special names requires a bit of homework, and the evidence can get a bit technical, but the results are essential for a proper evaluation of these ossuary inscriptions.

Yoseh is a shortened form, or nickname, of the more popular name Joseph (*Yehosef* in Hebrew). While the name Joseph is the second most common male name in the period, after Simon, this *nickname* Yoseh is rare.[8] The common name Joseph accounts for 8.6 percent of male names while Yoseh occurs only *seven* times on ossuary inscriptions and only *once* in Aramaic—here in the Talpiot Jesus tomb.[9] The remaining six ossuaries have the name in Greek, written as *Ioses* or *Iose*—translated in English Joses or Jose. That means Yoseh represents only .003 percent of male names, making it *exceedingly* rare. As we will see, this name alone drives the statistics on the probabilities of the cluster of these names occurring together in a single tomb off the charts.

The obvious question in considering whether this Talpiot tomb might be that of Jesus and his family is to ask whether there is anything in the New Testament gospels about someone with this rare nickname Yoseh.

Everyone familiar with the New Testament gospels knows of two Josephs—Joseph the husband of Mary, and Joseph of Arimathea, who took charge of Jesus' burial. They both go by the common full name Joseph.

Few people are aware that Jesus had four brothers. Their names are listed twice in the gospels—James, Joseph, Simon, and Judas. This gives us a *third* New Testament Joseph. James was the eldest and the second of the four was Joseph. We know nothing about him other than his name, whereas we have an abundance of historical sources on Jesus' oldest brother, James, who assumed leadership of the Jesus movement following Jesus' death.[10]

Levi Rahmani was the first to publish the Garden or Jesus tomb inscriptions, in his 1994 catalogue of ossuaries. He suggested that the Yoseh in the tomb was most likely the father of the Jesus buried there since the Jesus inscription says "Jesus son of Joseph." That is certainly possible, but then one would expect that the ossuary would have the name Joseph—not the rare nickname Yoseh. We have a different explanation for the Yoseh in the Jesus tomb.

James ran a computer search of the Greek texts of the New Testament for the name *Ioses*, the Greek form of *Yoseh*. To his surprise it did show up, but *only* in the gospel of Mark. According to Mark, Joses, or as some manuscripts have it, Yoseh, was the rare *nickname* of Jesus' second brother, Joseph (Mark 6:3).[11] Apparently this nickname was something Mark knew since Matthew, in listing the four brothers, seems to know only the full formal name Joseph (Matthew 13:55), though a few manuscript copies of Matthew also preserve the nickname Joses.

For our research this was a major milestone and so far as we know no one had noticed or pointed it out before. Thus we now have a significant linguistic link between the earliest New Testament gospel tradition about the brothers of Jesus and their names—or in this case, a nickname—and this rare form of the name Joseph on an ossuary

36. The Yoseh ossuary inscription.

from the Talpiot tomb. One of the things one tries to do in archaeology, when possible, is combine textual or literary evidence with the material archaeological evidence. One is always cautious that the text not be used to overinterpret the archaeological evidence or vice versa. In this case, where there appears to be a complete "fit" between text and artifact, we are in a good position to draw some reasonable conclusions. As we will see, when we explore why it is highly likely that Jesus' second brother, Joses, would be buried in the same tomb with him, our conclusions are further supported.

Of course it is hypothetically possible that there was another Yoseh in Jerusalem at the time of Jesus, and that he was related to some *other* Jesus with a father named Joseph. As we will see below, when you run the statistics on that possibility, it is extremely unlikely. But these are not the only factors that influence the probability.

The inscription *Mariamene Mara* is even more fascinating with regard to the mistaken assertion that the names in the Jesus tomb are common. Clearly it is some form of the common name Mary or *Mariam/Mariame* in Hebrew—but what about its strange ending? And what is the significance of *Mara*?

Of the six inscriptions from the tomb this is the only one in Greek. In contrast to the ossuaries of Jesus, Maria, and Yoseh, which are plain, this woman was buried in a beautifully decorated ossuary. Levi Rahmani deciphered her inscription in his *Catalogue of Jewish Ossuaries* published in 1994. For most of us Rahmani is the chief authority for the study of ossuaries and their inscriptions. His keen eye and uncanny ability to decipher some of the most obscure inscriptions are legendary.

Rahmani read the inscription as *Mariamene Mara*. No one questioned his judgment for thirteen years—until the story about the Talpiot "Jesus tomb" made headlines. Suddenly everyone was scrambling, it seemed, to come up with arguments against those Simcha had put forth for the first time in his 2007 Discovery Channel documentary *The Lost Tomb of Jesus.* There he had presented evidence that *Mariamene* was a unique form of the name Mary that was used by Jesus' first followers when referring to Mary Magdalene.

Several scholars have suggested that Rahmani misread the Greek, and that it should read *Mariame kai Mara*—Mary *and* Martha, referring to two individuals, perhaps even two sisters buried together in this one ossuary.[12] Since *Mariame* (without the final stem ending "n," or *nu* in Greek) is the most common form of the name Mary in Greek, any argument about uniqueness would thus evaporate. The Mary in the tomb might have been any Mary of the time and she would be almost impossible to identify further. And her sister Martha would be equally unknown.[13]

We find this new reading unconvincing and remain impressed with Rahmani's original transcription. The inscription itself appears to be from a single hand, written in a smooth-flowing style, with a decorative flourish around both names—pointing to a single individual who died and was placed in this inscribed ossuary. According to Rahmani, *Mariamene* is a diminutive or endearing variant of the common name *Mariame* or Mary.[14] *Mariamene,* spelled with the letter "n" or *nu* in Greek, is quite rare: only one other example is found on an ossuary—the one with the three fish on the front mentioned previously.[15] There are no other examples from this period—or as we were soon to discover, only two, in the *entirety* of Greek literature down through the late Middle Ages.

James ran an exhaustive computer search of the *Thesaurus Linguae Graecae*, a comprehensive digital database of Greek literature from Homer through 1453 CE. To his surprise he only found two ancient works that use *Mariamn*—with this rare "n" stem ending. Both texts specifically referred to Mary Magdalene!

The first text is a quotation from Hippolytus, a 3rd century Christian writer who records that James, the brother of Jesus, passed on secret teachings of Jesus to "Mariamene," that is Mary Magdalene.[16] There it was, in plain Greek—this *unusual* spelling of the name Miriame or Mary, precisely like the spelling on the ossuary. According to tradition Hippolytus was a disciple of Irenaeus, who was a disciple of Polycarp, who was a disciple of the apostle John—who of course knew both Mary Magdalene and Jesus. Perhaps it is this link of oral teaching, through three generations, that somehow had preserved this special name for Mary Magdalene. Its diminutive ending makes it a term of endearment—like calling someone named James "Jimmy," or an Elizabeth "Betty."

The second text that had the name Mariamene was a rare 4th century CE Greek manuscript of the *Acts of Philip,* dated to the 3rd or 4th century CE. Throughout the text Mary Magdalene is called Mariamene—again the precise form of the name found on the Talpiot tomb ossuary.

Some critics have questioned why one has to jump to the 3rd or 4th century to find a parallel to a 1st century name on an ossuary in order to argue that this name belongs to Mary Magdalene. Quite the opposite is the case. What the ossuary preserves is a rare endearing form of the common name *Mariame.* What should surprise us is that it shows up, out of the blue, in Hippolytus and the *Acts of Philip*—two centuries later, when referring to Mary Magdalene. They could not know anything about the ossuary or these inscriptions—so where did they get this tradition of the rare form of the name? That this rare form appears in these later sources strengthens rather than diminishes the argument in favor of associating this name with Mary Magdalene. If *Mariamene* is a late form of the name, found only in these 3rd and 4th century texts, as some have asserted, what is it doing on the Talpiot tomb ossuary?

It strains credibility to imagine that Rahmani, who was unaware of any association between his transcription of this ossuary inscription and identifications with Mary Magdalene in these later texts, would have mistakenly and accidentally come up with this exceedingly rare form of the common name Mary. Nor does it make any sense to think a *misreading* of the name in this inscription would end up producing two other instances for Mary Magdalene. The force of this evidence is so strong that a few scholars have even suggested that the text in Hippolytus somehow became corrupted. Again, it strains all credulity to maintain that mistakes, misreadings, and scribal errors would just happen to produce a match for an ossuary inscription in a 1st century Jerusalem tomb. What are the odds?

What about the second word in the inscription—*Mara*? Rahmani understood this as an alternative form of the more common name Martha and many scholars apparently agree.[17] He translated the full inscription: "[the ossuary] of Mariamene also known as Mara." His understanding was that this Mariamene was also called Mara—a kind of nickname equivalent to the more popular form Martha.

Readers will recall that one of the inscriptions we found on one of the ossuaries in the nearby Patio tomb also read "Mara." Is it just another form of the name Martha? In looking through all 600 ossuary inscriptions that are extant we discover that Mara is also quite rare, with only five examples other than the two in the Talpiot tombs.[18]

As explained before, we are convinced that *Mara* is an honorific title, not a proper name.[19] *Mara* and *Martha* are related; they both come from the Aramaic masculine word *Mar*, which means "Master" or "Lord" in English.[20] This is true still in modern Hebrew today. One can address a man formally as "Mar," meaning "Sir" or "Mister." It is a title not a name. If you add the feminine ending to *Mar* you get *Mara*. But English simply has no good translation for the feminine, while we use the masculine constantly. The followers of Jesus called him "Lord" or "Master," but how would we translate that title for a woman in English—perhaps one they also honored as his companion, partner, and wife? Probably our best equivalent in English is "Lady," the formal feminine form of the masculine Lord. When Catholics speak of "Our Lady," referring to Mary the mother of Jesus, they are preserving and echoing this very honorific title but they don't use it for Mary Magdalene. As we shall see she was vilified as a whore, as mentally unstable, or as both, and was written out of the dominant version of the rise and development of Christianity.

There are two other ossuary inscriptions discovered in Jerusalem that are relevant to a proper understanding of the *Mariamene Mara* inscription. The first refers to two males, a Matthew and a Simon, who are called "masters" of their tomb—meaning they own it. The word there for master is the plural of *Mar*. It is obvious that when it comes to males there is no hesitation to read *Mar* as a title. As mentioned, Jesus was referred to as *Mar* in the New Testament, in the early Christian Aramaic prayer "Mar-na-tha," meaning "our Lord come" (1 Corinthians 16:22).[21] The second inscription names a woman named Alexa, who is called Mara—just as in the Mariamene inscription. Rather than a second name, we take it as a title, so the inscription would read: "this is the ossuary of Alexa, [the] Lady." It is a title of honor.

The assertion that the names in the Jesus tomb are common simply does not stand up to scrutiny. Two of the inscriptions turn out to be quite rare (*Yoseh*) and unique (*Mariamene Mara*), and they both appear to have linguistic links with the names of individuals close to Jesus, his brother Joseph and Mary Magdalene.

RUNNING THE NUMBERS

We have looked at the names individually, but what about this particular cluster of names taken together? There have been some sophisticated attempts to do statistical analysis on the cluster of names, asking the question of the likelihood, given the frequencies of occurrence of each of these names, that they would appear in a tomb together. It is one thing to ask what are the odds of finding a "Jesus" in a tomb of this period, but quite another to ask, what about a "Jesus son of Joseph"? Each time we add a name, or a relationship, the odds change, based on how rare or common a particular name might be. Even fairly common names, as in our example above of the Beatles, carry a different statistical weight in a cluster.

The most formidable study is the peer-reviewed paper by Professor Andrey Feuerverger of the University of Toronto with a set of six responses. Since that paper there has been a series of further papers and responses with wildly differing results.[22] It has become clear that statistical results will differ according to the assumptions one uses in running the numbers. We have the data regarding the name frequencies of both males and females during the time of Jesus. What is impressive about this database is that a wider sample by Professor Tal Ilan, which includes all references, literary and inscriptional, from 200 BCE to 200 CE in the land of Israel, compares favorably with the name frequencies we find on the much smaller random sample of 600 inscribed ossuaries from tombs around Jerusalem in this period. In other words the tomb names are an accurate sampling of the larger society of the time. Based on this data, we can say with confidence that 3.9 percent of males had the name Jesus, 21.9 percent were called Mary, 6.5 percent were named Judah, and so forth. These numbers include all the forms of the names lumped together. For example, the count for Mary would include all Greek and Hebrew variants such as Mariame, Maria, Mariam, Marias, and so forth. The count for Jesus would include Yeshua, Yehoshua, Yeshu, Iesous, and other minor variants.

Some have questioned the statistical calculations of Feuerverger but his basic data and methods have been validated by subsequent studies.[23] The most impressive summary of the various studies, their variables, and the main issues at stake is the work of statistician Jerry Lutgen. His two papers, "The Talpiot Tomb: What Are the Odds?" and "Did the Set of Names from the Talpiot Tomb Arise by Chance?" set all the statistical studies in their proper context.[24]

The statistical studies ask how often this set of names would occur by chance if they were drawn randomly from the entire set of names in use during the period of time in question. As the probability of this set of names occurring by chance goes down, the probability that this is the family tomb of the New Testament Jesus goes up.

What Lutgen shows is that the numbers will vary significantly depending on how the names Jesus son of Joseph, Mariamene, and Yoseh are treated. If the latter two are taken as generic names for Mary and Joseph, two of the most frequent male and female names of the period, then the probability that this is the tomb of the family of Jesus comes out quite low.

For example, if Yoseh is taken as just another generic Joseph, you get a probability of only 3 percent, but if it is taken as the rare form discussed above, the probability rises to 47 percent. If you add a rare Mariamene with a generic Joseph you get 81 percent. But if you count *both* names as rare—which we believe they are—factoring in their rarity, the probability rises to 99.2 percent. This high percentage might not be intuitive, but it is mathematically sound, given the data we have on name frequencies.

We do not believe that statistics alone prove one way or the other that the Talpiot Jesus tomb is that of Jesus of Nazareth but the statistics do show that the oft-repeated assertion that lots of tombs in Jerusalem would likely have a similar set of names is false.

We have spent countless hours studying every entry in the ossuary inscription catalogues of Levi Rahmani and Hannah Cotton, the two major catalogues of ossuary inscriptions. We began to realize, after looking at tomb after tomb represented by all 600 inscriptions that have been found, that of the thousand or more known tombs that have been opened and examined in Jerusalem over the past hundred years there is not a single one other than this Talpiot tomb for which one could even make an argument that it might be the family tomb of Jesus. It is not as though there are a half-dozen or so other possible tombs that might fit Jesus and his family, and we have chosen to focus on this one. *There are no others.* The other tombs that have a Jesus inscription of any kind are clustered with names like Shelamzion, Chananiya, Shapira, Dositheos, Daniel, Menachem, or Sara, names that have no known association with Jesus of Nazareth or his family in our texts.

THE SECOND BURIAL OF JESUS

In trying to match the Talpiot Garden tomb with the historical record, we begin with what we know about the burial of Jesus of Nazareth from our earliest sources—the New Testament gospels. Although the apostle Paul (whose letters are even older than the gospels) knows the tradition that Jesus was "buried," he provides no narrative details that we might analyze historically (1 Corinthians 15:4). It is often assumed that the gospels report that Joseph of Arimathea took the corpse of Jesus and laid it in his own new tomb late Friday night, but a careful reading of our gospel accounts indicates that the tomb into which Jesus was *temporarily* placed did *not* belong to Joseph of Arimathea— as we discussed in chapter 1.

Mark implies that it was the pressing necessity of a quick temporary burial brought on by the nearness of the Sabbath that prompted Joseph of Arimathea to act in haste and approach the Roman governor Pontius Pilate for permission to bury Jesus' corpse (Mark 15:42–47). The gospel of John makes this point even more explicitly, stating plainly, "Now in the place he was crucified was a garden, and in the garden a new tomb . . . so because of the Jewish day of Preparation, *since the tomb was close at hand,* they laid Jesus there" (John 19:38–42).

This initial burial of Jesus by Joseph of Arimathea was a temporary measure because the Passover Sabbath was hours away. It was a burial of necessity and opportunity. This particular tomb was chosen because it was unused and happened to be near the place of crucifixion. The idea that this first tomb belonged to Joseph of Arimathea makes no sense. What are the chances that Joseph of Arimathea would just happen to have his own new family tomb conveniently located near the Place of the Skull, or Golgotha, where the Romans regularly crucified their victims?[25] Amos Kloner, who supervised the excavation of the Talpiot Jesus tomb, offers the following analysis:

> I would go one step further and suggest that Jesus' tomb was what the sages refer to as a "borrowed (or temporary) tomb." During the Second Temple period and later, Jews often practiced temporary burial . . . A borrowed or temporary cave was used for a limited time, and the occupation of the cave by the corpse conferred no rights of ownership upon the family . . . Jesus' interment was probably of this nature.[26]

Mark indicates that the intention of Joseph was to complete the full and proper rites of Jewish burial after Passover. Given these circumstances, one would expect the body of Jesus to be placed in a second tomb as a permanent resting place. This second tomb would presumably be one that either belonged to, or was provided by, Joseph of Arimathea, who had both the means and the formal responsibility to honor Jesus and his family in this way. Accordingly, one would not expect the permanent tomb of Jesus, and subsequently his family, to be near Golgotha, just outside the main gates of the city, but in a rock-hewn tomb elsewhere in the Jerusalem area, most likely where Joseph of Arimathea would have had a burial cave on his own estate.

James the brother of Jesus became leader of the Jesus movement following Jesus' death in 30 CE. Our evidence indicates that the movement was headquartered in Jerusalem until 70 CE when the Romans destroyed Jerusalem. The core group of followers banded around Jesus' family and the twelve apostles, who took up residence there as well, even though most of them were from Galilee.[27] This evidence points strongly toward the possibility of a Jesus family tomb in Jerusalem.

A JESUS FAMILY CLUSTER

Based on our earliest textual sources we propose the following list of individuals as potential candidates for burial in a hypothetical Jesus family tomb:

Jesus
Joseph his father
Mary his mother
His brothers, James, Joses, Simon, and Judas, and any of
      their wives or children
His sisters: Salome and Mary (if unmarried)
Any wife or children of Jesus (if he was married with children)

There are other names we simply do not know, such as the names of Jesus' brothers' wives or any of their children. These possibilities are based on our understanding of how family burial caves were populated in the period. If a woman was married, she would be in her husband's tomb, if not, she would be in her father's. A widow might be in her son's tomb.[28]

If we next ask which of these individuals might hypothetically be buried in a pre–70 CE Jesus family tomb in Jerusalem after the year 30 CE when Jesus was crucified, we have a specific chronological framework in which to test our hypothesis. Seventy CE is the year the Romans devastated Jerusalem and exiled much of the Jewish population. Normal Jewish life, including the common use of burial caves around the city, diminished.[29] Taking this date we come up with a more chronologically restricted list of potential candidates, since we would only include those in the family that we can assume might have died between 30 and 70 CE:

Jesus
Mary his mother

Joses and James, his brothers

Any wives and children of his dead brothers

Any wife and children of Jesus who died before 70 CE

We would eliminate Jesus' father, Joseph, because he seems to have died decades earlier, probably in Galilee, and we have no record of him in Jerusalem in this period (see Acts 1:14). Jesus' mother, Mary, given her age, could likely have died before 70 CE, and as a widow, according to Jewish custom, she could have been put in the tomb of her oldest son. Jesus' brothers Simon and Jude apparently lived past 70 CE, according to our records, so they should be eliminated from our list.[30] Jesus' brother Joses is a strong candidate for inclusion since he is the "missing brother" in our historical records. When James is murdered in 62 CE, it is Simon, the third brother, not Joses, the second, who takes over leadership of the movement—indicating that Joses had most likely died by that time. The New Testament letters of James and Jude testify to their influence, and we even have an account of the death of Simon by crucifixion, but nothing survives whatsoever regarding Joses. Given the culture it is likely that Jesus' sisters would have been married, and thus buried in the tombs of their husbands, so they are not prime candidates for the Jesus tomb. Since we have no textual record of wives and children of either Jesus or his two brothers who died before 70 CE we can only say hypothetically that if such people existed they might have been included.

As for the two Marys in the Talpiot tomb, there were three intimate "Marys" in Jesus' life: his mother, a sister, and Mary Magdalene. Indeed, it was Mary Magdalene, his mother, and his other sister, Salome, who attended to his burial rites (Mark 16:1). Family intimates carried out this important rite of washing and anointing the naked corpse for burial. As we will discuss later, our DNA tests on the bones from the Mariamene ossuary indicate the woman buried inside was not Jesus' sister or mother. It seems a logical possibility that she could be the "third" Mary, namely Mary Magdalene, his follower and close companion, based on her inclusion as a named intimate in our earliest records.

We find it striking that five of the six inscriptions correspond so closely to a hypothetical pre–70 CE family tomb of Jesus in Jerusalem as we might imagine it based on historical evidence—Jesus son of Joseph, Maria, Mariamene, Yoseh, and Judah the son of Jesus. The one inscription we can't account for in terms of what might be expected in our hypothetical Jesus family tomb is Matya or Matthew. The name is relatively rare, just 2.4 percent of males, as we have seen. We have noted that the name Matthew occurs more frequently than any other name in the family genealogy of Jesus (Luke 3:23–31), so it is quite possible that such a name would be given to a close relative. Although we might not be able to identify who this Matthew was, or his familial relationship to Jesus, it is a name that fits comfortably in the cluster.

We find this hypothetical "fit" between the intimate pre–70 CE family of Jesus of Nazareth and the names found in this tomb quite impressive and it argues strongly against an out-of-hand dismissal of the tomb as possibly, or even likely, associated with Jesus of Nazareth.

SUMMING UP THE OBJECTIONS

There have been five major objections put forth against the hypothesis that the Talpiot Jesus tomb is likely the family tomb of Jesus of Nazareth:

1. The names in the tomb are common.
2. Jesus had no wife or children.
3. Jesus and his family were too poor to have afforded a cave burial tomb.
4. Jesus would have been buried in Nazareth, not in Jerusalem.
5. Jesus' body was resurrected and taken up to heaven.

Each of these objections is in our view invalid. We have discussed the first and have shown that quite the opposite is the case. We will address the second in the following chapter. One major scholar has argued the third and we will consider it below. The fourth is simply not the case. All our textual evidence places the death and burial of Jesus in Jerusalem, not in Galilee. Since it was forbidden in Jewish law and custom to transport a corpse, the idea that Jesus' body would have been taken to a family tomb in Galilee is without any basis.[31] The final objection is theological, not historical, but since the Patio tomb shows evidence for faith in Jesus' resurrection by his earliest followers, adjacent to the Talpiot Jesus tomb, these original disciples obviously had a different understanding of the resurrection of Jesus from those who imagine it involved reviving a corpse and transporting it to heaven.

Were Jesus and his family—or even his group of close followers—too small, insignificant, and poor to have a family burial cave in Jerusalem?[32] The argument is made that whoever took the body from the initial cave burial would have buried him in a simple trench grave with no marker since the family was too poor to have afforded a rock-hewn tomb. This objection overlooks the fact that at least one follower of influence and means, Joseph of Arimathea, did in fact see to the initial burial in a rock-hewn tomb. Why would one assume that either Joseph, or other followers of means who were devoted to Jesus' messianic program, would not be able to provide a permanent tomb? We also have evidence that a group of wealthy and influential women, including Mary Magdalene, were supporting Jesus' movement financially, had followed him from Galilee, and were involved in the preparation of spices and ointments for his proper burial (Luke 8:1–3). The descriptions and circumstances all fit well with the idea of a body prepared for burial in a rock-hewn tomb with ossuaries.[33]

The Jesus movement, led by James his brother following his crucifixion, was headquartered in Jerusalem for the next forty years and its numbers and influence were sufficient to be noted by Josephus in the *Antiquities*.[34]

On more general grounds, this objection overlooks the extraordinary devotion that followers exhibit toward their spiritual and messianic leaders. Mark tells us that the followers of John the Baptizer went to collect his body and that they placed him in a tomb (Mark 6:29). The Syriac *Ascents of James* recounts how devout followers of James buried another murdered leader, known in some traditions as Stephen, in a tomb close to Jericho to which they made an annual pilgrimage.[35] The study of apocalyptic and messianic movements, both ancient and modern, makes clear that devoted groups have the collective means to support their leaders. It is an open and debated question in the field of Christian origins as to whether Jesus was poor and without means of any sort, but even if that were true, to rule out the likelihood that devoted followers of means would have provided him and his family with a place of burial is unwarranted.

The Talpiot tomb is quite modest in size and arrangement, measuring under three by three meters and less than two meters high. It is nothing like the more monumental decorated tombs closer to the city. Also, of the six inscribed ossuaries, four are "plain," and only two are "decorated" (Mariamene Mara and Yehuda bar Yeshua). We do not believe that the mere existence of a modest rock-hewn tomb of this type indicates high status and wealth. The comprehensive Kloner and Zissu survey of Jewish burial in and around Jerusalem in the period indicates little evidence of trench burials. Instead rock-hewn burial tombs were the norm for most of the population. As one moves away from the "front-row" seats near the Old City, the tombs south of Akeldama, around the Mount of Offense, and south into Talpiot are often more modest in form and size.[36]

THE TALPIOT TOMBS IN CONTEXT

The recent discoveries in the Patio tomb, which was likely located on a wealthy estate with two other tombs, one now destroyed, the other the Jesus family tomb, provides a completely new context for interpreting and understanding both the site and its possible connection to Jesus and his family. The latest advances in archaeological methodology have stressed that context is everything; nothing should be interpreted in isolation. Scholars call this method "landscape archaeology." What one attempts to do is re-create the larger context for a given archaeological site. For a cluster of tombs just outside an urban area this is particularly important. We have already stated that the original excavator of both tombs, Joseph Gath, notes in his reports that in the immediate vicinity of the tombs was an oil press, cisterns, the remains of a plastered installation that might have been a ritual bath, stone boundary walls, and terraces. Although some of these installations showed evidence of a later date, in the Byzantine period (4–5th centuries CE), Gath's descriptions indicate that they had been reused in later times. His conclusion was that these tombs in the time of Jesus were part of a large farm or wealthy settlement.[37]

Joseph of Arimathea was a wealthy Jewish leader, a member of the Sanhedrin, the highest Jewish court of the nation, who had enough status and influence to request Jesus' body from Pontius Pilate, the governor of Judea. Because the temporary tomb near the site of the crucifixion was found empty on Sunday morning, it is easy to miss the obvious point. Joseph of Arimathea was given charge of the proper burial of Jesus according to Jewish law and custom. Such a burial involved much more than temporary protection of the corpse from violation through the Passover festival and the Sabbath day. He had taken on the obligation to give Jesus a proper burial, a sacred responsibility in the Jewish tradition. The most likely hypothesis is that he would have provided a permanent place on his own land.

So far we have not found an inscription inside the Patio tomb linking Joseph of Arimathea to the site. But circumstantial evidence points in that direction. The designation *Arimathaia* in Greek (Mark 15:43) comes from the Hebrew word *rama*, meaning the "height." The Greek form *Arimathaia* seems to represent the Hebrew *Ramathaim*— meaning the "two heights." Everyone assumes this reference is to a city, based on Luke 23:51, but it more likely referred to a location with two prominent "heights."[38] Jerusalemites today refer to the Talpiot tomb area as Armon Hanatziv—the "Place of the High Commissioner," referring to the high ridge overlooking Jerusalem where the British high commissioner once had offices and today the United Nations has its headquarters. It is hard to imagine the area two thousand years ago as it is so built up with modern construction, but looking south from Jerusalem toward Talpiot, two prominent ridges are clearly visible.

The Jesus tomb is modest and quite small, with four plain ossuaries. The Patio tomb is clearly the more important tomb on the estate. It is much larger and the niches are nicely carved and gabled. Of the eight ossuaries originally in the tomb, only two are plain, the rest highly ornamented. One of the plain ones is the one with Jonah and the great fish. Since we now know it was first on the right, as one entered the tomb, it might well have been that of the master of the estate as we have noted. The obvious question is, why would a wealthy landowner with money to provide such ornate ossuaries choose such a plain one for himself and his family, fill it with bones, and have the "sign of Jonah" carved on the front? And why would someone of the family, whether the original master or not, incise a four-line testimony to God "lifting up" the dead? And who would write "Mara" on an ossuary, over a still unfinished rosette? Was it a female of the family named Mara, or was it someone wanting to honor the "Lady," perhaps even the one in the Jesus tomb nearby? Finally, writing the Divine Name—Jehovah, once in Greek, another time in Hebrew—on an ossuary, is not only unusual, it would be considered heretical by Jews of that time.

These are the sorts of anomalies that archaeologists look for. It is when we find the unexpected that we are able to advance and broaden our understanding of the culture and its diverse population. Most experts in the field see the followers of Jesus as Jews living like other Jews, and therefore leaving nothing behind that is distinctive or identifiable in the archaeological record. This might be true when it comes to food and drink, clothing, houses and ceramics, ritual baths, and most items of daily life, but we should not assume it is true in the case of burying the dead. Jesus' first followers were thoroughly Jewish, but they believed in a resurrection faith centered in their crucified Messiah that we should not assume went unmarked.

The Patio tomb seems to be Exhibit A in that regard. The two tombs mutually interpret one another. Taken in isolation each has its own fascinating tale, its anomalies to consider. Taken together we believe they tell a compelling and moving story, one of the most dramatic in history, of the tragic murder of Jesus, his burial and that of his family, and the developing resurrection faith of those who followed him. It is not hard or even overly speculative for us, to posit that the Talpiot tombs are a tiny but amazing glimpse into the life of Joseph of Arimathea, who makes his entrance and exit in the New Testament on a single page of the text.

We now turn to what is perhaps one of the most significant and far-reaching implications of these tombs, and particularly the Jesus family tomb: the question of whether Jesus was married and had a child. If the Talpiot tomb is indeed that of Jesus of Nazareth, it has already answered our question in the affirmative. But what else can be known or said about this subject that might help us understand what we find in the tomb?

CHAPTER FIVE

JESUS AND MARY MAGDALENE

Is it possible that Jesus was married? And that he could have fathered a child? These ideas so directly contradict our received tradition that they are hard to believe. Furthermore, there have been such sensational claims in the past, particularly in *The Da Vinci Code,* that it is important to be skeptical and to base any conclusions on solid evidence. It is for this reason that in his book *The Jesus Dynasty,* James said that he did not believe there was sufficient evidence to argue that Jesus was married to Mary Magdalene and that they had had a child. But to be a scholar is to remain open to new data and new interpretations and to be always willing to change one's position. Based on new evidence, James now believes that his earlier position was wrong.

The New Testament says nothing directly about Jesus being married or having a child. If Jesus had been married with a child would there not be some record, some hint somewhere in the gospels? There are times when the silence of a text speaks volumes. We are now convinced that the authors of the New Testament, written many decades after Jesus' life, were either unaware of Jesus' wife and child, or more likely, for theological reasons, decided to suppress this information. The Jesus of these gospels was the divine Son of God, ascended to heaven, and any "earthly," or sexual, ties to a mortal woman may well have been deemed inconceivable. His exalted heavenly status as the Son of God surely precluded him "leaving behind" such mortal remains. The New Testament gospels are male-dominated accounts in which the few women who do play a role in Jesus' life are marginalized and subordinated. They purportedly did not hold leadership roles equivalent to the male disciples. But the gospels are not devoid of references to Mary Magdalene's singular importance in Jesus' life. To the contrary, Mary Magdalene, along with Jesus' mother and his sister, prepared Jesus' naked corpse for burial, and she was the first witness to his resurrection from the dead. These stories show how central she must have been in his life. It is as though she could not be written out of the story—but her relatively isolated inclusion in such intimate and important ways hints at a larger role.

This silence, as we will see, is in sharp contrast to half a dozen other ancient texts that have been discovered in the last hundred years, including several "lost" gospels that are not included in the New Testament. In these texts, Mary Magdalene is mentioned very prominently, given a role superior to that of the twelve apostles, and presented as Jesus' intimate companion. These texts were written later than the New Testament gospels—most of them dating to the 2nd century CE—yet they bear witness nonetheless to an alternative role of Mary Magdalene in Jesus' life. As such they give voice to a suppressed history and a muted memory that correlates strongly with the evidence in the Talpiot tombs.

As mentioned earlier, the fact that the Talpiot tomb contains two ossuaries inscribed with names of women—*Maria* on one and *Mariamene Mara* on the second—plus a third ossuary *Judah son of Jesus*, strongly suggests that one of these two Marys is most likely the mother of the son, and thus the wife of the Jesus buried in this tomb. The DNA evidence, as we will see in chapter seven, shows that

Mariamene Mara is not Jesus' mother and most likely is the mother of the son.

Jesus of Nazareth had a mother named Mary, and apparently one of his sisters was also named Mary.[1] If Jesus' sister Mary were married, which seems likely given the norms of the culture, she would not be in his tomb but in the tomb of her husband. If the Talpiot tomb is that of Jesus and his family, the second Mary—Maria—is most likely his mother, unless she lived past 70 CE, which is very unlikely. Alternatively, the second Mary could perhaps be a wife of one of his brothers. That leaves Mariamene Mara as the most likely candidate to be the mother of his child. Based on the history that we can reconstruct as well as the linguistic fit of the name, Mary Magdalene is really the only viable candidate for that inscription in this tomb.

There is the related issue of the status of Mary Magdalene. The Mariamene buried in the Jesus family tomb is also known as Mara—the Lady, as we have seen. This title can potentially refer to her place of leadership and authority in the emerging Christian movement, a role that is hinted at by the evidence in the Talpiot tomb but never explicitly indicated in any of our sparse New Testament texts mentioning Mary Magdalene.

When we consider all the relevant ancient textual evidence regarding Mary Magdalene, both inside and outside the New Testament, with the new archaeological evidence from the Talpiot tombs, we find that there is an impressive correlation between much of this textual material and what we observe in the tombs.

MARY MAGDALENE IN THE NEW TESTAMENT GOSPELS

We begin with our earliest source on Mary Magdalene—the gospel of Mark, which, as we have said, most scholars consider to have been written before Matthew, Luke, or John. According to the gospels, Mary Magdalene is undoubtedly the most mysterious and intriguing woman in Jesus' life. She appears for the first time out of nowhere, without any introduction, watching the crucifixion of Jesus from afar. She is named *first*, surely giving her special priority, and she is associated with an entire group—one might even say, an *entourage of women* who had followed Jesus down from Galilee to Jerusalem just before the Passover festival began:

> There were also women looking on from afar, among whom were Mary Magdalene, and Mary the mother of James the younger and Joses, and Salome, who, when he was in Galilee, followed him, and ministered to him; and also many other women who came up with him to Jerusalem. (Mark 15:40–41).

Luke supplements this tradition of Mark, also emphasizing the many women from Galilee who were followers of Jesus. He names Mary Magdalene first, implying she has some kind of leadership role, but then identifies two others: a certain Joanna, who is the wife of Chuza, a household administrator in the court of Herod Antipas, king of Galilee; and Susanna, otherwise unknown. The implication is that these women are of high standing with financial means. Luke specifies that they provided for the Jesus movement (Luke 8:2–3).

In Mark's gospel it is Mary Magdalene, along with the other Mary, the mother of Joses, and presumably, although not mentioned, the mother of Jesus, who observes Joseph of Arimathea taking down the bloodied body from the cross, placing him temporarily in a nearby tomb, and sealing the entrance with a heavy stone, until the Passover was over (Mark 15:47).[2] As soon as the Sabbath day was over Mary Magdalene, accompanied by the other Mary and an unidentified woman named Salome, possibly Jesus' sister, bought spices so they might return to the tomb early Sunday morning to wash the corpse and complete the rites of burial. Mark relates that early on Sunday morning, the three women go to the tomb before the sun is risen, and find the stone rolled away and the body removed. Inside the tomb is a young man dressed in a white linen garment who informs the women that Jesus has been "raised up," that they are to go and tell his male disciples, and that he is going to meet them in Galilee (Mark 16:1–7).[3] According to Mark they flee from the tomb in fear and astonishment, saying nothing to anyone. In our oldest copies of Mark that is how the story ends—abruptly and mysteriously, with the promise to the women that Jesus will appear in Galilee in the future. The oldest copies of Mark have this abrupt ending with no "sightings" or appearances of Jesus to anyone. Later manuscripts or copies of Mark add one of three different alternative endings, composed by scribes to try to blunt the abruptness of Mark's original ending. They feared that Mark's account, if left as is, might leave doubt as to Jesus' resurrection.[4]

Washing and anointing a corpse for Jewish burial was an honored and intimate task. The body was stripped naked and washed from head to toe. This ritual was performed by the immediate family or those closely related. Although these narratives from Mark do not identify Mary Magdalene as the wife of Jesus, they cast her taking the lead in carrying out the burial rites for Jesus—an intimate task for a wife, mother, or sister. Matthew and Luke have Mark as their source, and although they relate the story of Jesus' burial slightly differently, they seem not to have independent information. It is also entirely possible, writing so many decades after the events, when all of the original witnesses were dead, that they know the tradition of Mary Magdalene's involvement in Jesus' burial and thus find it essential to include her, but have no idea who she was or why she was so prominent in the story they had been told.

In the gospel of John we seem to get an alternative narrative tradition, independent of Mark. John writes that Mary Magdalene *comes alone* to the tomb very early Sunday morning, while it is still dark. She sees the stone rolled away from the tomb and the body removed and she runs in panic to tell Peter and an unnamed disciple, otherwise identified as the "one whom Jesus loved" (John 20:2). What she exclaims to the men is most revealing: "They have taken the Master out of the tomb, and we do not know where they have laid him" (John 20:2).[5] In this account Mary Magdalene's logical assumption is that the body has been removed from the temporary tomb, which John has already emphasized was a tomb of convenience in an emergency, not a permanent burial cave (John 19:41–42). "They" refers to Joseph of Arimathea, assisted by another Sanhedrin member, Nicodemus, who John says assisted in the initial removal of the body from the cross.

What happens next is a story unique to John. Mary Magdalene returns to the empty tomb, weeping outside, then enters the tomb for the first time to look inside. She sees two angels dressed in white sitting inside. The Greek word translated "angel" (*aggelos*) can refer to a "messenger" and does not necessarily mean a nonterrestrial being. These two ask her why she is weeping. She repeats her take of the situation—"Because they have taken away my Master, and I do not know where they have laid him" (John 20:13). Just as she replies she turns and sees a man outside the tomb that she takes to be the gardener. He asks her the same question: "Woman, why are you weeping, whom do you seek?" She replies, "Sir, if you have carried him away, tell me where you have taken him, and I will take him away" (John 20:15). The man then addresses her by name—calling her *Miriam*, in the original Greek text, using the Hebrew form of her name. She apparently recognizes the voice and turns to face him, crying out in Hebrew, *Rabboni*—a diminutive term of endearment meaning "my dear Master." She recognizes it is Jesus but he tells her not to touch him, adding that he is ascending to heaven (John 20:16–17). For a woman to touch a man in this culture further implies a familial connection. Mary Magdalene returns to the male disciples and tells them what she has seen.

This remarkable story presents Mary Magdalene as the first witness to Jesus' resurrection. Unlike Mark, who has no appearances of Jesus following the empty tomb, or Matthew, who has Jesus encountering the eleven remaining apostles on a misty mountain in Galilee much later, or Luke, who relates that Jesus appeared physically to the disciples in a closed room, showing his wounds and eating a meal in front of them, John's story of Mary Magdalene's encounter stands in sharp contrast. John includes in his gospel additional appearances of Jesus to groups of men, but he alone preserves this Magdalene tradition.

Professor Jane Schaberg and others have interpreted this singular experience of Mary Magdalene as forming the core of the resurrection faith of Jesus' first followers.[6] It is a personal encounter prompted by an exchange of greetings—*Miriam* and *Rabboni*—as if those words signaled a flash of recognition based on personal intimacy. If one asks who can lay claim to the first appearance of Jesus after his death, John's story offers a clear answer—it was Mary Magdalene. Matthew knows a garbled version of the story in which the group of women encounter Jesus as they flee from the tomb, but without John's personal exchange between Mary and Jesus (Matthew 28:9–10). In Matthew's story the women are mere vehicles who carry the news to the male disciples, not independent witnesses whose testimony is valued. Jesus commissions the eleven remaining apostles, and the women are nowhere to be seen (Matthew 28:16–20).

Paul, who wrote in the 50s CE, just twenty years removed from the crucifixion, says explicitly that Jesus appeared first to Peter, then to the twelve apostles, then to James, and finally to five hundred brothers en mass (1 Corinthians 15:5). He either knows nothing of the Magdalene tradition, or given his view of women, considers it without merit. This was after all a time in ancient history when a woman's testimony in court did not carry the same weight as that of a man. Even in Luke the initial testimony of the women who first visited the tomb is dismissed as an "idle tale" (Luke 24:11). In a male-dominated movement how could a hysterical woman, weeping at a tomb, provide any kind of credible testimony?

There is evidence of criticism leveled against the developing Christian movement from the late 2nd century CE because of the involvement of women. Celsus, a pagan philosopher who wrote an attack of the Christians called *True Doctrine* around 178 CE, says:

> Jesus went about with his disciples collecting their livelihood
> in a shameful and importunate way . . . For in the gospels cer-
> tain women who had been healed from their ailments, among
> whom was Suzanna, provided the disciples with meals out of
> their own substance.[7]

Celsus does not specifically name Mary Magdalene but seems to have
her in mind:

> While he was alive he did not help himself, but after death
> he rose again and showed the marks of his punishment and
> how his hands had been pierced. But who saw this? A hysteri-
> cal female, as you say, and perhaps some other one of those
> (women) who were deluded by the same sorcery, who either
> dreamt in a certain state of mind and through wishful think-
> ing had a hallucination due to some mistaken notion (an
> experience which has happened to thousands), or, which is
> more likely, wanted to impress others by telling this fantastic
> tale, and so by this cock-and-bull story to provide a change
> for other beggars."[8]

Further on in the same narrative Celsus charges that Jesus "appeared
secretly to just one woman and to those of his own confraternity."[9]
This is without a doubt an accusation based on his reading of the account in the gospel of John. There is evidence that a number of other
pagan writers were critical of the female initiative that apparently was
central to Christianity's development.[10]

Is there any likely historical truth to the notion that the faith in
Jesus' resurrection began with this entourage of women led by Mary
Magdalene? Schaberg has argued that this singular account in John
20:1–18, where Mary Magdalene encounters and speaks to Jesus in the
garden tomb, preserves fragments of a tradition of Mary Magdalene
as *successor* to Jesus—and thus "first founder" of Christianity, in the

sense of authoritative witness to resurrection faith. Schaberg shows that the narrative structure of John 20 reflects an imaginative reuse of 2 Kings 2:1–18, where Elijah the prophet ascends to heaven, leaving his disciple Elisha as his designated witness and successor. This intimate personal appearance to Mary Magdalene, which focuses on an ascent to heaven rather than resurrection of the dead per se, stands in sharp contrast to the other formulations in the gospels that present indirect angelic encounters to a group of women. Upon this foundation Schaberg offers a preliminary sketch of what she rather boldly labels "Magdalene Christianity," both suppressed and lost in the New Testament gospel tradition, and particularly in Acts, much as the history of James the brother of Jesus and the Jerusalem community from 30 to 50 CE has been suppressed.

The notion of apostolic authority in early Christianity depended most of all on one's being a witness to Jesus' resurrection and receiving a commission.[11] Paul, for example, bases his own late addition to the apostolic roster upon his *visionary* experience of Jesus several years after he had been crucified: "Last of all, as to one untimely born, he appeared also to me. For I am the least of the apostles, unfit to be called an apostle, because I persecuted the church of God" (1 Corinthians 15:8–9). One should not take this modesty on the part of Paul as any indication that he thought he was in the least bit inferior to the apostles who were before him. He says of the other apostles: "But by the grace of God I am what I am, and his grace toward me was not in vain. On the contrary, I worked harder than any of them, though it was not I, but the grace of God, which is with me" (1 Corinthians 15:10). Apparently Paul did receive challenges to his rights to be called an apostle. Against such charges he adamantly defended himself, insisting that his apostleship was based squarely on his experience of having "seen Jesus our Lord" (1 Corinthians 9:1). Apostleship was not, in his view, something that was passed on from men, but was given by a "revelation of Jesus Christ" (Galatians 1:12, 16). But according to the book of Acts the main criterion in deciding who would replace Judas Iscariot as the twelfth apostle after he had betrayed Jesus and then killed himself was that the one chosen had been with Jesus in his lifetime and was a "witness to his resurrection" (Acts 1:21–22).

Not only did Mary Magdalene meet these criteria, but she had the additional status of being the first witness to Jesus' resurrection—even before Peter. The gospel of Luke explicitly rejects her status in this regard, characterizing the report of Mary and her entourage of women from Galilee and their claim to have "seen Jesus" as an "idle tale," using language that in the culture of that time was particularly associated with the testimony of women. Mary Magdalene's disqualification was based on her gender. Paul, for example, insists to his congregations:

> The women should keep silence in the churches. For they are not permitted to speak, but should be subordinate, as even the law says. If there is anything they desire to know, let them ask their husbands at home. For it is shameful for a woman to speak in church. (1 Corinthians 14:34–35)

This silencing and subordination of women was carried into the next generation, long after Paul was dead. One of his successors paraphrased Paul's position with even stronger language:

> Let a woman learn in silence with all submissiveness. I permit no woman to teach or to have authority over men; she is to keep silent. For Adam was formed first, then Eve; and Adam was not deceived, but the woman was deceived and became a transgressor. (1 Timothy 2:11–13)[12]

The remedy for this Adamic curse upon women was that they "be saved through bearing children" (1 Timothy 2:15).

A WOMAN CALLED MAGDALENE

Mary Magdalene is referred to by name only twelve times in the New Testament gospels and never again in any of the other New Testament writings. As we have seen, she appears at the death scene of Jesus, his burial, and the empty tomb, and then disappears from the record. If the New Testament writings were all we had, we would be hard-pressed to say anything more about her. Before we move to an alternative world of early Christian texts outside the New Testament that present an entirely different picture of her status and relationship to Jesus and the twelve apostles, we want to briefly examine why she might be called Magdalene, distinguishing her from the other Marys in the gospel narratives—including Jesus' mother and particularly, Mary of Bethany, the sister of Martha and Lazarus, with whom she has often been identified.

In the Greek texts of the gospels she is known by three slightly differing descriptions: *Maria the Magdalene, Miriam the Magdalene,* and *Maria the one called Magdalene.*[13] The majority of scholars understand the designation "Magdalene" to refer to the city of Magdala (or *Migdal* in Hebrew) located on the northwest shore of the Sea of Galilee about seven miles north of Tiberius. The Greeks called the city *Taricheia,* referring to the pickling of salted fish from the Sea of Galilee, exported throughout the Roman Empire. According to Josephus, the 1st century Jewish historian, Migdal was walled on the west side and had a large aqueduct system, a theater, hippodrome, and a market. Josephus describes it in some detail.[14]

Josephus fortified the city as his headquarters when he became commander of the Jewish forces in Galilee in the 1st Jewish revolt against Rome (66–73 CE). It was culturally and commercially diverse, opulent, and fully exposed to Greco-Roman culture. Shortly after the first Jewish revolt against Rome broke out in 66 CE, the Roman military commander Vespasian, who was later to become emperor, surrounded the city with three Roman legions and laid siege. He stationed 2,000 archers on the mountain to the west overlooking the city. There was a great naval battle at its port and thousands of Jews, defenseless in small boats, were slaughtered. Josephus, an eyewitness, reports that the Sea of Galilee was red with blood, with stinking corpses filling its shoreline for days to follow. The city finally surrendered and opened its gates while thousands of inhabitants who had fled south toward Tiberius were slaughtered or exiled.[15] 1,200 older people were executed, 6,000 of the strongest sent as a gift to the emperor Nero, and 34,400 were sent off as slaves.

The city was apparently more Romanized than the nearby Jewish cities of Capernaum or Chorazin with a cosmopolitan Greek atmosphere.[16] Ongoing excavations at Migdal, including the 2009 discovery of an ancient 1st century CE synagogue, will likely reveal much more as to what this important city was like.[17] If Mary's designation as "Magdalene" refers to her city of origin, placing her in that context gives us a glimpse into her possible background.

The Mariamene Mara ossuary in the Talpiot tomb, as well as that of Judah, the son of Jesus, are elaborately ornamented and the inscriptions are elegant and more formal in appearance than the graffiti-like name tags that many ossuaries exhibit. One is tempted to take Luke's tradition at face value and imagine her as a cosmopolitan woman of independent means who was able, with her connections reaching even into Herod Antipas's household, to head a sizable entourage of women who followed Jesus in Galilee and thus to wield considerable influence in the Jesus movement (Luke 8:1–3).

Even though the identification of Mary's name with the city of Magdala seems to carry the most weight there are two alternative interpretations of "Magdalene."

It is possible that "Magdalene" is a nickname, perhaps even given to Mary by Jesus. We know in the gospels that Jesus often gave his closest followers descriptive nicknames to characterize either their role in his movement or in some cases their personalities. For example, Simon son of Jonah, whom most people know as "Peter," was given the nickname *Cephas* or *Petros* (Peter) in Aramaic and Greek respectively—"the Rock" or "Rocky" (Matthew 16:18). The two fisherman brothers James and John, sons of Zebedee, were nicknamed *Boanerges*, meaning "sons of Thunder," apparently based on their aggressive personalities (Mark 3:17; 10:35–41; Luke 9:54). The apostle James was nicknamed "James the Less," or "James the Younger," either referring to his shortness of stature or his young age, and distinguishing him from the other James, son of Zebedee (Mark 15:40). Simon, another of the twelve apostles, was called "Simon the Zealot," either referring to his militant bent or to his zeal for a cause (Luke 16:15). Since the name Magdalene comes from the Hebrew or Aramaic word *migdal*, meaning tower, perhaps she was given this name "Mary the Tower" as a description of her status or her strong personality.

Finally, there is a third option, less well known but interesting to consider in the light of the Talpiot tombs. It is found tucked away in the Talmud, the ancient written collection of rabbinic oral tradition that was put together between the 5th and 6th centuries CE. There is a strange story about two women named Miriam: one is a hairdresser, presumably referring to Jesus' mother; the other is called Miriam the *Megadla*, meaning the "baby tender," or the one who "grows" the child.[18] We are convinced that these are cryptic references to Mary the mother of Jesus and Mary Magdalene.

One of the most fruitful new aspects of the study of the early development of Judaism and Christianity is the realization that Jews and Christians were living side by side both in the land of Israel and in the major urban centers of the Roman world between the 2nd century CE and the early Byzantine period (4th century CE). Both religions were thriving and both were seen by the dominant culture as strange and foreign due to their adherence to monotheism and their refusal to worship the emperor and participate in mainstream Greco-Roman religious and civic rites. Jews and Christians lived side by side and were in dialogue and debate with one another. For that reason there are many cryptic passages in the rabbinic literature of this period that refer to Jesus, his disputed paternity, his mother, his disciples, his teachings, and even his execution. These sharply polemical passages can seldom be taken as history per se, but they do reflect genuine debates and polemics between Jews and Christian in this time.[19] This material has often been dismissed or ignored because of its complexity. It is also very difficult to date. But it should not be overlooked, because most of the other sources we have on Christianity come from its adherents, written for the purpose of promoting the Christian faith. For example, the late 2nd century philosopher Celsus, mentioned above, says that he based his primary knowledge of the Christians on listening to a Jew who knew the "inside" story that the Christians were trying to repress. What we can begin to construct from the rabbinic materials is an alternative history by those who rubbed shoulders with Christians daily but strongly disputed their claims.

For this reason we believe that an interpretation of a more cryptic, coded meaning of Magdalene should be considered. Based on this tradition there were two Marys in Jesus' life—his mother and the one who "grew" the baby. Since this appears to be what we might have in our 1st century Jewish tomb, it may be the best explanation for the name.

Finally, as with the possibility that the surname means "the Tower," all three could be true. Nicknames often can have variant meanings and that is one reason they are so popular.

A MARRIED JESUS AND THE SILENCE OF THE NEW TESTAMENT

Even though there is no explicit reference to Jesus being married in any of the four gospels or other New Testament writings, the silence might turn out to be less deafening than one would suppose. There are several factors one must consider in making the judgment that he lived a celibate single life.[20]

First, it is important to realize that we know very little about the historical Jesus. What historians are absolutely sure about could be written down on a single piece of paper. What we have in the gospels are not biographies of Jesus—far from it. They are theological presentations regarding his preaching, healing, and in particular the significance of his death and resurrection. They contain almost no personal information. The gospel of Mark, for example, never names or mentions Jesus' father, while the gospel of John never names his mother. We have *one* childhood story, when he was twelve years old, and most scholars consider it a standard literary motif, not a historical account (Luke 2:41–52).[21] We know nothing of his life beyond that point, including his teens and twenties, when most Jewish males were expected to marry.

Second, in regards to the twelve apostles, no wife is named for any of them. None of their children is mentioned or named—how many, what they did, or any personal details about them. Most of the twelve, with the exception of Peter, hardly speak at all in our gospel accounts—a few lines at most.

This silence hardly means that none of them was married. In fact, there is a reference to Peter's mother-in-law, whom Jesus healed of a fever in Mark 1:30–31, but her name is never given. Paul refers to the wives of the other apostles and the brothers of Jesus, but again, no names are given (1 Corinthians 9:5). He even mentions that these women accompanied their husbands on their missionary travels. This is a culture in which countless women are largely forgotten and unknown, their voices muted by the dominant paternalism.[22]

Third, celibacy was not considered an ideal or valued lifestyle among Jews in the Greco-Roman period. Even though it is mistakenly believed that the Essenes, who wrote the Dead Sea Scrolls, valued and practiced celibacy, this notion is likely an invention. The Essenes were one of the three major Jewish groups of this period, along with Pharisees and Sadducees. This misunderstanding stems from the reports of Josephus the Jewish historian (37–100 CE); Philo of Alexandria, a Jewish Hellenistic philosopher (20 BCE–50 CE); and Pliny the Elder, a Roman official (23–79 CE) about the Essenes. Each of these writers projected his own admiration of celibate idealism onto the Essenes, though each of them was married. Josephus, for example, makes the following observation about women and marriage: "They [the Essenes] do not absolutely deny the value of marriage, and the succession of the human race is thereby continued; but they guard against the lascivious behavior of women, and are persuaded that none of them preserve their fidelity to one man."[23]

Such a negative attitude toward women by Josephus, who was married three times, has no basis in history. Philo writes: "[the Essenes] repudiate marriage; and at the same time they practice self-control to a remarkable degree; for no one of the Essenes ever marries a wife, because a wife is a selfish creature, addicted to jealousy and skilled at beguiling the morals of her husband and seducing him by her continued deceptions."[24] Pliny the Elder says that the Essenes "have no women and have renounced all sexual desire."[25] The Dead Sea Scrolls themselves tell a different story, and scholars give their testimony priority as primary sources.

The Dead Sea Scrolls, representing over six hundred texts of the period before and after the time of Jesus, were discovered hidden in caves along the northwest shore of the Dead Sea between 1947 and 1956. They never hint at celibacy; quite the opposite is true. Like other pious Jews of the time, they strictly adhered to the first commandment in the Torah: "Be fruitful, and multiply, and fill the earth" (Genesis 1:28). The Scrolls are full of instructions about marriage, divorce, and avoiding fornication, or sex outside of marriage.[26]

Jesus and John the Baptizer have been rightly connected to the apocalyptic and messianic ideas in the Dead Sea Scrolls. Though neither was likely a formal member of the Dead Sea community, they shared these common ideas. Since the Dead Sea community is most often identified as Essenes, and it is mistakenly assumed that the Essenes practiced celibacy, the argument is often made that Jesus' own celibacy arises out of this context.

It is the same with the rabbis that we know from this period. There are few explicit statements about rabbis being married in the rabbinic sources, but we can be sure that marriage was the norm and celibacy an anomaly. Entire tractates of Jewish law deal with marriage, divorce, and what is forbidden and allowed in terms of sexual behavior. We should assume that as a Jew of his time Jesus *was* married unless we have some evidence to the contrary.

Finally, the apostle Paul is the major Jewish figure of the time who does in fact commend, but not require, celibacy, based primarily on his notion that the end of the age has drawn very near (1 Corinthians 7:26, 29, 31). His was a "situational" celibacy, a practical choice one might make in view of the stressful times that he believed were imminent. Paul recommends celibacy for those who can handle a nonsexual life, but he knows most cannot and end up committing fornication (1 Corinthians 7:2).

It is entirely possible, even likely, that Paul had been married earlier in his life.[27] He says that he "advanced in Judaism beyond many of his own age," indicating that he had formal training as a Pharisee, presumably in Jerusalem (Galatians 1:14). Since for Paul the end of the age was at hand, he thought it inopportune to invest one's life in a gendered humanity that was soon to be transformed into a state where there would be "neither male nor female." Paul expected to live to see a cosmic transformation—a new creation in which birth and death, and mortal states of life in general would pass away.

One of the strongest indicators that Jesus was married comes from Paul directly. He quotes Jesus freely on the prohibition against divorce, but fails to use a celibate Jesus as his major model to support his position on celibacy (1 Corinthians 7:25). In fact he says quite the opposite, that when it comes to celibacy: "I have no command of the Lord, but I give my opinion as one who by the Lord's mercy is trustworthy" (1 Corinthians 7:25). Had Jesus been unmarried Paul would have undoubtedly said that all men should live like Jesus, following the celibate ideal espoused by the Lord, but he says nothing of the kind. In this case Paul's silence strongly implies that he did not think Jesus was unmarried. Given these considerations one can conclude that there are reasons to believe that Jesus was married. And married people at that time usually had children, as the First Commandment required.

The reason it is so difficult for people today to think of Jesus as a normally married Jew of his time and culture has little to do with the fact that his wife and child are not mentioned in our meager sources. This belief is based instead on an ideal of Christian asceticism that began to develop among the church fathers and mothers early in the 2nd century CE. This asceticism was not based on any historical memory of an unmarried Jesus but rather upon Paul's commendation of celibacy—now removed from its apocalyptic context. The celibacy these Christian leaders embraced was based on an aversion to the material world and the body, regarded as inferior to the unseen spiritual realities of the heavenly realms. Christians rejected the material world, even hated it with all its imperfections. They turned their attention wholly toward the heavenly, nonmaterial world. This dualistic view of the cosmos owes little to the historical Jesus the Jew and everything to Hellenistic philosophy and its ascetic ideal.[28] The negative view of women already so rife in the dominant cultural norms of the time was radically advanced by the Christian philosophers and theologians because women, and the sexual temptations they represented for men, were shunned as the ultimate obstacle to a higher spirituality. Tertullian, often called the "father of Latin Christianity," best represents this radically misogynistic trend that remains deeply ingrained in Western Christian culture to this day. Although he believed that even women could be saved by God's grace, he warned them that the whole responsibility for the human condition lay with Eve and her successors:

> You are the gateway of the devil; you are the one who unseals the curse of that tree, and you are the first one to turn your back on the divine law; you are the one who persuaded

him whom the devil was not capable of corrupting; you easily destroyed the image of God, Adam. Because of what you
deserve, that is, death, even the Son of God had to die.[29]

The brilliant 4th century church father Augustine of Hippo carried forward Paul's perspectives and pressed their implications to
the limit. He faced sexual temptations his entire life, even fathering
a child with his lover, but he sought to suppress his lust by choos-
ing a rigorously ascetic life. His famous dictim *inter faeces et uriname
nascimur*—"We are born between feces and urine"—yet with an immortal soul, lay at the root of his attraction and aversion to women.
Perhaps the most notorious example of this unfortunate development
in Christianity was the 5th century Latin theologian Jerome, the most
learned of the church fathers. His savage condemnation of women
and human sexuality was matched only by his disparagement of the
"Old Testament" law and those Jews who did not respond to Jesus. He
connected the two by arguing that the Old Testament was "carnal,"
of the flesh, whereas Christ was spiritual and pure, from above. The
virginal Christ, removed from the filth of sex, showed humankind the
way to escape their fleshly bonds and achieve heavenly perfection.
He even went so far as to state that a husband can best show his love
of his wife by abstaining from sexual intercourse. He opposed bath-
ing, makeup, and female adornment, and saw sex, symbolized by the
female temptress, as fit for pigs and dogs. Jerome wrote openly about
his bouts with sexual temptations.[30]

Given this dualistic orientation toward the heavenly world and
denigration of sex and birth—and therefore women as the vehicle
of both—one can readily see how Mary Magdalene, Jesus, Mary
the mother of Jesus, and even Joseph her husband *had* to be cast
as living nonsexual lives. This obsession with virginity is firmly
grounded in 2nd and 3rd century CE asceticism, not in Jesus' own
life and times.

MARY MAGDALENE AS SINNER AND WHORE

It is an easy step from this stream of dualistic misogynist thinking, the core of emerging 4th and 5th century Christianity, to recasting the New Testament figure of Mary Magdalene as a sinner and even a whore. None of eleven New Testament texts that mention her presents her in any negative light. On the contrary, as we have seen, she seems to be the leader of the band of faithful Galilean women who stand by Jesus at the cross. Even when the men have fled in fear, she prepares spices and perfumed oils in order to complete the Jewish rites of burial, and she becomes a first witness to the empty tomb and Jesus' resurrection. She enters and exits the scene in the space of a few pages of our texts—never to appear again in any New Testament text.

There are three scenes in Mark, Luke, and John respectively that recount how Jesus was anointed with a flask of costly scented oil by a woman. As they now stand in our texts they are not the same narrative, yet their core elements are so similar that they appear to be three versions of the "same" story, a woman anointing Jesus.

In the gospel of Mark the scene takes place in Bethany, a small village on the Mount of Olives just east of the city of Jerusalem, two days before Jesus' arrest and crucifixion (Mark 14:3–9).[31] Jesus is dining as a guest in the house of one called Simon the leper, otherwise unknown. A woman arrives with a flask of pure nard ointment, breaks it, and pours it over Jesus' head. Some at the dinner protest that such a costly ointment has been wasted and could have been sold and given to the poor for three hundred denarii—which would be a year's wages for a day laborer. Jesus defends the unnamed woman's action, saying, "You always have the poor with you. She has done a beautiful thing." He then declares: "She has done what she could. She has anointed my body for burying. And truly, I say to you, wherever the gospel is preached in the whole world, what she has done will be told in memory of her" (Mark 14:8–9).

The gospel of John seems to know a very similar story (John 12:1–

8; 11:1–3). Again the scene is in Bethany, but six days before the crucifixion, and at dinner in the house of the two sisters, Mary and Martha, and their brother Lazarus, whom Jesus had raised from the dead. Martha is serving but Mary took costly ointment of pure nard and anointed the feet of Jesus and wiped them with her hair. Judas Iscariot, who was to betray Jesus, objected that the ointment could have been sold for three hundred denarii and given to the poor. The text points out that he did this out of greed, not care for the poor, for he served as bursar of the group and used to pilfer the funds. Jesus replied: "Let her alone, let her keep it for the day of my burial. The poor you always have with you, but you do not always have me" (John 12:7–8).

In both texts the woman has a *prophetic* role—anointing Jesus' body beforehand as if he were already dead; she is commended for her actions, as if she somehow "knows" more than the others, perhaps without even realizing it herself, while the others miss the point of her actions entirely. In John the woman is named—Mary of Bethany, and her family has already been introduced (John 11). In Mark she is unidentified, with the irony that her story will be told perpetually "in memory of her." John's account is more shocking, since the anointing of the feet, and especially the wiping of the feet with her hair, either implies a shockingly inappropriate intimacy or a familial bond, since men and women who are not married would never touch in this way. The hair of a woman was considered sexually provocative and was to be covered, as in conservative Middle Eastern societies today, both Jewish and Muslim.[32] In that sense the story is scandalous, foreshadowing the attempt of Mary Magdalene to prepare spices and anoint the corpse of Jesus when he is dead. The problem is, Mary of Bethany is not Mary Magdalene—*or is she?* Mark had emphasized that Mary Magdalene and her entourage came from Galilee, whereas John introduces her at the crucifixion scene as an intimate family member, standing with Jesus' mother.

It is impossible to reconcile these differences. Mark and John clearly have the same story, but their details are different. The strong implication in John is that Mary of Bethany *is* otherwise known as Mary Magdalene, and that she is either married to Jesus or otherwise considered like a sister, a part of the family. Mark knows nothing of this and never mentions Mary of Bethany.

Luke's story recasts everything (Luke 7:36–50). The setting is Galilee, not Jerusalem, weeks if not months before Jesus' death. Jesus is dining at the house of a man named Simon, though it is not said he is a leper. A woman comes in off the street, unnamed, uninvited, and unannounced, but known to the village as a "sinner," which implies she was a whore. The diners are reclining, in Greco-Roman banquet style, and she stands behind Jesus at his feet and begins to weep, wetting his feet with her tears, kissing them, and anointing them with oil. Nothing is said about the cost of the oil and the objection is not the waste but that Jesus would permit himself to be touched by a sexually promiscuous woman and not realize, were he a prophet, her sinful status. Simon objects and Jesus rebukes him, commending the woman for her uninvited hospitality in welcoming him, washing his feet, and loving him. He declares: "Therefore I tell you, her sins, which are many, are forgiven, for she loved much; but he who is forgiven little, loves little." He then turns to the woman and says to her, "Your sins are forgiven." The dinner guests were even more scandalized that he could claim the right to forgive sins.

Some have doubted that the parallel accounts in Mark and John are related to this one, but most scholars, knowing that Luke is using Mark as his narrative source, are convinced he is deliberately recasting the scene. He drops the anointing scene entirely from the last days of Jesus' life, moves it to Galilee, and puts it much earlier. Why would he do this?

The answer is most likely that he wants to disparage Mary Magdalene. Immediately following his anointing story he introduces her by name but presents her as a terribly deranged woman, possessed of *seven demons* that Jesus had cast out! (Luke 8:2). Later, when he introduces the women from Galilee who stood by at Jesus' crucifix-

ion, he does not mention their names or put Mary Magdalene at their
head. He records no appearance of Jesus to Mary Magdalene at the
empty tomb, as do Matthew and John. Knowing how deeply embedded she is in early Christian tradition, Luke cannot write her out of
the story completely, so he minimizes her role. Later in his narrative, as a further way of distancing himself from the anointing story
in the gospel of John, he presents two sisters, Mary and Martha, but
has them living far outside of Jerusalem, somewhere in Galilee to the
north (Luke 13:22).

The Gospel of Peter, discovered in fragments in Egypt in the 1890s,
adopts and further appropriates Luke's marginalization of Mary
Magdalene. In this text Peter is prominent, narrating the events sur-
rounding Jesus' empty tomb, but no women are mentioned at Jesus'
crucifixion scene, standing faithfully while the men fled. Although
Mary Magdalene is mentioned, and even called a *mathetria*—a female
disciple of Jesus, who comes early Sunday morning with her friends to
mourn inside the tomb, most significantly Jesus never appears to the
women and they receive no commission to go and spread the good
news of the resurrection to the male disciples (*Gospel of Peter* 12:50).

Luke's strategy had a lasting effect. Readers of the gospels later
found it easy to conflate the stories. First, it became common and accepted to identify Mary Magdalene with Mary of Bethany, the sister
of Martha and brother of Lazarus. As early as the late 2nd century,
Tertullian had already described Mary Magdalene as the "woman
who was a sinner."[33] This salacious identification stuck. The image
of Jesus as the all-forgiving one—the friend of prostitutes and sinners—was sexually provocative. The idea of the sinful woman, like
Eve, seduced by the Devil, but now redeemed, could serve as the story
of all women.[34] It was Pope Gregory the Great (540–604 CE) who
sealed her fate. He conflated John's story of Mary of Bethany with the
sinful woman who anoints Jesus in Luke, and declared both women
were Mary Magdalene. He waxed on as to how Mary the whore, who
once perfumed herself to seduce men, flirted with her eyes, arranged

her hair, and made use of her lips, now turned all those elements in chaste service to the Lord—anointing him, weeping and wiping the tears with her hair, and kissing his feet.[35]

In the Middle Ages Mary Magdalene became wildly popular, with legends growing up regarding her missionary travels to Europe. She became the model of the hopeless sinner, transformed from a sexually fallen woman to a chaste and forgiven saint. All over Europe there are hundreds of shrines and churches dedicated to her with her supposed relics. Her feast days are among the most popular on the church calendar. It was not until the late 1970s that the Roman Catholic Church officially repudiated the connection between Luke's sinful woman and Mary Magdalene. Ironically, on a more popular level, the myth continues and most people still think of Mary Magdalene as the deranged whore whom Jesus redeemed. This view has been spurred on by films, plays, and books such as Martin Scorsese's *The Last Temptation of Christ* (based on Nikos Kazantzakis's novel), and of course Andrew Lloyd Webber and Tim Rice's *Jesus Christ Superstar*. It's an image too hard to resist—and yet if the Talpiot tomb is the tomb of the Jesus family and Mariamene can be identified with the historical Mary Magdalene, then the alternative, untold story is perhaps even more compelling.

MARY MAGDALENE AS THE APOSTLE OF THE APOSTLES

We have seen how Mary Magdalene, and in some cases her female entourage, are portrayed as "first witness" to Jesus' empty tomb and given the commission to tell the male disciples he is risen in the New Testament gospels. In Mark the women flee from the tomb and say nothing to anyone (Mark 16:8). In Luke they report to the eleven remaining apostles but their testimony is considered an "idle tale" (Luke 24:11). In Matthew, as the women flee the tomb they meet Jesus, grab hold of his feet, and worship him, and he directs them to tell the male apostles he will meet them in Galilee (Matthew 28:9–10). Finally, in

John, Mary Magdalene goes *alone* to the tomb and has her personal encounter and exchange with Jesus, thus becoming the *first witness* to Jesus raised from the dead and ascending to heaven (John 20:11–18).

In addition to the *Gospel of Peter* there are a dozen or so ancient texts, most of them discovered in the last hundred years, that present an alternative "lost" portrait of Mary Magdalene and her role as Jesus' female apostle extraordinaire—quite literally *the* apostle of the apostles and the successor to Jesus. Five of them were discovered in Egypt in 1945, buried in a jar in a field outside a village called Nag Hammadi. These texts are *The Gospel of Thomas, The Dialogue of the Savior, The First Apocalypse of James, The Gospel of Philip*, and *The Sophia of Jesus Christ*. Others, including *Pistis Sophia, The Gospel of Mary*, and the *Acts of Philip*, have turned up in various places, whether on the antiquities market, an archaeological dig, or lost or forgotten in ancient libraries. In these texts Mary Magdalene is Jesus' intimate confidante and companion, one who possesses unparalleled spiritual insights that she received directly from him. She is praised, but also at times opposed—especially by Peter, leader of the male apostles, who is threatened by her position and status based on her special relationship with Jesus. These texts originate outside the mainstream, that is, the male-dominated form of orthodox Christianity that began to take hold and triumph down to the time of Constantine, the first Christian emperor (circa 325 CE). The canonical New Testament, with its twenty-seven approved documents, was increasingly regarded as the only authorized text, inspired by God, while these other texts were marginalized, declared heretical, and eventually lost and forgotten. They are witness to the diverse mix of "Christianities" that were developing in the 2nd and 3rd centuries CE before a more singular orthodoxy, backed by Christian councils and creeds, took center stage.

Jane Schaberg has constructed a working profile of Mary Magdalene from these texts, isolating the major elements. Mary Magdalene is prominent among the followers of Jesus, she speaks boldly and is often in open conflict with the male disciples, she is an intimate companion of Jesus, and he praises her for her superior spiritual understanding and defends her.[36]

Each of these texts contains an assortment of these elements but one in particular, *The Gospel of Mary*, has them all. This is an extraordinary text. This is the only gospel of a woman, and not just any woman, Mary Magdalene. A fragmentary copy of *The Gospel of Mary* was purchased in Cairo in 1896. It is written in Coptic but was likely translated from a Greek original. It dates to the early 2nd century.[37] In this text Mary Magdalene is a beloved disciple of Jesus, taking center stage in leading the apostles and encouraging them. Peter is jealous of her, but admits her status as one closer to Jesus than anyone else, and more important, as one who received revelations that the male disciples were not privy to:

> Peter said to Mary: "Sister we know the savior loved you more than any other woman. Tell us the words of the savior that you remember, which you know but we do not, because we have not heard them." Mary answered and said, "What is hidden from you I shall reveal to you" (*Gospel of Mary* 10).[38]

As she begins to recount her visionary message both Peter and his brother Andrew express doubts about her veracity and question her authority. Peter objects: "Did he really speak with a woman in private without our knowledge? Should we all turn and listen to her? Did he prefer her to us?" (*Gospel of Mary* 18). Levi, who is better known as Matthew in the New Testament, defends her and rebukes Peter: "If the savior made her worthy, who are you to reject her? Surely the savior knows her well. That is why he has loved her more than us" (*Gospel of Mary* 18). The message Mary reveals, in this and many of these other texts, has been characterized as *Gnostic*, but most scholars consider the term to be problematic. It tends to lump them together as a monolithic whole.[39] In our analysis of these texts we are not so much interested in the theological content as the framework of the profile of Mary Magdalene and her prominent status alongside Jesus.

The Gospel of Philip is a beautifully written "gnostic" sermon by the followers of the brilliant 2nd century early Christian mystic and teacher Valentinus. Some have even suggested he is the author of the text. It refers to Mary Magdalene only twice, but both passages are noteworthy:

> Three women walked with the master: Mary his mother, [his] sister, and Mary Magdalene, who is called his companion. For "Mary" is the name of his sister, his mother, and his companion. (*Gospel of Philip* 59:6–10)

> The companion of the [savior] is Mary Magdalene. The [savior loved] her more than [all] the disciples, [and he] kissed her often on her [mouth]. The other [disciples] said to him, Why do you love her more than all of us? (*Gospel of Philip* 63:32–64, 9)

Translated, the word "companion" means his partner or consort. There is a worm hole in the papyrus right at the point where it says Jesus used to kiss Mary often on the . . . ? Most scholars have restored this to "mouth." Scholars have debated whether this relationship between the two involved sexual intimacy, but it most likely did. It was considered a "sacred union," but it was nonetheless physical.[40]

Pistis Sophia contains a series of questions asked of Jesus, and Mary Magdalene has the most prominent role among the disciples. She asks thirty-nine of the forty-six questions and offers elegant teachings about the nature of life in the world. Jesus extravagantly praises her: "Blessed Mary, you whom I shall complete with all the mysteries on high, speak openly, for you are one whose heart is set on heaven's kingdom more than all your brothers" (*Pistis Sophia* 18). Peter complains about her, telling Jesus "we cannot endure this woman," but Jesus praises her pure spiritual insights and declares her the most blessed of all women.

Scholars of these texts generally do not view them as historical accounts. However, they do generally agree that because she is the vehicle for alternative forms of emerging Christianity, her special role in the life of the historical Jesus, more muted in the New Testament gospels, reflects real history. Many of these documents come from the 2nd century CE and are accordingly not so far removed from the earlier Christian oral tradition and the canonical gospels.

MARY MAGDALENE AND THE TALPIOT TOMBS

We live in an age of rediscovery of long-lost texts and ancient manuscripts that are adding immensely to our understanding of early Christianity. Along with archaeological discoveries of ancient Jerusalem, we have new sources with which to evaluate the evidence found in the Talpiot tombs, especially with regard to Mariamene Mara and her role in Jesus' life and family.

Given the collective evidence, and particularly the unique tradition that the gospel of John adds to the core story of Mary Magdalene from Mark and Matthew, it seems plausible that the enigmatic figure of Mary Magdalene as first witness to Jesus' resurrection can be seen alongside the tradition of "Mary of Bethany," and the unnamed woman who anoints Jesus' head as well as his feet and dries them with her hair. These acts of intimacy, as is the preparation of his body for burial, are appropriate only for a wife, mother, or a sister. The fact that Mary Magdalene's first impulse, according to the gospel of John, on seeing Jesus resurrected was to touch him suggests further the intimate relationship between husband and wife. Taken together, these texts and the later 2nd century "gnostic" ones provide us with a broader context in which the evidence from the Talpiot tombs can be read in a new light. The archaeological evidence is clear—Jesus was married and had a son named Judah. To reject the finds of the

Garden tomb on the grounds that he could not have been married is a traditional bias based on misguided criteria.

The position of Mary of Bethany in the gospel of John also offers a new interpretive possibility for the names in the Talpiot tomb. If the traditions about her and about Mary Magdalene are confused, as they seem to be in the New Testament gospels, then Mary Magdalene might well have had a sister named Martha. As mentioned earlier, some scholars have read the *Mariamene Mara* inscription as *Mariam and Mara*—referring to two women named Mary and Martha. We are convinced otherwise, namely that *Mara* is more likely a title of honor for Mariamene, but having these two sisters, "Mary and Martha," buried together in a single ossuary, one the mother of Jesus' son, the other her unmarried sister, makes for an even closer fit with the thesis that the Talpiot Jesus tomb is the family tomb of Jesus. Interestingly enough, DNA evidence supports either possibility, as we will see in the final chapter, since sisters share the same mitochondrial DNA profiles.

We now turn to a consideration of a seventh inscribed ossuary, besides the six recovered by the IAA in 1980—namely the one inscribed "James son of Joseph, brother of Jesus." There is compelling new evidence that it also originated in the Talpiot Jesus family tomb. If that is the case, the probabilities of this configuration of names being the tomb of Jesus evolve into a virtual certainty.

CHAPTER SIX

THE MYSTERY OF THE JAMES OSSUARY

On October 21, 2002, the dramatic headline flashed around the world—*First Evidence of Jesus Written in Stone!* Hershel Shanks, editor of *Biblical Archaeology Review*, the flagship magazine of the nonprofit Biblical Archaeology Society, held a press conference packed with journalists at the Marriott hotel in Washington, D.C. He revealed that a limestone "bone box," an ossuary, reliably dated to the 1st century CE, had recently surfaced in Israel in the hands of an unnamed private collector. It was inscribed in Aramaic, *Ya'akov bar-Yosef akhui diYeshua.* English translation: *James son of Joseph brother of Jesus.* Shanks announced that scientists at the prestigious Geological Survey of Israel had verified the authenticity of the ossuary, and world-renowned Sorbonne epigrapher André Lemaire—an expert in ancient scripts—had also authenticated the inscription. Based on these verifications, and the statistical improbabilities of these names and relationships referring to anyone else in that time, Shanks asserted that this ossuary had once held the bones of James the brother of Jesus

37. The James ossuary with its inscription.

of Nazareth. If correct, this would be the first and only archaeological artifact from the time of Jesus to mention his name.

Major media throughout the world, including the *New York Times* and countless other newspapers, the major wire services, and all the major TV networks picked up the story. Shanks released photographs, passed out press releases, and the full story, including Lemaire's analysis, and that of the geologists, was published in the November–December issue of *Biblical Archaeology Review.*[1] Shanks and his coauthor, Professor Ben Witherington III, also published a book, *The Brother of Jesus: The Dramatic Story and Meaning of the First Archaeological Link to Jesus and His Family*, to coincide with the press conference.

Simcha was present throughout these dramatic events as he had contracted with Shanks to produce a TV documentary on the James ossuary that aired on the Discovery Channel, in over seventy countries, the following Easter, 2003.[2]

Shanks then dropped another bombshell—the ossuary itself was being flown from Israel and would be on display at the Royal Ontario Museum in Toronto, beginning November 15, 2002, just over a month away. The city and the date had been chosen to coincide with the annual professional meetings of the Society of Biblical Literature, the American Academy of Religion, and the American Schools of Oriental Research the weekend before Thanksgiving in Toronto. These meetings would bring together over ten thousand of the world's biblical scholars, professors of religion, and biblical archaeologists.

The orchestration of all of these related publications and activities could not have been more effective. The James ossuary was already being hailed as perhaps the greatest archaeological discovery of all time.

Simcha and James almost crossed paths in Toronto that November. James was attending the annual meetings and had been invited by Shanks to join him and a group of about thirty professors for a private after-hours viewing of the exhibit. Simcha was there to document the gathering and get the first live reactions of the scholars. A who's who of biblical scholars, experts in ancient inscriptions, and historians filled the exhibit hall that evening. Everyone present seemed genuinely moved by the ossuary itself and impressed with its authenticity, including the renowned epigraphers Frank Moore Cross, Jr., of Harvard, Joseph Fitzmyer of Catholic University of America, and P. Kyle McCarter of Johns Hopkins University. In addition to the viewing, there was a special plenary session with a panel discussion at the Society of Biblical Literature meeting that weekend. The only objection expressed on a panel that included André Lemaire and several leading historians and archaeologists was that giving such attention to an artifact that had been purchased on the antiquities market, and thus lacked any archaeological context that could serve to inform its interpretation, was less than ideal. This had also been the case for many of the Dead Sea Scrolls that first came to public view in 1947, because they were being offered for sale by Bedouin who claimed to have found them in caves on the northwest shore of the Dead Sea.

Sometimes valuable archaeological finds emerge from less than ideal circumstances. Because of this lack of context one has to always be cautious because a convincing forgery is always a possibility.[3]

By the time of the Toronto exhibit the name of the owner of the ossuary, Oded Golan, had been leaked. The IAA launched an investigation and by the summer of 2003, just a few months after Simcha's Discovery TV documentary had been released, a team of Israeli experts issued a report that concluded that although the James ossuary itself was authentic, Golan had forged part of the ossuary inscription in order to increase its value. Golan and four other co-conspirators were indicted on forty-four charges of forgery and antiquities trafficking, not only involving the James ossuary, but another inscribed artifact that had appeared on the black market in January of that year.[4] A criminal trial began in December 2004. On October 3, 2010, the prosecution and the defense concluded their cases. In the meantime charges were dropped against all but Golan. The ruling of the presiding judge is expected soon and based on some of his concluding remarks, some observers expect that the charges will be dismissed.[5]

Once the indictments were announced and the trial began in Jerusalem, a virtual bandwagon of opposition to the authenticity of the James ossuary inscription followed. This opposition included articles in the *New Yorker* and *Archaeology* magazines, a segment on *60 Minutes*, and stories in most major newspapers around the world, as well as countless blog and Internet posts. They concluded that Oded Golan was part of an extended forgery ring and that there was conclusive physical evidence that the James Ossuary inscription was a forgery.[6] Since then two major books have been published, one popular, the other scholarly, purporting to document the scandal and weighing in on the side of forgery.[7] The academic response on the whole has been harsh. One commentator put it this way: "the archaeological fact [is] that the inscription is a modern forgery."[8] The general public appears to have been convinced by this tsunami of criticism. Hershel

Shanks, an experienced lawyer, and his coauthor, Ben Witherington, have stood their ground but reserved final judgment. They argue that a convincing case for forgery has not been made. The scientists at the Geological Survey of Israel have not retracted their initial judgment as to the authenticity of the inscription and the ancient patina covering the ossuary, based on their initial physical tests. A few scattered academics have agreed but the mainstream believes the ossuary inscription to be a forgery.[9]

Despite the widespread perception that the inscription was forged, so far not a single qualified epigrapher has rejected the ossuary inscription on paleographic grounds—that is, the style of the writing and its integrity. Expert epigraphers can usually spot forgeries by examining the form and style of the letters and comparing them with inscriptions of the period in question that are known to be authentic from the archaeological contexts in which they were found. The Dead Sea Scrolls have been authenticated in this way despite their surfacing on the black market.

The IAA case for forgery was partly circumstantial, but primarily based on physical tests conducted by Yuval Goren. He concluded that the letters of the inscription cut through the original patina of the ossuary—the natural growth of chemical deposits that builds up over time on stone—showing that the incisions were made later, in modern times.[10] The indictment further charged that Golan had clumsily tried

38. A detailed drawing of the Aramaic inscription on the James ossuary.

to apply a fake patina over the inscription, once he had carved it, applying a pastiche he created. The case of the prosecution suffered a tremendous blow when it was shown by experts that although the ossuary inscription had been cleaned by its owner, there was nonetheless original, authentic patina in the grooves of the letters—demonstrating that it could not have been added later. The chief witness for the prosecution on the patina authenticity admitted under oath that this was the case.[11]

Professor Camille Fuchs has examined the prevalence of names of deceased Jewish male individuals in Jerusalem in the 1st century CE. He determined that there was a very high probability that between the years 45 and 70 AD not more than one adult male Jew with the name James who had a father named Joseph and a brother named Jesus is likely to have lived in Jerusalem.[12]

A MISSING OSSUARY

Early in our investigation of the Talpiot tombs, we began to consider the possibility that the unprovenanced James ossuary might have come from the Garden tomb. It was speculation at first, a hypothesis that if proven would substantiate the mounting evidence linking the Garden tomb with Jesus of Nazareth. If the James ossuary did come from the Talpiot Jesus tomb, its tie to Jesus of Nazareth could hardly be questioned.

Joseph Gath's initial report on the Garden tomb's excavation clearly states that there were *ten* ossuaries in the tomb. Here are Gath's own words:

> During the archaeological dig at the site 10 ossuaries were found in the different niches. No primary burial was found in the niches and only one niche was found without ossuaries (Niche no. 4). On the floor of the main room there were remains of bones, including skulls and limb bones below the burial shelves.[13]

In 2005, when James first visited the IAA storage warehouse in Beth Shemesh outside Jerusalem to examine the Talpiot Jesus tomb ossuaries, he was accompanied by Shimon Gibson who, as mentioned earlier, had been the surveyor for the excavation in April 1980. They were both astounded when the curator explained that only nine of the ten ossuaries from this tomb were listed on his tally. He apologized, stating that they had searched for the tenth but had no idea what had happened to it, even though it had been given a cataloguing number in 1980. His precise words were "The tenth ossuary is missing." Shimon rechecked the map he had drawn of the tomb at the time of the excavation—there was no doubt that the tomb had originally contained ten ossuaries.

James and Shimon began to search through the archive files of the IAA. There were clear photos of only nine ossuaries, but nothing in the records about a tenth. They checked the 1996 published report on the tomb prepared by Amos Kloner, who was Gath's supervisor and had overseen the excavation. Kloner described each of the first nine ossuaries in detail along with the original photographs. At the end of his roster he listed the tenth, but with a one-word description and no photo: "10. IAA 80.509: 60 x 26 x 30 cm. Plain." From this one line we knew that the ossuary had been given a catalogue number but no one seemed to have any idea what had happened to it. The curator explained that it should have been photographed as part of the routine registration process.

Later we noticed that the Rahmani catalogue of ossuaries in the Israeli state collection also included only nine (nos. 701–9), with the comment that the tenth was plain and broken and was not retained.[14] James had noticed that the dimensions of the James ossuary were officially published as: 56.5 x 25 x 30.5—close but not exactly the same as the missing tenth ossuary. Simcha subsequently asked his associate Felix Goluber to measure the James ossuary under IAA supervision, using the standard template indicating where to take length, width, and height measurements. It was 56.5 x 25.7 x 29.5—a bit closer to the dimensions Kloner had published. Felix noted that the James ossuary was not rectangular in shape but trapezoid, so that its dimensions would vary slightly, depending on which side or end was measured.[15] For us the "fit" was close enough that we did not think that the *possibility* that the James ossuary was the missing tenth from the Talpiot tomb should be dismissed. Obviously, there would need to be much more evidence.

Subsequently James met with Joe Zias in Jerusalem. Zias was the anthropologist at the IAA in 1980. James asked Joe what might have happened to the tenth ossuary. Joe explained that with millions of artifacts from thousands of excavations, things regularly go missing, but often they show up again. Joe was quite sure the missing tenth ossuary had nothing to do with the James ossuary and told James he thought his speculation in that regard was irresponsible and misleading.

A BROTHER NAMED JAMES

When the news of the James ossuary first was announced, the major challenge was to explain to the public that Jesus even had brothers and sisters, much less a brother as prominent as James, who history shows succeeded Jesus as head of the movement after his crucifixion. Even though two of our gospels, Mark and Matthew, list the brothers of Jesus by name, and Paul in his letters refers to meeting "James the Lord's brother" and acknowledged his leadership of the Jerusalem church, James remains one of the least-known characters in the history of the early Christian movement (Mark 6:3; Matthew 13:55; Galatians 1:19). The reasons for this are twofold; one is a matter of simple name confusion, the other of deeply ingrained theological dogma.

This name confusion is understandable. Although the name James—Jacob in Greek and Hebrew—is an uncommon male Jewish name in the time of Jesus (1.6 percent of all named males), there are two Jameses listed among the twelve apostles. One is James the fisherman, the brother of John and the son of Zebedee, while the other is James the son of Alphaeus (Mark 1:19; 3:17–18). There is also "James the Less," or perhaps "James the Younger," who may or may not be identified with either of the two Jameses in the list of the twelve (Mark 15:40). Jesus' brother named James may or may not be identified with James the son of Alphaeus or James the Younger, so we have anywhere from two to four men named James who are prominent in the life of Jesus. There have been various proposals as to how to sort through these different figures, but scholars are not in agreement.[16]

Throughout Europe and in most countries where Christianity is the dominant religion, there are countless churches and cathedrals named for St. James. Some honor James the fisherman, others James the Younger, and a few, especially in the Armenian and Eastern traditions, James the brother of Jesus. Almost every city has a church dedicated to St. James, but most people would be hard-pressed to identify which James is the namesake.

The theological problem is a more difficult one. Sorting through the various men named James in the gospels is one thing, but asserting that Jesus had a natural brother, born of the same mother, is quite another. Some Christians consider this concept to be heresy. It strikes at the deeply felt emotions of millions of devout Christians who believe in the Blessed *Virgin* Mary—and for them this means *perpetual* virginity. According to this understanding, not only did Mary become pregnant without a man, by the Holy Spirit, but she also remained a chaste virgin the rest of her life. According to this belief, it would be impossible for Jesus to have had actual *brothers* (and sisters) no matter what the gospels report.

For the same reasons that the emerging Christian church desperately wanted to cast Jesus as a lifelong celibate, it became even more essential that his mother be one. She became *the* preeminent symbol of an ideal woman in the early Christian church: pure and holy, entirely dedicated to spiritual things. As we discussed previously, *female* sexuality was seen as much more threatening than male sexuality. Once one insists that "the blessed Virgin Mary" was "ever-virgin," then there has to be some explanation for the fact that two of the gospels name four brothers as well as mentioning at least two un-named sisters. The conflict arises when later forms of ascetic piety and assumptions about "holiness" are imposed on a culture for dog-matic or political reasons. In that process we lose the historical reality of Mary—or to use her Jewish name, Miriam—as a Jewish married woman with a family of at least six children.

Matthew and Luke both relate the story of Mary's virginal preg-nancy. Matthew adds that after Joseph discovered her condition, he went ahead with the marriage but "knew her not *until* she had borne a son, and he called his name Jesus" (Matthew 1:25). The notion of the perpetual virginity of Mary is not found in any of our New Testament documents, and her virginal conception of Jesus is found only in Matthew and Luke. It is never mentioned—by Paul, Mark, John, or any other New Testament writer. What's more, it was not even an ele-ment in the earliest Christian creeds.

The first official mention of Mary's perpetual virginity only ap-pears in 374 CE, from a Christian theologian named Epiphanius.[17] Until then most of our early Christian writings take for granted that the brothers and sisters of Jesus were the natural-born children of Joseph and Mary.[18]

By the late 4th century CE the church began to handle the prob-lem of Mary's sexual life with two alternative explanations. One is that "brothers" is not meant literally but is a general term referring to "cousins." This became the standard explanation in the West.[19] In the East, Greek-speaking Christians favored a different view—the broth-ers were sons of Joseph by a previous marriage. It was imagined that Joseph was much older than Mary, that he had been married with four sons and at least two daughters before he met Mary, and that his wife, the natural mother of these six children, had most likely died. That would mean that these other children, whether brothers or sis-ters, had no blood ties to Jesus or his mother.[20]

Another related problem developed over the next century or two in the West. If Jesus was a lifelong celibate and his mother a perpetual virgin, then surely Joseph, the reputed father, must also have been celibate—otherwise how could the sexual purity of the mother and son be associated with someone not celibate?

The solution became obvious—Joseph, husband of Mary, must have been a lifelong ("perpetual") virgin as well. That way the Holy Family, Jesus included, could be fully and properly "holy" and re-moved from the corruptions of the flesh. Such a belief views sex dimly.

The idea took hold and had irresistible power. It became incon-ceivable for Christians, particularly in the West, to imagine Mary or Joseph as a normal sexual couple, or for that matter even living a "bodily" life at all. There were even serious discussions of whether any of the three of them—Jesus, Mary, or Joseph—shared normal bodily functions with the rest of humankind. Since the theologians knew it was important to emphasize that Jesus was "fully human" as well as "fully God," it was generally agreed that they used the toilet, bathed, and experienced all normal bodily functions—but one gets the idea it was best not to think of such things. The same kind of extreme dual-ism of flesh and spirit, of earth and heaven, of "below" and "above," was now projected onto the entire "family" of Jesus—which by any definition was no longer a normal family.

That is one reason the Talpiot tombs are so important. If they are related to the *historical* Jesus, as a Jew in his own culture and time, they jolt us back to reality. They help us recover not just Jesus, but his mother, his brothers, and perhaps his wife and child, as real human beings who walked and breathed and lived and died—as we all do. There is something incredibly sobering about ossuaries, bones, and tombs, reminding us that this world, with its realities of death and the decay of the body, is our shared human experience.

Over the past five years we have been in many Jerusalem tombs of this period trying to learn firsthand about Jewish burial. We have never failed to enter a tomb without a sobering and moving sense of the shared humanity that the tomb so tangibly represents. The day we first entered the Talpiot Jesus tomb together in December 2005 it was hard to say much at all. After all our research discussions, we were suddenly speechless. We gazed at the piles of holy books that the rabbis had buried inside and it was eerily still and quiet. We could hear the voices of the film crew outside, but for a few moments we felt joined to this family that we had studied so intensely in a way we had not imagined. It was one of those moments in life, seldom duplicated and never forgotten.

JAMES THE JUST

Paul, as we have noted, mentions visiting James *the brother of Jesus* in his letter to the Galatians (Galatians 1–2). Although Paul stresses the independence of his personal "revelation of Jesus Christ" from those who were apostles before him, his acknowledgment that James had become the leader of the movement following the death of Jesus is clear. Although Peter is remembered as the titular leader of the apostles, our earliest New Testament sources tell a somewhat different story. Paul refers to the three "pillars" of the church, naming James, Peter (whom he calls by his Aramaic name, Cephas), and John—but James is always listed first (Galatians 2:9). The book of Acts, written by the author of the gospel of Luke, underscores James's leadership. It is James the brother of Jesus who presides over the first council of the church, held around 50 CE in Jerusalem. Peter is of course present, and is invited to speak, but James presides and at the end of their meeting declares *his* decision—to which the body of "apostles and elders assembled agree" (Acts 15:19). Several years later, when Paul returns to Jerusalem, under criticism from some in the movement that he was abandoning his Jewish observance of the Torah, it is before "James and all the elders" that Paul appears to defend himself and it is James again who pronounces his decision, to which Paul agrees (Acts 21:17–26). There is even a book of the New Testament that may have been written by James and another by Jesus' brother Judas.

In texts and traditions outside the New Testament, ranging from the 2nd through the 4th centuries, no one disputes that it was James who was left in charge of the movement Jesus had begun, governing things from the mother church in Jerusalem.[21]

Clement of Alexandria, who wrote in the late 2nd century CE, confirms this succession of James. At one point he wrote: "Peter and James and John after the Ascension of the Savior did not struggle for glory, because they had previously been given honor by the Savior, but chose James the Just as Overseer of Jerusalem."[22] In a subsequent passage Clement elaborated: "After the resurrection the Lord [Jesus] gave the tradition of knowledge to James the Just and John and Peter, these gave it to the other Apostles, and the other Apostles to the Seventy."[23] This passage preserves for us the tiered structure of the leadership that Jesus left behind: James the Just as Successor; John and Peter as his advisers; the rest of the twelve; then the Seventy, who were called "Elders."

Eusebius, the early 4th century CE Christian historian, commented on this passage: "James whom men of old had surnamed 'Just' for his excellence of virtue, is recorded to have been the first elected to the *throne* of the Oversight of the church in Jerusalem."[24] The Greek term *thronos* refers to a "seat" or "chair" of authority and is the same term used for a king or ruler.

Eusebius also preserves the testimony of Hegesippus, a Jewish Christian of the early second century CE, who he says is from the "generation after the Apostles": "The succession of the church passed to James the brother of the Lord, together with the Apostles. He was called the 'Just' by all men from the Lord's time until ours, since many are called James, but he was holy from his mother's womb."[25] The Greek word that Hegesippus used here, *diadexomai* ("to succeed"), is regularly used for the passing of inherited leadership, as when Philip, king of Macedonia, passes on his rule to Alexander the Great.[26]

An archaeological discovery has added to and reinforced these texts on the importance of James. In a chance find made in 1945 in Upper Egypt, the Coptic *Gospel of Thomas* was discovered along with eleven other Coptic texts that we now call the Nag Hammadi library. Five of these texts we mentioned in the previous chapter as giving a new and important role to Mary Magdalene. Although *The Gospel of Thomas* dates to the third century, scholars have shown that it preserves, despite later theological embellishments, an original Aramaic document that comes to us from the early days of the Jerusalem church.[27] It provides a rare glimpse into what scholars have called "Jewish Christianity," that is, the earliest followers of Jesus led by James the brother of Jesus. *The Gospel of Thomas* is not a narrative of the life of Jesus but rather a listing of 114 of his "sayings" or teachings. Saying 12 reads as follows: "The disciples said to Jesus, 'We know you will leave us. Who is going to be our leader then?' Jesus said to them, 'No matter where you go you are to go to James the Just, for whose sake heaven and earth came into being.'"

Here we have an unambiguous statement from Jesus that he is handing over the leadership and spiritual direction of his movement to James his brother. *The Gospel of Thomas* in its present form dates from a later period when disputes of succession and authority had become quite heated. The phrase "no matter where you go" implies that the authority and leadership of James are not restricted to the Jerusalem church or even to the land of Israel. According to this text James the brother of Jesus had been put in charge over *all* of Jesus' followers. The phrase "for whose sake heaven and earth came into being" reflects a Jewish notion that the world exists and is sustained because of the extraordinary virtues of a handful of righteous or "just" individuals.[28] James acquired the designation "James the Just" both to distinguish him from others of that name and to honor him for his preeminent position. *The Gospel of Thomas* provides us with our clearest evidence that James succeeded Jesus as leader of the movement.

Another more recent discovery is the Syriac text known as *The*

Ascents of James. This document is embedded in a later corpus known as the *Pseudo-Clementine Recognitions,* which reflects some of the earliest traditions related to the Jerusalem church under the leadership of James the Just.[29] It records events in Jerusalem seven years following the death of Jesus, when James is clearly at the helm: "The church in Jerusalem that was established by our Lord was increasing in numbers being ruled uprightly and firmly by James who was made Overseer over it by our Lord."[30] The Latin version says much the same: "Wherefore observe the greatest caution, that you believe no teacher, unless he bring from Jerusalem the testimonial of James the Lord's brother, or of whosoever may come after him" (4:35). *The Second Apocalypse of James,* one of the texts found with *The Gospel of Thomas* at Nag Hammadi, stresses the intimate bond between Jesus and James. In this text Jesus and James are said to have "nursed with the same milk" and Jesus kisses his brother James and says to him "Behold I shall reveal to you everything my beloved" (50:15–22). Here he seems almost a counterpart to Mary Magdalene. *The Gospel of the Hebrews* puts James at the Last Supper, thus implying he was one of the twelve. Although we don't have the entire text, and it exists only in quotations by the 4th century Christian writer Jerome, this gospel was originally written in Hebrew.

Josephus, the Jewish historian, an outsider to Christianity, nonetheless reports the death of James at Passover in the year 62 CE. It is his text that allows us to date James's death with some precision:

> He [Annas] convened the judges of the Sanhedrin and brought before them James the brother of Jesus (called Christ), and some others, on the accusation of breaking the law and delivered them to be stoned. And those inhabitants of the city who were considered the most fair-minded and who were strict in observance of the law were offended at this.[31]

We also have a more detailed account of the death of James than Josephus' reference here to his stoning. Hegesippus reports that before James was stoned, he was pushed over the southeast wall of the Temple complex and fell into the Kidron Valley. Barely alive, he was then stoned and beaten to death with a club. Hegesippus says that James was buried in that area, not far from the Temple.[32]

DID THE JAMES OSSUARY COME FROM THE TALPIOT TOMB?

There are several problems with the claim that the James ossuary came from the Talpiot Jesus tomb. First, if the James ossuary was in fact the tenth and missing ossuary from the tomb, even though it has disappeared, it was definitely catalogued by the authorities at the IAA, apparently measured, and given a registration number. Oded Golan says that he purchased the ossuary from an antiquities dealer in Jerusalem. It is difficult to construct any kind of hypothetical scenario in which the ossuary would have been removed from the IAA collection to end up on the market. Second, even though the dimensions of the missing ossuary and that of the James ossuary are close, the ossuary is described as "plain and broken" by Rahmani in his catalogue. Although in 2002 the James ossuary was broken while in transport to the Royal Ontario Museum and subsequently repaired, it was not broken when Golan acquired it. While not elaborately ornamented, it does have faint traces of the beginnings of rosette designs on the side opposite the inscription, so it is not "plain." Rahmani, known for his keen eye and detailed descriptions, would not likely have missed this feature. Third, Golan has testified that he obtained the ossuary sometime *before* 1978, providing photographic evidence that seems to support his story, whereas the Talpiot tomb was not excavated until April 1980.[33] Although it is possible that the ossuary had been looted from the tomb sometime previous to 1980, we don't know whether the entrance to the tomb was visible to passersby before the construction blast that obliterated its outside front entrance or porch. Finally, since Hegesippus reports that the tomb of James was visible in the Kidron Valley, not far from the southwest corner of the Old City, how and when would James's ossuary have been moved to the Talpiot tomb?

In contrast, new evidence has come to light that not only supports the case for the James ossuary originating in the Talpiot tomb, but addresses these major objections in an unanticipated way.

Recently a group of scientists headed by Amnon Rosenfeld of the Israel Geologic Society published a summary of their work on the authenticity of the patina inside the inscribed letters of the James ossuary. Rosenfeld was on the original team at the IGS that had authenticated the patina on the ossuary in 2002. They conclude:

> The most important indication that the inscription "Ya'akov Son of Josef Brother of Jesus" is authentic is the beige patina that can be found inside the letters, accreting gradationally into the inscription. The patina can be observed on the surface of the ossuary continuing into the engraving . . . These minerals and the circular pitting within the thin layers of the beige to gray patina were found on the surface of the ossuary and, more importantly, within the letters of the inscription. They indicate biological activity and are the product of airborne and/or subaerial geo-bio activity that covers all surfaces of the ossuary . . . indicative of slow growth over many years.[34]

The team then turned to an evaluative analysis of the scientific tests done in 2006 on the comparative chemical composition of the patina accretions on ossuaries taken from various ancient tombs in the Jerusalem area. The premise of the tests was that ossuaries accumulate distinctive and measurable biochemical "signatures" based on the cave environments in which they have spent the past two millennia.[35] Patina samples were taken from the James ossuary, three ossuaries from the Talpiot Jesus tomb (Jesus son of Joseph, Mariamene, and Matthew), and ossuaries from thirteen other burial caves in the area. By comparing these signatures one can determine whether the

James ossuary had developed its patina in that particular "tomb" environment:

> Among the examined 14 burial caves was also the Talpiot cave. Six Talpiot tomb wall and ceiling patinas were sampled December 14th, 2006 (op. cit.). The elemental spectra of the samples were examined by SEM-EDS in the Suffolk Crime Lab (NY). Each sample was analyzed (SEM-EDS) in at least 3 different locations. The differences between tombs were easily discerned by the elemental fingerprints. The quantitative variability of the elements (patina fingerprint) within an individual tomb (wall patina, ceiling patina, ossuary patina) were small, 5% or less.[36]

Even tombs that shared a similar rock formation in close proximity to one another nonetheless had their own distinctive chemical signatures. The results showed that the James ossuary shared the same chemical signature as the three other ossuaries from the Talpiot Jesus tomb that were tested as well as with the walls and ceiling of that tomb. In contrast, the James ossuary patina signature differed considerably from the chemical composition of ossuaries from the other thirteen burial caves.[37]

Rosenfeld and his colleagues suggest that based on these patina fingerprints the James ossuary was more likely a looted *eleventh* ossuary, rather than the missing *tenth* ossuary that had been catalogued by the IAA in 1980 and discarded or misplaced. They observed that the James ossuary was weathered intensively with massive pitting and striations. None of the other nine ossuaries from the Talpiot tomb show this kind of weathering. They concluded, on the basis of this weathering, that the James ossuary had been exposed to the elements for at least two hundred years. Since we know that the blocking stone was missing from the Garden tomb when it was examined in 1980, and the tomb itself was filled with the local terra rossa soil to a depth of two feet, covering the tops of the ossuaries in the niches, the James ossuary may have been nearer the exposed doorway of the tomb, where the fill was more shallow. When or how the James ossuary would have been taken from the Talpiot tomb we cannot determine. It might have been a number of years before the 1980 excavation of the tomb, or it could have been looted the first night when the front entryway of the tomb was blown open and exposed, before the IAA officials arrived to begin their work. If the ossuary was close to the entrance it may have been the only ossuary seen inside by looters since the others were covered with soil.

During the trial Oded Golan presented photos taken in 1976 in his parents' apartment showing that he possessed the James ossuary with its full inscription at that time—well before the excavation of the

39. Photo from 1976 of the James ossuary in the apartment of Golan's parents.

Talpiot tomb in 1980. A photographic expert, a former head of the Department of Photography and Documentation at the FBI, found no possibility that the photos were made at a later time.

If the James ossuary inscription is authentic and if it has probably come from the Talpiot Jesus tomb, what about the report by Hegesippus that the tomb of James was visible in the Kidron Valley? We suggest that there well might have been some kind of monument to James in that area. We also must observe that Hegesippus spent his career in Rome. We can't assume that he is reporting an eyewitness account. Today there are several monumental tombs in the Kidron Valley dating to the late Hellenistic period (200–100 BCE) that are variously identified as the "Tomb of the Blessed Virgin Mary," the "Tomb of Zechariah," the "Pillar of Absalom," and a tomb inscribed as that of a priestly family, which is sometimes identified as the "Tomb of James." These sites have no historical connection to these figures.

40. The Talpiot Jesus tomb before excavation, the ossuaries covered with soil.

They are part of hagiographic traditions that Christians developed in the late Byzantine period down through the Crusades.

Even though we had initially suggested the possibility of the missing tenth ossuary being that of James, based on the similar dimensions and the patina fingerprints that seemed to place it in the Talpiot tomb, we must always adapt our views to new evidence.[38] Shimon Gibson had suggested this theory of a missing *eleventh* ossuary to us back in 2006, when he recalled that the ten ossuaries inside the niches and removed to the Rockefeller Museum had been covered with soil. When the IAA archaeologists arrived on Friday morning, March 28, 1980, the first day of the excavation, they took photos and there is no evidence of any ossuaries having been dug out of the niches. But it is entirely possible, since patina tests show the James ossuary spent much of its history over the past two millennia in the Talpiot tomb environment, that this ossuary was near the door, less covered with soil, and thus easy to carry off. By whom or when we will likely never know. What we do know is that the mystery of the James ossuary is closer to being solved than ever before, and that whether it is the tenth or eleventh ossuary, it likely supports the Talpiot tomb's links to Jesus, his family, and the early Christians who believed in his resurrection.

CHAPTER SEVEN

RESURRECTION, LOST BONES, AND JESUS' DNA

The two major new discoveries in the Patio tomb—the epitaph and the Jonah image—provide for the first time in history tangible *archaeological* evidence related to the resurrection faith of Jesus' first followers. As we have explained earlier, the "Jonah ossuary" that until 1980 was located right in the front of the first niche on the right as one entered the tomb most likely belonged to the father of the family. Since it was filled to the top with bones it probably held the remains of his wife and children as well. Also in that niche were two additional ossuaries, filling it to capacity, as if later family members wanted to be as close as possible to whoever was in the Jonah ossuary. The Jonah ossuary, in our view, is by far the most unusual ossuary ever found. It has no parallels in all of Jerusalem.

Although this ossuary has no names inscribed on it and no standard ornamentation, it offers something infinitely more valuable and interesting. The drawing of Jonah and the big fish might be considered crude, even amateurish, with its awkward stick figure with a circular head emerging from the fish's mouth. It might even seem unbecoming to the tomb of the wealthy man who owned the estate upon which this and two other tombs are closely clustered.

In contrast, the tomb itself is simple but elegant. Its symmetrically carved gables boast lovely ornamented painted ossuaries, as elaborately carved as any in the Israel state collection. This family could afford to have any kind of ossuary it might have desired, which makes the Jonah ossuary stand out all the more. It tells a story, expressing a faith in resurrection that might have been inspired by direct and personal contact with Jesus of Nazareth. On one end we find just the tail of a big fish, the rest of the fish cut off at the bottom edge of the ossuary as if it were diving into the deep. At the other end some kind of doorway, with double crossed panels or bars. We cannot be sure of the intended narration but it surely has something to do with "entering" the watery deep, perhaps the gates of death, being taken under, but then miraculously being spit out of the jaws of death onto dry land—alive and rescued.

Cave burial in this period represents at the same time a kind of dreadfulness as well as love. When we bury our dead deep in the ground, there is a sense in which we have a symbolic token of the deceased, the grave site. We have removed them from the living. They are truly gone from our presence. In a family burial cave, generation after generation enters the tomb for rites of burial and mourning. The bones are visible, whether gathered in a central pit or placed in ossuaries. The living family is quite literally in the physical presence of the dead. The stark reality of death and decay cannot be ignored or forgotten. When the patriarch Jacob knew he was dying he called his twelve sons together—the sons who became the twelve tribes of Israel—and told them: "I am to be gathered to my people; bury me with my father in the cave that is in the field of Machpelah . . . which Abraham bought . . . to possess as a burying place" (Genesis 49:30). This notion of being gathered to the fathers is the central expression about death in the Hebrew Bible or Old Testament. Abraham, Moses, all the prophets die and are buried, joining those who went before them—quite literally "gathered" together.

We have described the emotions we felt when we first entered the Jesus tomb. For over thirty years it has been empty of the remains of those once buried there, filled only with discarded holy books and cemented over with a heavy cover. The Patio tomb was a quite different experience. Even though some of the ossuaries had been moved to different niches in the brief 1981 examination by the IAA archaeologists, the tomb is largely intact. The bones in the five niches without ossuaries are undisturbed and still in place, just as they must have been left when the bodies were laid to rest. Since our entry into this tomb was accomplished remotely, it was as if we were somehow there but not there, observing but not disturbing, catching a tiny glimpse of the expressions of faith and life the tomb represents, but still separated in time and space.

We have entered dozens of excavated tombs in Jerusalem in the course of our five-year investigation to learn what we could about Jewish burial in this time. This was different. We were visiting this tomb while leaving it intact. It is hard to describe the emotions involved. The experience transcended the academic, the cerebral, and even the technical challenges before us. Everyone on our team felt this. We were privileged to discover a link, if not a bridge, between this thoroughly Jewish tomb and an emerging Christian faith that had barely begun to express itself. Like time travel or some high-tech spectral presence, we were witnessing the birth of Christianity and the once strong, familial link between Judaism and Christianity that existed among Jesus' earliest followers.

The four-line inscription just a few feet away on the elaborately decorated face of the ossuary next to the Jonah ossuary was equally revealing to us. This time we were decoding words, not drawings, but the message appears to be related. In 1980 this ossuary was in the second niche on the right, maybe indicating it came from a slightly later time. It is hard to know when the tomb was dug but we are fairly sure that like other Jerusalem burial caves, it went out of use around 70 CE, when the Romans brutally crushed the Jewish revolt and killed or exiled the inhabitants of the city. The normal life cycles of death and burial were shattered and disrupted. It is possible that any family members who survived the war never return to their ancestral homes. The exposed bones in the niches offer silent testimony to this devastation, which likely prevented family members from completing the Jewish burial rites for their relatives.

We can estimate that two or three generations of the family might have buried their dead in this tomb. If the Patio tomb was the family tomb of Joseph of Arimathea, as we propose, the person who scratched these four lines in Greek wanted to give mute testimony to that same faith in Jesus' resurrection that the Jonah ossuary represents. This epitaph is not a professionally executed inscription in formal script. It is legible but shows individual intent—*the Divine [or Wondrous] Jehovah raises up* . . . We do not think the inscription is a testimony to a generic faith that God will "lift up" the dead, even though many Jews in this time did believe that God would raise the dead at the end of the age. We are convinced that each discovery must interpret the other and both must be seen in the context that the other provides. The sign of Jonah is clear and unambiguous. The connection to Jesus is direct and explicit. That Jonah became the preeminent symbol of the resurrection of Jesus for 3rd and 4th century Christians testifies to its simple power. The inscription affirming that God either has lifted up or will lift up bones from the dead is most likely connected as well to a resurrection faith grounded in the family's encounters with Jesus—not the Jesus of texts and oral tradition, but the *human* Jesus whose physical remains we believe were reverently treasured and remembered by this family that had had the privilege of attending to his burial. The ossuaries, the bones, the inscriptions, and the tombs themselves became for us silent testimonies to lives once lived. They sparked our imagination.

James and Mariamene are written about in our surviving texts, but we know next to nothing about the son, Judah, and precious little about the mother, Mary—if the Mary ossuary is indeed that of Jesus' mother. The gospel of John does not even name her. Matthew, Mark, and Luke mention her only at Jesus' birth and his death. There are some legendary traditions about Jesus' mother going to Asia Minor with the apostle John, but they make no sense historically. They are built on the mistaken idea, in our view, that John the fisherman, one of the twelve apostles, is the mysterious unnamed "beloved disciple" mentioned five times in the gospel of John, to whom Jesus gave charge of his mother as he was dying on the cross.[1] This seems highly unlikely, as if his brother James would have abandoned his responsibilities as the older brother, or for that matter, his wife, Mariamene, who apparently was very close to Mary, based on the evidence in the gospels.[2] The last we hear of Jesus' mother in the New Testament is that she was mentioned with the rest of the group, along with his brothers, living in Jerusalem (Acts 1:14). She is not even named. She is apparently a widow. Joseph is never mentioned in the gospels after the birth of Jesus. Jesus is called "the son of Joseph" twice and the "son of the carpenter [*tekton*]," translated "builder," in Matthew 13:55. We should not expect Joseph to be buried in this tomb. If Mary died before 70 CE she would be gathered with her sons. Depending on how Joses died, perhaps all three were martyred for what was called "the hope of Israel."

Judah's parents gave their son a proud Maccabean surname—after Judas Maccabee, the brave hero who led a revolt against the forces of the brutal Greek occupier Antiochus Epiphanes in 167 BCE and set up an independent Jewish state that lasted until the Romans arrived in 63 BCE. His was a common male name (6.5 percent), popular in this period for those who wanted to show solidarity for the freedom of Israel. Two of the twelve apostles are named Judas—one infamous, the other virtually forgotten (Mark 3:13–19). Judas the Galilean was the most famous "Judah" of that generation. He led a revolt in the year 6 CE, in Galilee, when Jesus would have been about ten years old. Josephus relates his story, calling him the founder of the "4th philosophy," after the Pharisees, Sadducees, and Essenes—the Zealots.[3] He is also mentioned in the book of Acts (5:37). Like Mary, he had sons named James and Simon, and like Mary, his sons were slain by the agents of Rome. We will likely never know what Judah son of Jesus's life was like, or how he died. His ossuary is not undersized (55 x 23 x 27 centimeters), so he was not a child when he died. It is nicely ornamented and the inscription of his name, "Judah son of Jesus," is the only one that is formally carved.

What about the resurrection faith of these families? Why were they, of all the Jews buried in this time, the only ones to inscribe on their ossuaries testimonies to God raising the dead? In our minds there is no doubt why. Theirs was not a generic faith in "life after death" but faith in the resurrection of their Teacher.

41. The Judah son of Jesus ossuary with its ornamentation and inscription.

CAN THESE BONES LIVE?

When one thinks about our concepts of death and the afterlife in the Western world the questions most people have are questions of individual survival—whether there is "life" after death. The nature of that life or survival can be thought of in a variety of ways, but the fundamental question is, What happens to me when I die? Is there something or is there nothing? Those who believe in "life after death" are affirming, in some manner, the idea that some essence of the individual self, the person we sense ourselves to be, survives the death of the body. It is the survival of the "I," the ego self that is in question. It is assumed that the biological self or body returns to dust or ashes, but the inner self lives on in some way. These questions come to us intuitively on the level of personal experience anytime someone we love dies. The heart stops, respiration ceases, and the person is pronounced dead. The person becomes a "corpse" and it is easy to think of the now-decaying body as merely a "house" or vehicle for the inner self or soul—but not the *person* we knew in life. We dispose of the body according to our cultural customs and personal choices, respectfully but also realistically, knowing that this body is irretrievable.

This view of the human person as both a mortal physical body and an immortal soul or spirit is deeply rooted in our Western religious and philosophical past. For most, without belief in some sort of life after death, there could be no viable spiritual faith. The alternative is seen as *materialism*—that we are just a functioning biological organism made wholly of matter.

In the writings of Plato Socrates summed it up best as he drank the fatal hemlock, having been condemned to death by the Athenian elders. He told his disciples to weep not for him but for themselves, for he was returning "home" while they would remain for a time in the house or prison of the body, until their time of release came.[4] The Roman philosopher and statesman Cicero, who lived in the 1st century BCE, explained this view more fully: "Strive on indeed, and be sure that it is not you that is mortal, but only your body. For that man whom your outward form reveals is not yourself; the spirit is the true self, not that physical figure that can be pointed out by the finger" (6:24).[5] This Platonic body/soul dualism became the standard belief in Greco-Roman antiquity, even among some Hellenized 1st century Jews, such as Philo and Josephus.[6] Celebrated early Christian theologians such as Clement of Alexandria, Origen, and Augustine considered Plato a kind of honorary "pre-Christian" and reshaped their exposition of the Christian faith almost wholly in Platonic categories.

Because of this Platonic influence it is extremely difficult for people today, whether Christian, Jewish, Muslim, or any other spiritual tradition, to conceive of life after death other than through the lens of Plato—the body perishes and the immortal soul passes on to an unseen realm of the spirit.

Given this perspective we must ask, what could bones possibly have to do with any idea of life after death? Although the term *resurrection* has become rooted in our Jewish-Christian-Islamic cultures, most are confused about how two ideas—immortality of the soul and resurrection of the body—relate to one another. If one attends a funeral and the rabbi, priest, minister, or imam stands before the corpse, right before lowering it into the grave, or in front of an urn of ashes, while reading words of scripture declaring that the "dead shall rise," people are often confused about what is being affirmed. Are they to believe that the body, destined to the dust or turned to ashes, is somehow to be revived or re-created? Is "resurrection" to be taken literally, or is it just a metaphorical or symbolic way of saying, "We believe the essential human person survives death." Is there such a thing as "spiritual" resurrection?

Resurrection of the dead is affirmed in our Western religious creeds. Jews recite the Thirteen Principles of Maimonides, the last of which says, "I believe in the resurrection of the dead." Christians affirm the "resurrection of the body" in the Apostles' Creed, the oldest confession of its type. Muslims affirm that God will raise the dead for judgment on the Last Day—also called the "Day of Standing Up" (*Surah* 2:79).

The original core idea of "resurrection of the dead," at least for Christians and Jews, whose understanding is rooted in the Hebrew Bible, is best illustrated by Ezekiel's vision of the dry bones. The prophet Ezekiel sees a valley full of dry bones and God asks him, "Son of man, can these bones live?" Ezekiel answers, "O LORD God you know." Then God tells him to address the bones: "Thus says the Lord GOD to the bones: Behold I will cause breath to enter you, and you shall live. And I will lay sinews upon you and will cause flesh to come upon you, and cover you with skin, and put breath in you, and you shall live, and you shall know that I am the LORD." (Ezekiel 37:5–6) Resurrection of the dead in this passage is a reconstitution of the physical body, a miraculous revival of the entire person, living and breathing again in this world. Here the concept of resurrection of the dead involves a *bodily* return to this world, contrasted to the concept of the immortal soul that undergoes a transition from the body to a higher state in another realm.

The language of both the Hebrew Bible and New Testament bears out this core idea. In Hebrew one speaks of God literally "making live" the dead. The Greek word for resurrection (*anastasis*) mean literally "to stand up." Thus "lifting up" or "raising up" is a way of affirming that the person represented by the bones will *return to life*. But what kind of life—and in what kind of body?

In the Bible, when the bones are buried, the spirit or soul descends into the "world of the dead," called Sheol in Hebrew and Hades in Greek. Sheol is described as a land of silence and forgetfulness, a region gloomy, dark, and deep (Psalms 115:17; 6:5; 88:3–12; Isaiah 38:18). All the dead go down to Sheol, and there they make their bed together— whether good or evil, rich or poor, slave or free (Job 3:11–19). The dead in Sheol are mere shadows of their former embodied selves; lacking substance they are called "shades" (Psalms 88:10).[7] There is one "séance" story in the Hebrew Bible in which the infamous medium of Endor conjured up the "shade" of the dead prophet Samuel at the insistence of King Saul, who wanted to communicate with him. When Samuel appears, rising up out of the earth, he asks Saul, "Why have you disturbed me by bringing me up?" (1 Samuel 28:8–15). But even Samuel must then return to Sheol. Death is a one-way street; it is the land of no return: "But man dies, and is laid low; man breathes his last, and where is he? As waters fail from a lake, and a river wastes away and dries up, so man lies down and rises not again; till the heavens are no more he will not awake, or be aroused out of his sleep." (Job 14:10–12)

There are three stories of the resuscitation of the dead in the Hebrew Bible. Elijah raises the son of a widow; his successor, Elisha, raises the child of a wealthy woman; and a dead man put in the grave of Elijah, touching his bones, "lived and was raised to his feet" (1 Kings 17:17–22; 2 Kings 2:32–37; 2 Kings 13:21). Jesus raises three people from the dead in the gospels: a twelve-year-old girl; a young man, son of a widow; and Lazarus, brother of Mary and Martha (Mark 5:41–43; Luke 7:11–17; John 11:43–44). Matthew says that at the death of Jesus many of the dead came out of their graves and walked about in the city (Matthew 27:52). Peter raises a widow and Paul revives a young man who fell from a window (Acts 20:9–12).

What is important to note about all these stories of "resurrection" is that these people returned from death to live again, but they subsequently died again. This notion of a temporary return from death, basically a revival of a corpse, is not the view of resurrection of the dead that Jews in the time of Jesus believed and that followers of Jesus affirmed about him.

The Hebrew Bible says very little about resurrection of the dead in this more extended sense. The single unambiguous passage is from Daniel, one of the latest books, but it is a key to understanding the concept at its core:

And there shall be a time of trouble, such as never has been since there was a nation till that time; but at that time your people shall be delivered, everyone whose name shall be found written in the book. And multitudes of those who sleep in the dust of the earth shall awake, some to everlasting life, and some to shame and everlasting contempt. And those who are wise shall shine like the brightness of the firmament; and those who turn many to righteousness like the stars forever and ever. (Daniel 12:1–4)

The metaphor of "sleeping in the dust of the earth" and then awakening captures precisely the core idea of resurrection of the dead. The bodies of the dead have long ago decayed and turned to dust, so this is no resuscitation of a corpse, nor is it even Ezekiel's vision of re-clothing dry bones with sinew and skin. This is an entirely new concept that has begun to develop in Jewish thought. Jews like Jesus, as well as the Pharisees, believed that on the "last day" the dead would be raised. People confuse this notion with the *literal* idea of resuscitation or the "standing up" of a corpse. The Jewish idea of resurrection at the end of days does not involve collecting the dust, the fragmentary decaying bones, or other remains of the body and somehow restoring their form. According to the book of Revelation, even the "sea" gives up the dead that are in it—which can hardly mean one must search for digested bodies that the fish have eaten and eliminated, as unpleasant as the thought may be (Revelation 20:11–15). Corpse revival is not resurrection of the dead.

The fully developed view of resurrection of the dead among Jews in the time of Jesus was that at the end of days the dead would come forth from Sheol or Hades—literally the "state of being dead"—and live again in an embodied form. The question was, what kind of embodied form? It was there that the debates began. The Sadducees, who denied the resurrection, poked fun at the Pharisees, who affirmed it. How could God raise the dead? What if a woman had had seven husbands in her life, each of whom died—in the resurrection whose wife would she be? Jesus was confronted with this question in the gospels (Luke 20:34–40). His answer was clear and unambiguous: when the dead come forth they will be in a transformed body, much like the angels, not the literal physical bodies that they once inhabited. There will be no "marriage or giving in marriage," as there will be no "male or female" in terms of physical gender. There will be no birth, no death, but a new transformed life.

Paul is clear on this point. Some of his converts in the city of Corinth were denying the resurrection of the dead. They were most likely thinking along the lines of Plato—if the immortal soul is freed from the prison of the body at death, why would it ever return to the body? And yet that is precisely what Paul defended—a return to a body. But as he makes clear, it is not a natural or "physical body"— the one he calls the body of "dust"—but a spiritual body, literally "wind body" (*pneumatikos*), that is transformed and not subject to death (1 Corinthians 15:42–50).

Resurrection of the dead, according to both Paul and Jesus, has nothing to do with one's former physical body. Paul's objectors taunted him—"How are the dead raised? In what kind of a body will they come forth?" He called them fools because they had no idea about the concept of resurrection, mistaking it for corpse revival (1 Corinthians 15:34). Paul says that Jesus had become what he calls a life-giving spirit. The difference between this idea and that of the Greek notion of the immortal soul is difficult to understand, but in the Hebraic view of things the distinction was important. Simply put, in Greek thought death was a friend that released one from the bonds of the lower, mortal, decaying, material world. In Hebrew thought the created world is good—even very good—and death is an enemy, but one that can be conquered. Paul writes that the "last enemy to be destroyed is death," and then the creation, which is good, will be "released from its bondage to decay" (1 Corinthians 15:26; Romans 8:21).

The whole concept turns on the notion of how the created world is viewed—as something to abandon and escape (the Greek view) or something to be transformed and changed (the Hebrew view). That is why the Bible speaks of "new heavens and a new earth," rather than leaving this earth to go to heaven (Isaiah 65:17; Revelation 21:1). The kingdom of God arrives when the will of God is done *on earth as it is in heaven*. In both the Hebrew Bible and the New Testament the ideal future arrives when God *comes down* to the renewed creation, not when we leave a hopeless world to join God in heaven (Revelation 21:3).

Paul makes clear that in Christian resurrection the *body is left behind* like a change of clothing, to turn to dust, and the spirit is "reclothed" with a new spiritual body. He compares the physical body to a temporary tent, but the new body is a permanent house (2 Corinthians 5:1–5). He even throws in a polemic against the Greek Platonic view of the "unclothed" or disembodied immortal soul. He says our desire is not to be naked, which is the state of death *before* resurrection, but to be clothed again!

Paul reflects the earliest Christian view of Jesus' resurrection, the resurrection hope his followers had, and that our Talpiot tombs affirm. That is why the presence of bones—even if they are the bones of Jesus—do not contradict the faith in resurrection of Jesus' followers.

THE FIRST CHRISTIANS AND RESURRECTION

What we have found in the Talpiot tombs is primary evidence of what the first Christians believed about resurrection faith. It is not theology, but it is firm archaeological testimony that helps us to reconstruct what early Christians believed. The tomb evidence agrees with the teachings of both Jesus and Paul about the new spiritual body. The confusion in the gospels has come because of a fundamental misunderstanding of the empty tomb. There *was* an empty tomb, but it was the first tomb, the temporary one in which Joseph of Arimathea placed the corpse of Jesus until the Passover and Sabbath were past. The Talpiot Jesus tomb was not empty—the "Jesus son of Joseph" ossuary held his bones, and we have even been able to do DNA tests on those remains.

Discovering remains of the body of Jesus is no threat to the original resurrection faith of Jesus' followers; it is actually an affirmation of that faith. Paul knows nothing of that first empty tomb. He knows that Jesus died and was *buried* and on the third day he was *raised up*. He then appeared to his followers not as a resuscitated corpse, but in Paul's words, as a "life-giving spirit" (1 Corinthians 15:3–8). These words of Paul are our earliest testimony to faith in Jesus' resurrection—until now. We now have testimony by Jesus' original followers that possibly *predates* Paul, and predates the gospels by many decades. Mark, Matthew, Luke, and John were written between 70 and 100 CE. The names on the books are traditional. They are not included in the text but were added to the manuscripts later as "titles." In other words, Mark does not begin, "I Mark, having witnessed these things, do hereby write . . ." Nor does Matthew, Luke, or John. In that sense all four gospels are pseudonymous—we don't know their real authors.

If you take the gospels in order, beginning with Mark, there are no appearances of Jesus after his death, just the statement that he will "go before them to Galilee."[8] Several scholars understand this as a reference to his second coming. In Matthew the women at the tomb see Jesus and later the eleven apostles encounter him on a misty mountaintop—*but some doubted.* Jesus gives them their commission to take the gospel to the world (Matthew 28:18–19). Here we have clearly left the world of history and entered the world of theology. The "Great Commission" is Matthew's view of the Christian mission until the end of the age. Scholars do not regard these words as spoken by the historical Jesus. Luke first introduces the idea that Jesus came back in a physical body—wounds and all, asking for food to eat. He tells a story of Jesus appearing to two men on the road to Emmaus, and then appearing to the eleven apostles and other disciples. They mistake him for a ghost, but he lets them know that he has "flesh and bones" and is not a spirit. He then eats fish in front of them (Luke 24:39). John, like Luke, affirms this same view—that Jesus shows his wounds to Thomas and later meets a group of the apostles on the Sea of Galilee and cooks fish on the shore on a charcoal fire (John 20:24–25; 21:9–14).

What Luke and John introduce, namely that Jesus appeared in the *same body* that had been placed in the tomb, represents a major departure from early Christian resurrection faith. This later understanding of Jesus' resurrection has led to endless confusion on the part of sincere Christians. These stories are secondary and legendary. Mark, who wrote decades earlier, does not know them, and Paul, who writes even earlier, says plainly that the new resurrected body is not "flesh and blood" (1 Corinthians 15:50).

These accounts of Luke and John were written for apologetic purposes against pagan critics like Celsus who charged that the "appearances" of Jesus to his followers were merely hysteria and delusion. By the time Luke and John wrote, at the turn of the 1st century or even later, Christians were disputing with pagans and Jews who did not accept a Jesus born of a virgin or raised from the dead. The pagans charged that the resurrection appearances were delusional but within Jewish tradition it was reported that the body was moved. Matthew's polemic against this view, protesting that it was a *Jewish lie*, actually testifies to its partial truth (Matthew 28:11–15). Matthew, in his typical anti-Semitic fashion, charges that the Jews were easily bribed for money and willing to spread a lie, saying, "The disciples came and stole him away." Part was true—they did come by night and take the body away, but they hardly stole it. Joseph of Arimathea had been given permission to take care of the burial by the Roman governor himself—Pontius Pilate. When Matthew says the "story is spread among the Jews to this day," that is likely also partially true. Jews who lived in Jerusalem knew that Jesus' body had been moved, and reverently buried by his family and his followers. One has to remember that the gospel writers, removed five or six decades from the events, know nothing of the Christianity that thrived and grew in Jerusalem even before Paul came along. Jesus died around 30 CE, Paul writes in the 50s CE, and the gospels, again, were written between 70 and 100 CE, or even later. The gospel writers are far removed from the original followers of Jesus, most of whom were dead, including Paul, Peter, and James.

The Q document that was a source for Matthew and Luke, and the letter of James wholly concentrate on the ethical teachings of Jesus. They contain *no* Christian theology at all. James mentions his brother Jesus only twice, both times in passing. Paul, on the other hand, begins the development of what we come to know as classic Christian teachings—Jesus as the incarnate divine Son of God, his death and resurrection for sins, forgiveness through his blood, baptism as a mystical rite of union, and the Eucharist as eating the body and blood of Christ. Paul, though, still has the notion of resurrection of the dead straight and he says he *received* what he passes on in this regard—presumably from the first witnesses (1 Corinthians 15:1–8). Although we believe that Paul's theology is far removed from that of Jesus' first followers, his view of Jesus' resurrection comes directly from them—and it did not involve bones or corpses being revived. Paul is our best link to the Talpiot tombs.

We realize it is hard to imagine, given the confusion the later gospel accounts have introduced, that early followers of Jesus would have visited the Jesus family tomb, honoring and remembering their revered Teacher, the one they believed was the messiah, and declaring their resurrection faith. But when one understands the Jewish culture and context of the time, that is precisely what one would expect. Within Judaism the tombs of the *zadikim*—the righteous ones—are honored, remembered, and considered holy.

LOST BONES AND JESUS' DNA

The question we have most been asked since the Talpiot Jesus tomb was first brought to the attention of the public is, "What happened to the bones in the ossuaries?" A second related question we are asked is, "Why don't you run DNA tests on all the bones in all the ossuaries?" The answer to the first question is, We don't know. Our assumption, as we have explained, is that the bones were taken to the Rockefeller Museum, still in the ossuaries, where the custom at that time was to have them examined by an anthropologist. We know that was the case a year later with the one ossuary that Amos Kloner removed from the Patio tomb. The official IAA photo, taken before it was cleaned, shows the skeletal materials inside.

It would truly be a boon to our knowledge if we had a proper bone report on the remains inside all the ossuaries. One would think there would at least be written records confirming their receipt. Such materials are registered and signed for if normal procedure is followed. After all, if the Jesus son of Joseph ossuary contained the remains of Jesus of Nazareth, assuming the bones were not too deteriorated, a skillful anthropologist might have been able to identify marks from crucifixion

42. The small ossuary from the Patio tomb full of bones.

or other evidence of trauma. We would have known the sex and age of the various individuals if more than one person's bones were in a given ossuary, and a wealth of additional forensic information might have become available. Regrettably, this information appears to be missing.

Because burial is such a central ritual to the Jewish faith, there has been mounting tension over the past few decades between archaeologists and segments of the Orthodox Jewish community over the fate of human remains uncovered in archaeological digs. This controversy stems from the fact that some Orthodox groups believe that archaeological excavations of human tombs and ossuaries are a defilement of ancient Jewish graves. Conversely, archaeologists argue that excavation is an essential tool in the understanding of ancient cultures and religions, and in the advancement of archaeology as a science.

The 1978 Antiquities Law, sometimes referred to as the "dry-bones law," distinguished human remains from the category of antiquities in an attempt to resolve this conflict. Established by the Israel Antiquities Authority, the Antiquities Law made it illegal to excavate known burial sites, whether Jewish or non-Jewish. Therefore, if archaeologists accidentally uncover human bones, the bones are to be turned over promptly to the Religious Affairs Ministry. In 1994, legislation was passed so that archaeologists had to discern on site whether bones found during excavations were humans or not. Remains could be moved to the lab for analysis only if it was impossible to distinguish on site whether bones were human or nonhuman. Due to this legislation all human materials were ordered removed from the Rockefeller labs and turned over to the Orthodox authorities. How this law might have affected the bones from the Talpiot Jesus tomb we have no way of knowing.

One has to remember that the archaeologists involved in the tomb at that time, Amos Kloner and Shimon Gibson, as well as Joe Zias, the anthropologist at the Rockefeller, have stated repeatedly that the Talpiot Jesus tomb is of no particular scientific or historical interest. In other words, there is nothing more to be said about

it beyond Amos Kloner's 1996 published report. In their judgment
we have spent six years of our time, not to mention huge sums of
money, investigating something unimportant. The statistical studies,
paleographic analysis, patina and soil analysis, and DNA tests are unwarranted. The constant refrain, now repeated endlessly from every
quarter, has been that the names are common; they mean nothing. As
we have seen, this is simply false, and a growing number of historians
and archaeologists realize this fact.[9]

Until recently, DNA tests were not done on skeletal materials
from tombs, so far as we know. The tensions with the Orthodox authorities have also had some bearing on DNA analysis, as some of the
rabbis understand the value of such tests for identifying the dead
while others are opposed to any handling of human bones.

What is called paleo-DNA or ancient DNA (abbreviated aDNA)
is a relatively new and developing science that has only recently been
able to meet the challenge of extracting DNA from degraded materials. What can be done today is quite amazing and the techniques are
improving continually.[10]

We were able to order DNA tests on bone materials from the
Jesus and the Mariamene ossuaries. In these ossuaries we found

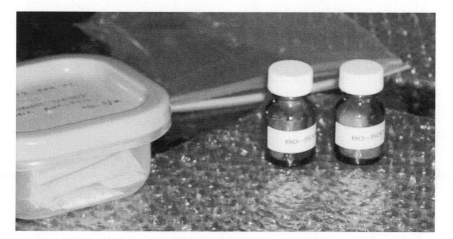

43. Bone samples from the Talpiot Jesus tomb prepared for DNA testing.

only tiny bone chips. As we have explained, the other ossuaries had been cleaned. We would have gladly had tests run on *any* remains we could have obtained. The DNA samples we had tested were collected in a proper manner and the risk of modern contamination, as with all aDNA tests, is a part of the procedure. DNA control samples are taken of anyone who had any contact with the materials, outside or inside the lab, even if the containers remained closed, to ensure that no modern DNA is sequenced with the ancient DNA.

The small bone chips we found contained no marrow. We shipped them to the Paleo-DNA Laboratory at Lakehead University in Thunder Bay, Ontario, on March 26, 2004. The lab had great difficulty getting any kind of useful results. The samples went through several extractions, as attempts were made to "amplify" the DNA sequences, then further clone the results. The lab attempted to gather everything it could, including mitochondrial DNA (mtDNA) as well as genomic DNA (gDNA), also known as nuclear DNA. The mtDNA is found in every cell of the body. Humans with the same mother share the same mtDNA, so it can be very useful for determining sibling relationships. Nuclear or gDNA is much more difficult to work with unless one can extract undamaged material that has not been desiccated. It is the gDNA that can determine paternity.

We received our first results in July 2006. The tests, though exceedingly difficult, were successful beyond our expectations. Even though there was no possibility of nuclear or gDNA with these samples due to their degradation, there were readable DNA results for both samples—the bone fragments in the Yeshua ossuary and those in the Mariamene one. The DNA tests map out the mutations in the mitDNA strands that differ from the norm, thus allowing one to match up a mother and any of her children since those specific mutations are shared between them. Two children from the same mother would accordingly carry these identical mutations from their mother.

Our Lakehead University tests gave us three clear mutations from each sample, and the differences established that the Mariamene in the tomb was neither the mother nor the sister of Yeshua—they had no blood relationship. This would not, of course, prove that she was a wife of Yeshua and the mother of his child Judah, but it would leave open that possibility. Had she been either his mother or his sister, our interpretation of her identification based on the unique name Mariamene and the designation *Mara* as Mary Magdalene would have been disproven.

More recently, in May 2011, we decided to retest the bone samples that we had saved for future analysis at the ancient DNA laboratory at the University of California at Davis. Their results, using an even more sophisticated battery of tests, confirmed our previous results but also added several new mutations to the three we already had. Not only does that give us a more complete DNA profile for both Yeshua and Mariamene, it establishes beyond any reasonable doubt that they have no family blood link to one another. Here for the first time we are publishing the mutations that offer the unique DNA identification of both the Yeshua and the Mariamene found in the Jesus family tomb:

mitDNA Base position	16051	16172	16223	16255	16278	16292	16519
Standard sequences	A	C	T	G	C	C	T
80.503/ Jesus	No result	C	T	A	T	T	No result
80.500/ Mariamene	G	T	T	G	C	T	C

The top line gives the base position number with the standard sequences of A C T G that most human beings share.[11] The rows labeled "Jesus" and "Mariamene" then give the distinctive mutations that each of them share. Note the differences between them. If Mariamene was either the mother or sister of Yeshua, these mutations or variations from the standard sequence would match, which they do not.

It is unfortunate that we were not able to conduct full DNA tests of all the bones found in all the ossuaries from the Jesus tomb. Ideally that would have allowed one to construct a kind of provisional "family tree," at least in terms of the familial genetic relationships between those individuals buried therein. Since the bones themselves were never examined scientifically and no one is even sure what happened to them, that opportunity is forever lost. There is much more we would like to know from such tests, but even to be able to say that the Jesus son of Joseph in the tomb was not a brother or son of the woman called Mariamene Mara does nonetheless contribute to our understanding. It also correlates with the evidence that we have presented in this book that she is very possibly Mary Magdalene, the mother of Judah, the son of Jesus.

Finally, if this tomb is indeed that of Jesus of Nazareth and his family then to have even a limited DNA sequence from the skeletal remains of Jesus himself is an amazing historical discovery. It is not that the DNA information tells us much we can make much use of in terms of scientific information, but the literal connection those bone fragments make between us and the historical figure of Jesus is profoundly moving, however one might understand the earliest faith in his resurrection. What we have presented in this chapter is what we are convinced was the earliest resurrection faith of his first followers, now witnessed to so clearly in the discoveries of both tombs. Taken with all the other evidence, those tiny bone fragments serve as a silent witness to the faith of those who buried their Teacher and continued to live their lives in hope of the kingdom of God.

THE FIRST CHRISTIANS AND CHRISTIANITY TODAY

The greatest story ever told is still being discovered. This book describes the earliest example of Christian art ever discovered, pushing back the date of any pictorial image related to Jesus by at least 150 years. Adjacent to the Jonah image, just inches away, we have also documented the earliest inscription related to faith in resurrection of the dead. Both discoveries date to the lifetimes of the generation of Jews who heard Jesus preach and witnessed his death. These finds constitute what historians call *primary* evidence, unfiltered by the complexity of traditions that developed around Jesus during the first hundred years after his death. This first archaeological evidence of a teaching of Jesus—the cryptic saying, attributed to him by Matthew, regarding the "sign of Jonah,"—is revolutionary. These discoveries offer us a glimpse into the very birth of Christianity.

These extraordinary finds in the Patio tomb, near a tomb that is likely the family burial chamber of Jesus and his family, provide us a glimpse of earliest Christianity. These discourses can inform Christian faith by bringing us closer to understanding Jesus and his first followers than we have ever been before. These discoveries allow us to bypass the accumulated traditions that have obscured Jesus and the earliest beliefs about him for so long. They allow us to see him with new eyes, as he truly was in his time and place. The collective evidence found in the two Talpiot tombs should be good news for all who can look beyond theological dogma and interpretation and recognize the value in *recovering* this significant glimpse into the faith of Jesus' first followers. It is rare for any archaeological discovery, short of a written text, to tell so much. Prior to our discoveries the only direct archaeological link to Jesus was the "James son of Joseph brother of Jesus" ossuary. That artifact, which we believe also came from one of the Talpiot tombs, has advanced our evidence by light years. We can now reconsider *all* the other ossuaries that scholars have dismissed as having anything to do with the Jewish followers of Jesus. We can say with assurance that followers of Jesus were expressing evidence of their faith in the various ways they inscribed their ossuaries. This is a major advance in the field of biblical archaeology.

We truly live in a privileged time as witnesses to these archaeological discoveries from Jerusalem, the place of Christianity's birth. These are not collective communal interpretations, but singular testimonies of specific individuals who lived and died in Jesus' own time. This gives them a special value beyond even a formally written text. Historians covet evidence of this sort—whether epitaphs, personal letters written on papyri, even receipts or graffiti. They represent the forgotten voices of individuals who left testimony of their thoughts, activities, practices, or beliefs. In the case of the Jonah ossuary a picture is worth much more than a thousand words. Taken in its wider context it requires us to reread the gospels, in light of these finds, and not the other way around.

THE QUEST FOR THE HISTORICAL JESUS

For the past 175 years scholars have been trying to learn more about Jesus based on the accepted methods of historical critical inquiry.[1]

Prior to the 19th century few had distinguished between the Jesus of history and the Christ of faith. The theology of the Christian church, as defined in the major Christian creeds, had treated faith in Christ as the preexistent divine Son of God who had died and been resurrected from the dead to bring salvation to the world as if it were historical fact. The quest for the historical Jesus represented a new approach to the gospels that involved reading them critically and trying to separate theological belief in Christ from the story of Jesus the human being—a 1st century Jew in his own culture and time.[2] What those pioneers of the 19th century quest for the historical Jesus lacked was the textual and archaeological discoveries of the 20th and 21st centuries. It is hard to imagine writing about the historical Jesus without the Dead Sea Scrolls, the many "lost" gospels that have been found, and most important, the emerging archaeological record of Galilee and Judea that continually informs our own historical quests.

Scholars have long recognized that the four New Testament gospels are theological portrayals of Jesus rather than historical accounts. This is not to say that they contain *no* history. It is rather recognition that each of the gospel writers portrays a theological *interpretation* of Jesus with specific agendas and points of view relative to the times in which he wrote—fifty to a hundred years after Jesus' death. Even the names associated with the gospels—Matthew, Mark, Luke, and John—are attributions that were added later. The original texts do not name their authors. They are anonymous works written to promote diverse theological visions of Jesus, his teachings, and the significance of his death and resurrection.

As we have seen, Mark, our earliest gospel, mentions *no* appearances of Jesus after his death. The oldest copies of Mark end at chapter 16, verse 8: the women flee from the empty tomb and say nothing to anyone. The implications are enormous. Mark could write a gospel in the 70s CE, more than forty years after Jesus' death, and it could circulate without anyone saying, "Wait, I thought Jesus appeared to Mary Magdalene, or to the women at the tomb, or to a gathering of disciples in Jerusalem that same day, or to the disciples who had returned home to Galilee." Mark believed that his story was *the* gospel—as he say clearly in his opening line: "The beginning of the Gospel of Jesus Christ" (Mark 1:1). At least according to Mark, the story of Jesus did not involve resurrection appearances of the type found in Matthew, and especially in Luke and John, who move closer toward the idea of the resuscitation of a corpse—misunderstanding the "empty tomb" and why it was found empty that Sunday morning.

In Matthew Jesus does not appear to the eleven male disciples in Jerusalem at all, but only much later in Galilee, and even then some of them doubted (Matthew 28:16–20). The latest gospels, Luke and John, further expand the traditions, with Jesus appearing in *physical form*—eating fish and showing his wounds in his hands, feet, and side. He invites the disciples to touch him, saying that he is not a ghost, but flesh and bones (Luke 24:39–43; John 20:26–29). These appearances take place both in Jerusalem and Galilee. This is a vastly expanded tradition over that of Mark, who better represents the original faith of Jesus' followers. These writers have lost the original view of resurrection, defended by Paul much earlier, in the 50s CE, in which the flesh and bones were left behind, but the spirit was "lifted up" to God. It was only decades later that people found Mark's abrupt ending unacceptable and attempted to amend it to conform to these later accounts (Mark 16:9–20).

In contrast, the 2nd century CE gospel of Peter, discovered in Egypt in the 1890s, supports Mark's earlier tradition. Unfortunately we only have fragments but the text ends abruptly with the disciples weeping and mourning for seven days, being grieved at Jesus' death and the discovery of the empty tomb. They return to their homes in Galilee and resume their normal lives. Peter and his brother Andrew go back to their fishing (*Gospel of Peter* 15:58–60). It is possible the text ended with them seeing Jesus; we don't know, since it breaks off, but either way, this tradition that they wept and mourned the whole week of Passover and then returned home, contrasts sharply with the accounts in Luke and John. There is no way to reconcile these views from a historical point of view. They show a theological development away from the evidence in the Talpiot tomb, in which the flesh and bones of "Jesus son of Joseph" are put in the cave, and subsequently in the ossuary, but his followers maintained faith in his resurrection—his being lifted up to the "holy place."

Mary Magdalene is another example of the necessity of separating theology, myth, and tradition from history. Mark mysteriously mentions Mary Magdalene, like a character who appears out of nowhere, at the cross and then at Jesus' tomb, but she plays no role in terms of witnessing to Jesus' resurrection. *The Gospel of Peter* does the same. Mary visits the tomb, finds it empty, but then flees in fear, saying nothing to anyone. Luke seems reluctant even to mention her name, although she is clearly identified in Mark, who is his main source. Luke says only that "the women who had followed him from Galilee" saw his death and his temporary burial—leaving them unnamed (Luke 24:49, 55). When he finally does name them, it is to dismiss them as witnesses of Jesus' resurrection in favor of Peter and the male disciples (Luke 24:10–11). In contrast, John names Mary Magdalene as the intimate "first witness" of Jesus' resurrection (John 20:1–18). In half a dozen later gospels, as we have seen, Mary Magdalene is the most prominent of the disciples of Jesus, even ahead of the twelve, causing Peter to be jealous of her intimacy with Jesus. The archaeological findings of the Talpiot tombs put in perspective the theology and tradition that began to marginalize her and, in the gospel of Luke, even damn her as a fallen woman. The Jesus tomb speaks volumes, even through its six simple inscriptions. Here we find Mariamene Mara buried side-by-side next to Jesus and what we believe to be their child Judah—together in death as in life. These archaeological facts are quite touching and moving in terms of their implications once one can clear away the theological dogma and mythological notions of bodies—bones, flesh, and all—being taken up to heaven. To find oneself in the presence of *the historical Jesus* and the tomb of his family takes one beyond issues of faith or religious orientation. For us it was experiencing history, the history of the man who was one of the most influential human beings who ever lived.

It is the same with the brothers of Jesus. Mark names all four brothers, including Joses, the nickname of Jesus' second brother, whereas Luke, recording the same scene, omits the brothers as well as Jesus' mother (compare Mark 6:1–3 and Luke 4:22–23). John presents the brothers of Jesus as hostile to him (John 7:3–5). Not one of the four gospels records the fact that James the brother of Jesus assumed leadership of the twelve after Jesus' death, yet, as we have seen, multiple sources confirm that this was the case.

The case of Joses is particularly fascinating to consider. He is the second brother of Jesus, born after James, but other than his name listed in Mark's gospel, and nowhere else, his very existence has been muted—until now. We don't know how he died but that he is interred in an ossuary before 70 CE means that his life was likely somehow cut short. Perhaps he too, like Jesus and James to follow, went up against the corrupt religious establishment and was killed. We will never know his story but his ossuary is an amazing testimony to his life. Had he lived he would likely have succeeded James in leading the Jesus movement. Instead the third brother, Simon, took over.[3]

These differences, and there are many more, are not a matter of minor details. Although some scholars have tried to reconcile these diverse traditions, it is impossible. The gospel writers are not recording history but a series of competing traditions and emphases that developed fifty to a hundred years after Jesus' death.

The letters of Paul were written earlier than the gospels (50s–60s CE) and in some ways they bring us closer to Jesus' first followers— certainly in terms of chronology. In other ways, because Paul never met Jesus and insisted that his visions of the heavenly "Christ" were superior to the physical contact that James, Peter, and John had with Jesus before his death, they too can be much more theological than historical. Paul never mentions Mary Magdalene, and his denigrating insistence that women be silent and submissive to men shows he would not have accepted her status as Jesus' intimate and most trusted follower. Alternatively, he is our best witness for the leadership of James over the Jesus movement, and since he directly encountered James, Peter, John, and the rest of the apostles, even if in conflict, we can take James's prominence as an established historical fact. This correlates well with the other sources we have, outside the New Testament gospels, which give James this leadership role as "successor" to Jesus.

In the same way Paul's clear interpretation of Jesus' resurrection from the dead as leaving behind the physical body, and being re-clothed in a spiritual incorruptible body, has to be given priority over the views of Luke and John, who stress a resuscitated physical corpse.

According to Paul, the new resurrection body will not be "flesh and blood," but rather a transformed *immortal spirit*—clothed in a new spiritual body (1 Corinthians 15:35–50). In the gospels, Jesus says much the same thing. He condemns the literal-minded Sadducees who rejected the idea of resurrection of the dead as an absurdity because they took it to mean that God must reassemble bodies long perished. Jesus responded clearly—in the "resurrection of the dead" there is no longer male or female, no marriage or birth or death. Resurrection is a completely transformed state, though an embodied one (Luke 20:27–36).

The evidence of the Talpiot tombs correlates Paul's view of resurrection of the dead as well as that of Jesus with the archaeology of his first followers.

As the Christian theological tradition developed, the early Christian fathers took the accounts of Luke and John even further and formulated an idea not found anywhere in the New Testament, which they called the "resurrection of the *flesh*."[4] They argued that Jesus' physical body was revived and he walked out of his tomb in a transformed state that was still flesh and bones, but somehow that *body* was *not* physical, even though it looked and functioned as if it were. They claimed that Jesus' body was ethereal and immortal. Some of the church fathers, such as the 3rd century theologian Tertullian, went so far as to argue that God, who created the world, would gather the *very flesh* of those long dead, including those who had turned to dust, ashes, or been lost in the sea. He went on to say that those in the resurrection would have the capacity to eat and have sex but would have no desire for such things.

This flatly contradicts Paul, Jesus, and our new archaeological evidence from these two tombs. Jesus' first followers believed that Jesus had been "raised up from the dead," but as we see in the Greek inscription in the Patio tomb, they believed in his exaltation in heaven. Anthropomorphic language is common throughout the Bible. These early Christians believed Jesus "sat at the right hand of God," but they were not so naïve or literal as to believe in thrones or seats upon which an embodied God the Father and Jesus Christ his son sat side by side. Affirming the resurrection of the dead, before the theologians elaborated the notion, meant that one affirmed that Jesus was "raised up" or "lifted up" into the holy realms. It was an affirmation of triumph and glory, not a statement about the revival of a physical corpse.

For centuries Christians have looked to the past to inform the present. They have been convinced that by exploring the origins of Christian faith they could transcend many of the theological accretions that have accumulated over the centuries. This was the spirit of the radical Protestant reformers, but over the past hundred years, Catholics have taken up the same challenge—to draw as close to the beginnings as one can, given our sources. It is not a matter of imitating the past. We know that Christianity today, with its history, traditions, and modern cultural contexts, cannot replicate the faith of the first Christians but it cannot help but be enriched by drawing closer to its authentic history.

The Jesus Discovery documents a long journey that we hope will be a beginning, not an end. We want to promote the kind of fruitful historical inquiry and discussions that advance our understanding of

Jesus of Nazareth. Whether Christian, Jewish, Muslim, or any other faith, or no faith, we have all been affected deeply and significantly by the life and death of this man. For billions of people he continues to be the focus of faith and adoration, the hope of both life and death. Whatever one's view of Jesus, we should always remember the lessons of the Enlightenment and the very foundation of our academic and scientific culture—good history is never the enemy of informed faith. As has ever been the case through the ages it is dogma, ignorance, and bias that should ever remain our common enemy. Our hope is that our decade-long investigation of the Talpiot tombs will serve to dispel those ancient stumbling blocks so that responsible history and informed faith can dwell together in peace.

NOTES

PREFACE

1. We use the designations BCE (before the Common Era) and CE (the Common Era) rather than the conventional designations of BC and AD. The dates remain the same in either system.

2. See http://www.rushprnews.com/2007/02/25/holy-film-see-the-lost-tomb-of-jesus-on-the-discovery-channel, as well as Simcha Jacobovici and Charles Pellegrino, *The Jesus Family Tomb: The Evidence Behind the Discovery No One Wanted to Find*, rev. pbk. ed. (New York: HarperOne, 2007).

3. See Jack Finegan, *The Archaeology of the New Testament*, rev. ed. (Princeton, NJ: Princeton University Press, 1992), pp. 359–74, for a summary of the positive case. Not all scholars agree. James Strange offers an assessment of the evidence for and against; see "Archaeological Evidence of Jewish Believers," in *Jewish Believers in Jesus: The Early Centuries*, ed. Oskar Skarsaune and Reidar Hvalvik (Peabody, MA: Hendrickson, 2007), pp. 710–41. For other dissenting views see Joan Taylor, *Christians and the Holy Places* (New York: Oxford University Press, 1993), as well as Gideon Avni and Shimon Gibson, "The 'Jewish-Christian' Tomb From the Mount of Offense (*Batn Al-Hawa'*) in Jerusalem Reconsidered," *Revue Biblique* 115 (1998), 161–75.

CHAPTER ONE: THE DISCOVERY

1. Robin Margaret Jensen, *Understanding Early Christian Art* (London and New York: Routledge, 2000).

2. See Byron R. McCane, *Roll Back the Stone: Death and Burial in the Time of Jesus* (New York: Trinity Press International, 2003), pp. 39–47. On the practice of Jewish burial in Jerusalem more generally in this period, see Eric M. Meyers, *Jewish Ossuaries: Reburial and Rebirth*, Biblica et orientalia 24 (Rome: Pontifical Biblical Institute Press, 1971); Pau Figueras, *Decorated Jewish Ossuaries*, Documenta Et Monumenta Orientis Antiqui 20 (Leiden: Brill, 1983); and especially the comprehensive work of Rachel Hachlili, *Jewish Funerary Customs, Practices and Rites in The Second Temple Period*, Supplements to the *Journal for the Study of Judaism* 94 (Leiden: Brill, 2005).

3. See Byron R. McCane, " 'Let the Dead Bury Their Own Dead': Secondary Burial and Matt 8:21–22," *Harvard Theological Review* 83 (1990): 31–42.

4. See http://www.antiquities.org.il/article_Item_eng.asp?sec_id=42&subj_id=228&autotitle=true&Module_id=6.

5. See the Israel Antiquities Authority website for its policy on "salvage" archaeology: http://www.antiquities.org.il/article_Item_eng.asp?sec_id=41&subj_id=227&id=205&module_id=#as.

6. See Jerome Murphy-O'Connor, *The Holy Land: An Oxford Archaeological Guide*, 5th ed. (Oxford: Oxford University Press, 2008), for a survey of major sites and their periods.

7. See the comments of L. Y. Rahmani, *A Catalogue of Jewish Ossuaries in the Collections of the State of Israel* (Jerusalem: Israel Antiquities Authority, Israel Academy of Sciences and Humanities, 1994), p. 23. Rahmani's catalogue is abbreviated herein as *CJO* with specific ossuaries designated by a number.

8. The reason these numbers are imprecise is that many of these tombs have been destroyed or were never recorded and hundreds of the estimated ossuaries have disappeared or been lost over time. See Hannah M. Cotton et al., eds., *Corpus Inscriptionum Iudaeae/Palaestinae*, vol. 1.1 (Berlin: De Gruyter, 2010), pp. 8–9, and Amos Kloner and Boaz Zissu, *The Necropolis of Jerusalem in the Second Temple Period*, Interdisciplinary Studies in Ancient Culture and Religion, vol. 8 (Leuven, Belgium; and Dudley, MA: Peeters, 2007), pp. 30–31. Zissu was able to locate 793 cave-tombs within two miles of the Old City of Jerusalem. Cotton's *Corpus* is abbreviated *CIIP* herein with specific ossuaries designated by number.

9. Cotton, *CIIP*, pp. 65–609. Most of these inscribed ossuaries are in the Israeli State Collection though various ecclesiastic institutions and even private individuals in and around the Old City of Jerusalem have their own collections. Rahmani's older catalogue of ossuaries in the Israel State Collection up through 1989 lists 227 inscribed ossuaries of a total of 897, or 25 percent; see *CJO*, p. 11.

10. Typically 60 percent are Hebrew/Aramaic, 30 percent are Greek, and 10 percent are mixed Greek and Hebrew.

11. See Rahmani, *CJO*, pp. 25–28. For typical examples of Greek funerary epitaphs see http://religiousstudies.uncc.edu/people/jtabor/dualism.html.

12. Cotton, *CIIP* 324, pp. 344–46. The names are inscribed in three different places on the ossuary, on the front and back sides and on the lid, as: Alexandros Simon; Simon Ale[xandros]; Alexandros *of* Simon, and *of* Alexandros. The possessive can refer to the ossuary *of* the person named, meaning it belongs to them, in which case this ossuary could have well held the bones of both son Alexander and father Simon.

13. See Tom Powers, "Treasures in the Storeroom: Family Tomb of Simon of Cyrene," *Biblical Archaeology Review* (July–August, 2003): 46–51, 59. A version of Powers' analysis can be read at: http://israelpalestineguide.files. wordpress.com/2010/06/alexander-son-of-simon-ossuary-illustrated-2010-edit.pdf. See the official publication by Nahman Avigad, "A Depository of Inscribed Ossuaries in the Kidron Valley," *Israel Exploration Journal* 12 (1962): 1–12, as well as his encyclopedia entry "Tomb South of the Village of Silwan," in *The New Encyclopedia of Archaeological Excavations in the Holy Land*, vol. 2, p. 753. Avigad doubted that this inscribed ossuary could be identified with the Alexander son of Simon mentioned in the New Testament.

14. There was no Rufus buried in this tomb but the single inscriptional example of this Latin name, rare in Jerusalem but known in Cyrene, was found in another tomb in 1954 in another area of Jerusalem, see Cotton, *CIIP*, no. 385, pp. 405–6.

15. Cotton, *CIIP*, nos. 461, 462, pp. 481–85. See Zvi Greenhut, "Burial Cave of the Caiaphas Family," *Biblical Archaeology Review* 18:5 (September–October 1992): 29–36, 76 and Ronny Reich, "Caiaphas Name Inscribed on Bone Boxes," *Biblical Archaeology Review* 18.5 (1992):40–44, 76.

16. See http://www.time.com/time/world/article/0,8599,2064920,00.html and http://www.jpost.com/NationalNews/Article.aspx?id=216355. Simcha's paper

on these two missing nails is archived at http://jamestabor.com/2011/06/22/simcha-jacobovici-responds-to-critics-of-his-nails-of-the-cross-film/.

17. Passover fell on Tuesday, March 1, in 1980 with Easter the following Sunday, March 6. A year later, in 1981, Passover was on Sunday, April 19 and Easter was the same day. Given the differences in the Jewish and Gregorian calendars, Passover and Easter can fall as much as a month apart since Passover is determined by the lunar calendar, falling on the fifteenth day of the Jewish month of Nisan, while Easter, in the Roman Catholic tradition, is the first Sunday following the full moon after the Vernal Equinox (March 20, 2011). This can be any Sunday between March 22 and April 25.

18. Scholars continue to debate the year of the crucifixion and have made credible arguments for each year from 30 to 36 CE. See Jack Finegan, *Handbook of Biblical Chronology: Principles of Time Reckoning in the Ancient World and Problems of Chronology in the Bible*, rev. ed. (Peabody, MA: Hendrickson, 1998), pp. 353–68. The majority has agreed on 30 CE so we have adopted this date in this book.

19. There are three published reports on the tomb, each tantalizingly sparse in details with some differences among them: Amos Kloner, *Excavations and Surveys in Israel 1982*, vol. 1, nos. 78–81 (October 1982), p. 51; Amos Kloner, *Survey of Jerusalem: The Southern Sector* (Jerusalem: Israel Antiquities Authority, 2000), p. 84; Kloner and Zissu, *Necropolis of Jerusalem*, p. 342, which contains a map by Kloner. The IAA files contain one memo dated August 2, 1981, plus some photographs. An April 17, 1981, memo that Kloner wrote right after his team finished their work is referenced in the August 2 memo but is nowhere to be found. One early Roman period cooking pot was catalogued by the IAA as from this tomb, although excavators remember other items being removed. There is no copy of the excavation license. These are unfortunate losses and perhaps these and other materials will be recovered in the future.

20. See Amos Kloner and Shimon Gibson, "The Talpiot Tomb Reconsidered: The Archaeological Facts," in *The Tomb of Jesus and His Family? Exploring Ancient Jewish Tombs Near Jerusalem's Walls: The Fourth Princeton Symposium on Judaism and Christian Origins*, ed. James H. Charlesworth and Arthur C. Boulet (Grand Rapids, MI: Eerdmans, 2011). We thank Professors Kloner and Gibson for making a prepublication copy of their paper available to us. The ossuary Kloner removed is now catalogued as

IAA 81-505. See Rahmani, *CJO,* no. 741, p. 229, and plate 106. Curiously, the Rahmani catalogue lists this ossuary from a nearby site, the Mount of Offense, east of the Old City of Jerusalem, and calls it a "chance find," but Kloner has identified it as the one he removed and the IAA files show it was examined and photographed at the Rockefeller Museum.

21. See *Excavations and Surveys in Israel 1982,* vol. 1, nos. 78–81 (October 1982), p. 51. Curiously, Kloner reports that "three of the *kokhim* contained seven ossuaries" and does not mention removing an eighth one from a fourth niche; see *Survey of Jerusalem: the Southern Sector* (Jerusalem: Israel Antiquities Authority, 2000), p. 84. Kloner later published a sketch of the tomb showing the locations of all eight ossuaries, distributed in four of the niches; see Kloner and Zissu, *Necropolis of Jerusalem,* p. 342.

22. See Kloner and Zissu, *Necropolis of Jerusalem,* p. 342, and Kloner and Gibson, "The Talpiot Tomb Reconsidered."

23. The tag reads: 1050/1981-2162, dated April 16, 1981.

24. Kloner reports this in a handwritten August 2, 1981, memo now in the IAA archives that includes a color sketch of the pillar with the vent running up through it. Oddly, Kloner puts the wrong tomb license number—1053—in this memo, which is the permit number for a tomb north of Jerusalem having nothing to do with Talpiot.

25. The following description of the discovery of the tomb and its excavation is based on eyewitness interviews with the participants who are still alive as well as original files from the Israel Antiquities Authority archives, an official report published in 1996 by Amos Kloner, "A Tomb with Inscribed Ossuaries in East Talpiot, Jerusalem," *Atiquot* 29 (1996): 15–22, and Kloner and Gibson, "The Talpiot Tomb Reconsidered."

26. In 1980 what is now known as the Israel Antiquities Authority (IAA) was called the Israel Department of Antiquities and Museums (IDAM), founded in 1948. The department was reorganized and renamed in 1999. In this book we generally use the present designation IAA for sake of clarity.

27. Going from west to east the niches contained respectively groupings of two, two, none, one, two, and three ossuaries. See Shimon Gibson's map, p. 29.

28. Ouriel's account of his discovery of the tomb is available as a blog entry at http://www.tapuz.co.il/blog/ViewEntry.asp?entryid=930249&r=1, posted March 9, 2007.

29. See Michael Balter, "Archaeologists and Rabbis Clash Over Human Remains," *Science* 7 (January 2000): 34–35.

30. So far as we know, the first extensive DNA tests done on a Jerusalem tomb from this period were commissioned by Shimon Gibson, Boaz Zissu, and James Tabor on the skeletal remains of a looted Hinnom Valley tomb in 2000. See http://www.plosone.org/article/info%3Adoi %2F10.1371%2Fjournal.pone.0008319 for the published results.

31. See Kloner and Gibson, "The Talpiot Tomb Reconsidered."

32. In Gath's original typed report, dated April 15, 1980, he does not mention inscriptions but on his handwritten "dig card," dated the same day he noted, "So far about four inscriptions were found on the ossuaries."

33. It is catalogued as S 767 and appears as No. 9/Plate 2 in the Rachmani catalogue. Sukenik found it in a basement storage area of the Palestinian Archaeological Museum (today the Rockefeller) in Jerusalem in 1926. It is today on display in the Israel Museum. When Sukenik published a report about the ossuary in January 1931, the news that such an inscription existed, the only one ever found inscribed "Jesus son of Joseph," created no small stir in the world press, particularly in Europe. See L. H. Vincent, "Épitaphe prétendue de N.S. Jésus-Christ," *Atti della pontificia: Academia romana di archaeologie: Rendiconti* 7 (1929–30): 213–39.

34. Gath published a short preliminary report in 1981, but before the ossuary inscriptions had been deciphered; *Hadashot Arkheologiyot* 76 (1981): 24–26. See Rahmani, *CJO* 701, p. 222.

35. "My husband knew it was Jesus' tomb," by David Horovitz, *Jerusalem Post*, January 17, 2008 and "Widow: Archaeologist kept 'Jesus tomb' discovery secret for fear of anti-Semitism," by Jonathan Lis, *Haaretz*, January 17, 2008. Rahmani thanked Joseph Gath as the excavator for permission to publish his finds in the *CJO* volume, p. 222. This acknowledgment likely indicates that Rahmani discussed the inscriptions with Gath in the late 1980s when the catalogue was being prepared.

36. London *Sunday Times*, March 31, 1996, p. 1.

37. Amos Kloner, "A Tomb with Inscribed Ossuaries in East Talpiyot, Jerusalem," *Atiquot* 29 (1996): 15–22.

38. See Kloner and Gibson, "The Talpiot Tomb Reconsidered," where they express their views quite emphatically.

39. Tabor, *The Jesus Dynasty,* p. 4.

40. See http://www.jesusfamilytomb.com/; Jacobovici and Pellegrino, *The Jesus Family Tomb;* and James D. Tabor, "Testing a Hypothesis," *Near Eastern Archaeology* 69: 3–4 (2006): 132–36, and "The Talpiot 'Jesus' Tomb: A Historical Analysis," in *The Tomb of Jesus and His Family? Exploring Ancient Jewish Tombs Near Jerusalem's Walls: The Fourth Princeton Symposium on Judaism and Christian Origins,* ed. James H. Charlesworth and Arthur C. Boulet (Grand Rapids, MI: Eerdmans, 2011).

41. Typed report of Gath dated April 15, 1980, now in the IAA archive files for License 938.

42. Compare Matthew 27:57–61, Luke 23:50–56, John 19:38–42.

43. Matthew's assertion that this temporary tomb belonged to Joseph is clearly an interpolation added for theological reasons (Matthew 27:60). It lacks any historical basis or even likelihood. What would be the chances that Joseph, who took charge of Jesus' burial, just happened to own a tomb adjacent to the place the Romans used to crucify criminals? A major theme of Matthew's gospel is to show how Jesus fulfilled prophecies of the Hebrew Bible as the messiah. Here he has in mind Isaiah 53:9, which he interprets as requiring the "suffering servant" to be buried in a rich man's tomb. None of the other gospels make this claim and John, in explaining the circumstances for the choice of this temporary tomb, flatly contradicts Matthew.

CHAPTER TWO: TWO TALPIOT TOMBS

1. Shimon Gibson, *The Cave of John the Baptist: The Stunning Archaeological Discovery That Has Redefined Christian History* (New York: Doubleday, 2004), and the review in *Biblical Archaeology Review* archived at http://www.bib-arch.org/reviews/review-cave-of-john-the-baptist.asp.

2. Gibson, Tabor, and some UNC Charlotte students, who had been excavating at Suba, were hiking in the area of Akeldama, the ravine just south of Jerusalem's Old City, in July 2000. The tomb turned out to have the remains of the only ancient burial shroud ever found in Jerusalem, confirmed by carbon-14 tests as dating to the 1st century CE.

3. Andre Lemaire, "Burial Box of James the Brother of Jesus," *Biblical Archaeology Review* 28:6 (November–December 2002): 24–33, and Hershel Shanks and Ben Witherington III, *The Brother of Jesus: The Dramatic Story*

& Meaning of the First Archaeological Link to Jesus and His Family (San Francisco: HarperSanFrancisco, 2003).

4. The authenticity of parts of the inscription, particularly the phrase "brother of Jesus," was questioned by some. See Neil Asher Silberman and Yuval Goren, "Faking Biblical History," *Archeology* 56:5 (September–October 2003): 22–30. A protracted legal battle charging the owner of the ossuary, Oded Golan, with forgery, is nearing an end as we write this book. The evidence seems to show rather conclusively that the entire inscription is authentic; see http://bibleinterp.com/articles/authjam358012.shtml. We will cover this subject in detail in chapter 6.

5. See http://ancientdna.com.

6. Oded says he is not sure just when he acquired the James ossuary and initially, in 2002, he said "fifteen to twenty years ago." Later, with further checking, he put the date back as early as 1978.

7. Simcha Jacobovici and Charles Pellegrino, *The Jesus Family Tomb: The Evidence Behind the Discovery No One Wanted to Find*, rev. pbk. ed. (New York: HarperOne, 2007)

8. See http://www.jesusfamilytomb.com/movie_overview/decoders.html for background on the initial participants in the Talpiot "Jesus tomb" research.

9. In the course of the investigation for the 2007 film *The Lost Tomb of Jesus*, dozens of additional academic experts were brought into the investigation, all of whom signed a standard nondisclosure agreement. Among the principals were François Bovon (historian of early Christianity, Harvard University), James H. Charlesworth (biblical scholar, Princeton Theological Seminary), Frank Moore Cross (Hebrew Bible scholar and epigrapher, Harvard University), John Dominic Crossan (New Testament scholar, DePaul University), Shimon Gibson (archaeologist, Albright Institute), Andrey Feuerverger (statistician, University of Toronto), Tal Ilan (Jewish studies, Freie University, Berlin), Amos Kloner (archaeologist, Bar Ilan University, Israel), Israel Knohl (Hebrew Bible, Hebrew University, Jerusalem), Jerome Murphy-O'Connor (New Testament, École Biblique in Jerusalem), and Stephen J. Pfann (University of the Holy Land, Jerusalem). Each contributed in his or her area of expertise without necessarily assenting to the main thesis of the film. See http://www.jesusfamilytomb.com/experts.html for biographical details.

10. *Acts of Philip* 8:16, 21; 13:1–2, 4. See François Bovon, "Mary Magdalene in the *Acts of Philip*," in E. Stanley Jones, ed., *Which Mary? The Marys of Early Christian Tradition*, Symposium Series, SBL 19 (Atlanta: Society of Biblical Literature), pp. 75–89.

11. The Aramaic name *Marta* (Martha) is derived from *Mar/Mara*. Some argue that *Mara* is just an alternative form of Martha but as we explain in chapter 5, such is not the case.

12. In a short published report Kloner specifically says that "two of the ossuaries bore names incised in Greek." Amos Kloner, *Excavations and Surveys in Israel 1982*, vol. 1, nos. 78–81 (October 1982), p. 51.

13. See "The Aftermath" and "The World Reacts" in *The Jesus Family Tomb*, pp. 213–18, 219–34.

14. A director's cut version is available on DVD and through Netflix: http://www.amazon.com/Lost-Tomb-Jesus-Simcha-Jacobovici/dp/B000OHZJSC and http://movies.netflix.com/Movie/The-Lost-Tomb-of-Jesus/70064836#height1991. The website is http://jesusfamilytomb.com/. http://dsc.discovery.com/convergence/tomb/tomb.html. Of the hundreds of websites that address the subject of the Talpiot Jesus tomb the best and most balanced in our opinion is http://talpiottomb.com/.

15. Louis Lapides, *Burying the Jesus Tomb Controversy: Errors and Conclusions Found in the Lost Tomb of Jesus* (Agoura Hills, CA: Scripture Solutions, 2007), Dillon Burrows, *The Jesus Family Tomb Controversy: How the Evidence Falls Short* (Ann Arbor, MI: Nimble Books, 2007), Don Sausa, *The Jesus Tomb: Is It Fact or Fiction? Scholars Chime In* (San Ramon, CA: Vision Press, 2007), Gary R. Habermas, *The Secret of the Talpiot Tomb: Unraveling the Mystery of the Jesus Family Tomb* (Nashville, TN: Holman Reference, 2008), René A. López, *The Jesus Family Tomb Examined* (Springfield, MO: 21st Century Press, 2008), *The Jesus Tomb Unmasked,* DVD (Brigham City, UT: Living Hope Ministries, 2009).

16. The main objections are addressed based on what we knew in 2007 by James Tabor in an epilogue to the paperback edition of *The Jesus Family Tomb*, pp. 219–34.

17. The volume is now in press: *The Tomb of Jesus and His Family? Exploring Ancient Jewish Tombs Near Jerusalem's Walls: The Fourth Princeton Symposium on Judaism and Christian Origins,* ed. James H. Charlesworth and Arthur C. Boulet (Grand Rapids, MI: Eerdmans, 2011).

18. A summary and analysis of the results of the conference by James Tabor is archived at http://sbl-site.org/publications/article.aspx?articleId=749.

19. For the rigorous requirements for an IAA license see http://www.antiquities.org.il/about_eng.asp?Modul_id=108.

20. http://walterklassen.com.

21. See Rahmani, *CJO,* p. 34.

22. See Rahmani, *CJO,* pp. 31–32.

CHAPTER THREE: DECODING THE MYSTERIOUS SIGN OF JONAH

1. See Bart Ehrman, *The New Testament: A Historical Introduction to the Early Christian Writings,* 5th ed. (Oxford: Oxford University Press, 2011).

2. Quotations from the Bible are from the Revised Standard Version, with some revisions by the authors for accuracy and clarity.

3. Here in Mark 4:9, 23 but also compare Matthew 11:15; 13:9, 15–16, 43; Luke 8:8; 14:35.

4. The Q hypothesis, often referred to as the "two source" hypothesis (Mark and Q being the two sources), was first expounded in 1838 by C. H. Weisse.

5. For a reconstruction and translation of Q in English see http://homes .chass.utoronto.ca/~kloppen/iqpqet.htm.

6. John Kloppenborg, *Excavating Q: The History and Setting of the Sayings Gospel* (Minneapolis: Fortress Press, 2000).

7. Based on prophecies in the Hebrew Bible there developed an expectation for the arrival of a native king or "messiah" who would be a bloodline descendant of King David (Jeremiah 23:5). See Tabor, *The Jesus Dynasty,* pp. 144–48.

8. Scholars have debated for centuries how to fit "three days and three nights" into the period from Friday sundown until Sunday/Easter morning—which is obviously two nights and hardly three days. There is good evidence that Jesus was in fact crucified on a Thursday, not a Friday, before the Sabbath of Passover, not the weekly Sabbath. If such is the case then Matthew's saying about the three days and three nights will fit the narrative—Thursday, Friday, and Saturday nights, followed by the empty tomb on Sunday. See Tabor, *The Jesus Dynasty,* pp. 198–207.

9. See Simon Chow, *The Sign of Jonah Reconsidered: A Study of Its Meaning in the Gospel Traditions,* Coniectanea Biblica: New Testament Series, vol. 27 (Stockholm: Almqvist & Wilsell International, 1995), pp. 27–44.

10. *Lives of the Prophets* 10:1–3; 2 Maccabees 6:8.

11. The original is lost and most date the Armenian translation to the 6th century CE. See Michael E. Stone, *Apocrypha, Pseudepigrapha, and Armenian Studies: Collected Papers,* Orientalia Lovaniensia Analecta (Leuven: Peeters, 2006). See Hans Lewy, *The Pseudo-Philonic De Jona. Part I: The Armenian Text with a Critical Introduction* (London: Christophers, 1936).

12. Translation by Jacob Neusner, *The Mishnah: A New Translation* (New Haven, CT: Yale University Press, 1991). The Mishnah is one of the earlier collections of rabbinic interpretations of the Torah, put together in the early 3rd century CE but often reflecting earlier traditions.

13. Jacob Neusner, *Christian Faith and the Bible of Judaism: The Judaic Encounter with Scripture,* Brown Judaic Studies, 208 (Atlanta: Scholars Press, 1990), pp. 4–9.

14. Erwin R. Goodenough, *Jewish Symbols in the Greco-Roman Period*, vol. 2, Bollingen Series 37 (New York: Pantheon Books, 1953), pp. 225–27.

15. Rachel Hachlili, *Ancient Jewish Art and Archaeology in the Land of Israel* (Leiden: Brill, 1988) and *Ancient Jewish Art and Archaeology in the Diaspora* (Leiden: Brill, 1998).

16. Graydon F. Snyder, *Ante-Pacem: Archaeological Evidence of Church Life before Constantine* (Macon, GA: Mercer University Press, 2003), p. 87.

17. Robin Jensen, *Understanding Early Christian Art* (New York and London: Routledge, 2000), pp. 173–77.

18. See Chow, *The Sign of Jonah Reconsidered*, pp. 176–93, for a survey of texts.

19. *Dialogue with Trypho* 107.

20. *Acts of Paul* 3:29–31.

21. *b. Hullin* 67b; *b. Baba Batra* 74a; 2 Esdras 6: 49–53, 1 Enoch 90:7–9.

22. See Kloner and Zissu, *Necropolis of Jerusalem*, pp. 110–11.

23. See Cotton, *CIIP*, nos. 460, 359, 375, 451.

24. See the discussion of Rahmani, *CJO*, no. 455, and Cotton, *CIIP*, no. 93.

25. In the 3rd century CE at Bet She'arim brief expressions of encouragement and consolation occur on 40 out of the 220 inscriptions at the site; see Rahmani, *CJO*, p. 17.

26. Hundreds of dedicatory inscriptions all over the Mediterranean world have been found that read "To the Most High God." See Stephen Mitchell, "The Cult of Theos Hypsistos between Pagans, Jews, and Christians," in *Pagan Monotheism in Late Antiquity,* ed. Polymnia Athanassiadi and

Michael Frede (Oxford: Clarendon Press, 1999), pp. 81–147. These use the superlative *hupsistos*, which means "most high" and is related to the verb found in our inscription, *upsoo*, "to lift up."

27. For additional examples see Cotton, *CIIP,* nos. 84, 112, 113, 284, 383, 509, and 606.

28. Diodorus Siculus, *History* 1.94; Irenaeus, *Against Heresies* 2.35.3; Clement of Alexandria, *Stromata* 5.6; Origen, *Commentary on John* 2.1. The expanded form IAIO occurs on a magical curse tablet from Carthage; see David R. Jordan, "Notes from Carthage," *Zeitschrift für Papyrologie und Epigraphik* 111 (1996): 115–23.

29. It would be either a third-person aorist or future but unlikely present in this context since that would require a first-person subject.

30. See the extensive treatment on *HUPSOS* in *Theological Dictionary of the New Testament*, ed. Gerhard Kittel and Gerhard Friedrich, trans. and ed. Geoffrey W. Bromiley, vol. 8 (Grand Rapids, MI: Eerdmans, 1979), pp. 602–20.

31. *Thanksgiving Hymns* (1QH 6:34; 11:12).

32. Pau Figueras, "Jewish and Christian Beliefs of Life After Death in the Light of the Ossuary Decoration" (Ph.D. diss., Hebrew University, 1974). His more comprehensive work is *Decorated Jewish Ossuaries*, Documenta Et Monumenta Orientis Antiqui 20 (Leiden: Brill, 1983).

33. Rahmani, *CJO*, no. 140.

34. Cotton, *CIIP*, no. 546.

35. See Rahmani, *CJO*, pp. 25–28, for a negative evaluation of the theories of E. R. Goodenough, Bellarmino Bagatti, Emmanuele Testa, and Pau Figueras with bibliography.

36. Rachmani, *CJO*, no. 108; Cotton, *CIIJ*, no. 133.

37. Tal Ilan, *Lexicon of Jewish Names in Late Antiquity, Part I, Palestine 330 BCE–200 CE,* Texts and Studies in Ancient Judaism 91 (Tübingen: Mohr Siebeck, 2002).

38. E. L. Sukenik, "The Earliest Records of Christianity," in *American Journal of Archaeology* 51 (1947): 351–65. There has been an extensive discussion and critique of Sukenik's proposals; see the bibliography in Cotton, *CIIP*, p. 502.

39. See a summary of the discussion with analysis by J. P. Kane, "By No Means 'The Earliest Records of Christianity'—with an Emended Reading of

the Talpioth Inscription IHΣOYΣ IOY," in *Palestine Exploration Quarterly* 103 (1971): 103–8.

40. See Cotton, *CIIP,* no. 247, and Gideon Avni and Shimon Gibson, "The 'Jewish-Christian' Tomb From the Mount of Offense (*Batn Al-Hawa'*) in Jerusalem Reconsidered," *Revue Biblique* 115 (1998): 161–75, who argue this tomb and its markings have nothing to do with early Jewish-Christianity. Joan Taylor, *Christians and the Holy Places: The Myth of Jewish Christian Origins* (Oxford: Clarendon Press, 1993), pp. 5–12.

41. See R. H. Smith, "The Cross Marks on Jewish Ossuaries," *Palestine Exploration Quarterly* 106 (1974): 40–49, for the arguments.

42. See Cotton, *CIIP,* no. 263.

43. Cotton, *CIIP,* nos. 425, 546, 547, 548, 583.

44. See Cotton, *CIIP,* nos. 139, 195, 206, 239, 247, 267, 295, 320.

45. See Cotton, *CIIP,* nos. 36, 109, 489.

CHAPTER FOUR: RETURNING TO THE JESUS FAMILY TOMB

1. Kloner and Gibson, "The Talpiot Tombs Reconsidered."

2. Two of the decorated ossuaries had inscriptions (IAA 80.500: *Maramenon (he) Mara* [Gk] and IAA 80.501: *Yehuda bar Yeshua*) and four of the "plain" or undecorated ones (IAA 80. 502: *Matya/Matah;* IAA 80.503: *Yeshua bar Yehosef;* IAA 80.504: *Yoseh;* and IAA 80. 505: *Maria/Marya*). See Rahmani, *CJO,* pp. 222–24.

3. The statistics on name frequencies are drawn from Tal Ilan, *Lexicon of Jewish Names.* She finds a total of 2,538 occurrences of male names and 320 of female but from a four-hundred-year period, 200 BCE to 200 CE. Hachlili, *Jewish Funerary Customs, Practices and Rites in the Second Temple Period,* offers a somewhat different tabulation from a more limited chronological sample, namely 30 BCE to 70 CE. See p. 200 for a convenient summary chart that breaks down male and female names and their percentages according to Hachlili's methods. Both offer comprehensive surveys of all male and female Jewish names, in the periods specified, drawn from all sources, not just from ossuary inscriptions. The percentages of ossuary name frequencies are generally in line with the wider compilations by Tal Ilan and Hachlili. The ossuary names represent a random sampling that tends to hold up statistically since the number of inscriptions, 650 total, is quite large.

4. See Rahmani, *CJO*, pp. 15–16.

5. Even today in Israel, if one fills out a legal document (visa application, court forms, contracts, etc.) the name of one's father is given. The custom also prevails in Jewish prayers and liturgy, where individuals are identified as "so-and-so, the son-of or daughter-of so-and-so."

6. See Rahmani, *CJO*, pp. 16–17.

7. See chapter 1, note 33.

8. In later rabbinic texts the nickname Yosi becomes quite popular but it never occurs on any ossuary in this period and it is decidedly different from Yoseh. See the comprehensive study of Eldad Keynan, "A Critical Evaluation of the Occurrences of Common Names, Rare Names, and Nicknames: The Name YOSEH (יוסה) from the Talpiot tomb as a Test Case," in *The Tomb of Jesus and His Family? Exploring Ancient Jewish Tombs Near Jerusalem's Walls: The Fourth Princeton Symposium on Judaism and Christian Origins*, eds. James H. Charlesworth and Arthur C. Boulet (Grand Rapids: Eerdmans, forthcoming, 2011).

9. Cotton, *et. al., CIIJ* no. 116 suggests a reading of "Maria Yoseh" for one additional ossuary but this is unlikely, see Rahmani, *COJO,* no. 8. According to Tal Ilan, Joseph is represented as 217 out of a total of 2,538 named males. *Yoseh* in Aramaic does show up in two other non-ossuary sources, making a total of three known occurrences.

10. See James Tabor, *The Jesus Dynasty*, pp. 243–304 for a survey of what is known about James the brother of Jesus.

11. Several manuscripts of Mark have *Yoseh* (Ιωση), which is much closer to the Aramaic, but *Joses* (Ιωσης) is the preferred reading.

12. See S. J. Pfann, "Mary Magdalene Has Left the Room. A Suggested New Reading of Ossuary CJO 701," *Near Eastern Archaeology* 69: 3–4 (2006): 130–31. Pfann's reading is accepted by Jonathan Price and others, see Cotton, *et. al., CIIP*, no. 447.

13. Even though we do not accept the reading "Mariam and Martha" it is worth pointing out that those two names come up in the gospels for two sisters who live in Bethany, near Jerusalem, along with their brother Lazarus (John 11:1). According to our records Jesus is quite close to this family, so ironically, the names "Mary and Martha" are not alien to the Jesus tradition of intimates. Some have even suggested that Mary of Bethany is Mary Magdalene.

14. See Rahmani, *CJO*, no. 701 as well as his introductory comments, p. 14. The Greek is in the genitive case in a diminutive form of Μαριαμηνη. This form of the name is rare and is found also on one other ossuary, Rahmani #108. Di Segni supports Rahmani's reading (as per private e-mail correspondence with the author in 2007).

15. See Rahmani, *CJO*, no. 108. It is interesting to note that Jonathan Price, who disputes Rahmani's reading of the Talpiot tomb as Mariame*ne*, accepts tentatively his reading of this second ossuary as Mariame*ne*—and yet the inscriptions are almost identical, see Cotton, *et. al.*, *CIIP*, no. 133, as well as the representations in Rahmani of the inscriptions themselves.

16. Hippolytus, *Refutation of All Heresies* 5.7.1.

17. See Cotton, *et al.*, *CIIP*, no. 97.

18. Cotton, *et al.*, *CIIP*, nos. 97, 200, 262, 517 and 563. We do not accept that no. 543 is using Mara for a male named Joseph. A close examination shows a line break that would indicate this man is being called Mar—the son of Benaya, son of Yehuda. See the limited examples of the use of Mar/Mara in Aramaic and Greek in Tal Ilan, *Lexicon of Jewish Names in late Antiquity*, pp. 422–23.

19. See Cotton, *et. al.*, *CIIP*, no. 262 where Jonathan Price writes that although Mara is short for Martha it can be a title.

20. *Mara*, which comes from the Aramaic masculine word *Mar*, is the absolute feminine, whereas *Marta* (Martha) is the emphatic feminine. They both come from the same masculine noun and mean the same thing, but Martha evolved into a name and is common (eighteen examples on ossuaries), whereas Mara functions more as a title and is rare.

21. Paul translates the Aramaic into Greek as *maranatha*.

22. Andrey Feuerverger, "Statistical Analysis of an Archaeological Find," *Annals of Applied Statistics* 2 (2008): 3–54, followed by six discussion papers in response and a final rejoinder by Feuerverger, pp. 66–73, 99–112.

23. Since Feuerverger's publication the statistical discussion and its variables have been considerably advanced by Kevin Kilty and Mark Elliott, "Probability, Statistics, and the Talpiot tomb," http://www.lccc.wy.edu/ Media/Website%20Resources/documents/Education%20Natural%20 and%20Social%20Sciences/tomb.pdf and "Inside the Numbers on the Talpiot tombs," http://www.lccc.wy.edu/Media/Website%20Resources/documents/ Education%20Natural%20and%20Social%20Sciences/tombNumbers.pdf.

24. "The Talpiot Tomb: What Are the Odds?" http://www.bibleinterp.com/articles/tomb357926.shtml and http://talpiottomb.com/common_names_v4.3b.doc.

25. The assumption that Joseph owned this tomb is based on a theological interpolation of Matthew, who adds two words to his source Mark, "he laid it in *his own* new tomb" (Matthew 27:60), to make Jesus' burial fit the prophecy Isaiah 53:9, that the grave of God's "Servant" would be "with a rich man."

26. Amos Kloner, "Did a Rolling Stone Close Jesus' Tomb?," *Biblical Archaeology Review* 22:5 (1999): 23–29, 26. Kloner cites several rabbinic texts to support his assertion. Compare his fuller academic treatment, "Reconstruction of the Tomb in the Rotunda of the Holy Sepulchre According to Archaeological Finds and Jewish Burial Customs of the First century CE," in *The Beginnings of Christianity: A Collection of Articles* (Jerusalem: Yad Ben-Zvi, 2005), pp. 269–78.

27. See Jeffrey Bütz, *The Brother of Jesus and the Lost Teachings of Christianity* (Rochester, VT: Inner Traditions, 2005), pp. 95–99, for a survey of a growing scholarly consensus that James, the brother of Jesus, had likely already taken up residence in Jerusalem prior to Jesus' crucifixion.

28. See Eldad Keynan, "The Holy Sepulcher, the Court Tombs, and the Talpiot Tomb in the Light of Jewish Law," in *The Tomb of Jesus and His Family? Exploring Ancient Jewish Tombs Near Jerusalem's Walls: The Fourth Princeton Symposium on Judaism and Christian Origins,* ed. James H. Charlesworth and Arthur C. Boulet (Grand Rapids, MI: Eerdmans, forthcoming, 2011).

29. See Rahmani, *CJO,* p. 23; Cotton, *CIIP,* pp. 10–17.

30. For the historical records of what happened to Jesus' brothers and the disastrous impact of the 70 CE Roman destruction of Jerusalem see Tabor, *The Jesus Dynasty,* pp. 284–304.

31. On Jewish law and burial customs see Keynan, "The Holy Sepulcher, the Court Tombs, and the Talpiot tomb in the Light of Jewish Law." There is a very late, 16th century CE rabbinic tradition from the Kabbalistic Rabbi Isaac ben Luria that the grave of Jesus is in the north, in Galilee, outside the city of Tsfat (Safed); Tabor, *The Jesus Dynasty,* pp. 238–40.

32. See Jodi Magness, "Has the Tomb of Jesus Been Discovered?" SBL Forum, n.p. (cited February 2007), http://sbl-site.org/Article.aspx?ArticleID=640, as well as the response of James D. Tabor, "Two Burials of Jesus of Nazareth

and the Talpiot Yeshua Tomb," SBL Forum, http://sbl-site.org/Article
.aspx?ArticleID=651.

33. See Luke 8:2–3; 23:55–56.

34. *Antiquities* 20.200–1.

35. See Syriac, *Recognitions* 1.43.3 as reconstructed by Robert E. Van Voorst,
The Ascents of James: History and Theology of a Jewish-Christian Community,
SBL Dissertation Series 112 (Atlanta: Scholars Press, 1989).

36. Amos Kloner and Boaz Zissu, *The Necropolis of Jerusalem in the Second
Temple Period*, Interdisciplinary Studies in Ancient Culture and Religion 8
(Leuven, Belgium; and Dudley, MA: Peeters, 2007).

37. *Hadashot Arkheologiyot* 76 (1981).

38. Luke's source is Mark and his explanation that it is a city might be his
own expansion. His gospel is not geographically accurate.

CHAPTER FIVE: JESUS AND MARY MAGDALENE

1. According to early Christian tradition the names of Jesus' two sisters, not
given in the New Testament gospels (see Mark 6:3), were Mary and Salome.
See Epiphanius, *Panarion* 78.8–9 and compare *Gospel of Phillip* 59:6–11 with
Protoevangelium of James 19–20.

2. For the arguments for identifying this second Mary as Jesus' mother see
Tabor, *The Jesus Dynasty*, pp. 73–82.

3. Salome is likely Jesus' sister, or perhaps the mother of the sons of Zebedee,
the fishermen James and John (Matthew 27:56). Luke adds that Joanna, the
wife of Herod's assistant, was with them. Even though the verb used for
"lifted up" can just mean to pick up or carry, in this context it seems to refer
to being lifted up from the dead—in other words, resurrected.

4. See Tabor, *The Jesus Dynasty*, pp. 223–41. The main appended ending
(Mark 16:9–20) does not appear in our two oldest manuscripts, Sinaiticus
and Vaticanus, dating to the early 4th century AD. It is also absent from
about one hundred Armenian manuscripts, the Old Latin version, and the
Sinaitic Syriac. Even copies of Mark that contain the ending often include
notes from the scribe pointing out that it is not in the oldest manuscripts.

5. We have translated "Lord" here as Master, which has fewer theological
connotations and fits with what follows in the story where Mary Magdalene
addresses Jesus as Rabboni—my Master.

6. See Jane Schaberg, *Mary Magdalene Understood* (New York: Continuum

Press, 2006), pp. 122–26. Schaberg's full study is *The Resurrection of Mary Magdalene: Legends, Apocrypha, and the Christian Testament* (New York: Continuum, 2004).

7. *Contra Celsum* 1.65. Celsus's critique is preserved by the church father Origen, who wrote a defense against him around 248 CE. He apparently knows the passage in Luke 8:1–3 that mentions Joanna. There is a summary of his critique in his own words at http://www.bluffton.edu/~humanities/1/celsus.htm.

8. *Contra Celsum*, 2.55.

9. *Contra Celsum* 2.70.

10. See the study of Margaret Y. MacDonald, *Early Christian Women and Pagan Opinion: The Power of the Hysterical Woman* (Cambridge: Cambridge University Press, 1996).

11. See Ann Graham Brock, *Mary Magdalene, The First Apostle: The Struggle for Authority*, Harvard Theological Studies 51 (Cambridge, MA: Harvard University Press, 2003).

12. Although the New Testament letters of 1 and 2 Timothy and Titus are attributed to Paul, scholars are universally agreed that they are "deutero-Pauline," written by some of his followers in the generation after his death. See Ehrman, *The New Testament*, pp. 395–407.

13. Matthew 27:56, 61; 28:1; Mark 15:40, 47; 16:1; Luke 8:2; 24:10; John 19:25; 20:1, 18.

14. Josephus, *Wars* 3:462ff.

15. Ibid., 3:462–505, 532–42.

16. Rami Arav and John J. Rousseau, *Jesus and His World: An Archaeological and Cultural Dictionary* (Minneapolis: Augsburg Press, 1995), p. 189.

17. See http://www.antiquities.org.il/article_Item_eng.asp?sec_id=25&subj_id=240&id=1601&module_id=#as and http://edition.cnn.com/2009/WORLD/meast/09/11/jerusalem.synagogue/index.html.

18. *b. Chagiga* 4b. In another story in the Talmud, Jesus' mother is referred to as the "hairdresser" who was seduced by a Gentile named "Pandeira" (b. Shabbat 104b). There is a play on words here, likely referring to two Miriams, one who "grows" the hair, the other who "grows" the child. In the story the angel of death strikes the wrong Mary—in this case Miriam the Megdala, getting the names confused. See Burton L. Visotzky, "Mary Maudlin Among the Rabbis," in *Fathers of the World: Essays in Rabbinic and Patristic Literatures* (Tübingen: J. C. B. Mohr/Paul Siebeck, 1995), pp. 85–92.

19. See Peter Schaeffer's comprehensive study of all the major passages, *Jesus in the Talmud,* 3rd ed. (Princeton, NJ: Princeton University Press, 2007).

20. For a typical defense of the idea that Jesus was not married by an evangelical Christian writer see http://www.beliefnet.com/Faiths/Christianity/2003/11/Was-Jesus-Married.aspx.

21. Josephus mentions a similar story about his own precociousness at age fourteen, see *Life* 9.

22. See Sarah Pomeroy, *Goddesses, Whores, Wives, and Slaves: Women in Classical Antiquity* (New York: Schocken Books, 1995).

23. Josephus, *Wars* 2.121.

24. Philo, *Hypothetica* 11.14.

25. Pliny the Elder, *Natural History* 5.73.

26. See the excerpt on celibacy among the Essenes by Lawrence H. Schiffman, *Reclaiming the Dead Sea Scrolls,* Anchor Bible Reference Library (New York: Doubleday, 1995), pp. 127–44, available at http://cojs.org/cojs wiki/Celibacy_of_the_Essenes,_Lawrence_H._Schiffman,_Reclaiming_ the_Dead_Sea_Scrolls,_Jewish_Publication_Society,_Philadelphia.

27. Like Jesus, Paul forbids divorce, reflecting a primordial ideal, but his assertion that a Christian abandoned by an "unbelieving" mate was free from the bonds of marriage might well reflect his own experience (1 Corinthians 7: 12–16).

28. See Daniel Boyarin, *A Radical Jew: Paul and the Politics of Identity* (Berkely: University of California Press, 1997), pp. 158–79.

29. Tertullian, *On the Dress of Women* 1.1.

30. Elizabeth Clark, *Women in the Early Church* (Wilmington, DE: Michael Glazier, 1983).

31. Matthew 26:6–13 has the same story, based on his source Mark, but he specifies that the objection to the waste came from "the disciples."

32. See Paul's insistence on covering the hair in 1 Corinthians 11:2–16.

33. Tertullian, *Against Marcion* 4:18.9, 16–17.

34. See Gregory of Nyssa, a 4th century bishop, who equated Mary Magdalene with Eve, *Against Eunomius* 3.10.16.

35. *Homily* 33 on Luke 7.

36. Schaberg, *Mary Magdalene Understood*, pp. 71–97.

37. Karen L. King, *The Gospel of Mary of Magdala: Jesus and the First Woman Apostle* (Santa Rosa, CA: Polebridge Press, 2003) is the most thorough study

of this text with a full introduction and translation. Since the discovery of the Coptic manuscript two additional fragments in Greek have turned up. King includes them as well in her analysis.

38. Translations of these Mary Magdalene–related texts are those of Marvin Meyer, *The Gospels of Mary: The Secret Tradition of Mary Magdalene the Companion of Jesus* (New York: HarperSanFrancisco, 2004).

39. It is generally agreed that the term *gnostic* with a small *g* is more appropriate. See Schaberg's observations in *Mary Magdalene Understood,* pp. 68–71.

40. See April D. DeConick, "The Great Mystery of Marriage: Sex and Conception in Ancient Valentinian Traditions," *Vigiliae Christianae* 57 (2003): 307–42.

CHAPTER SIX: THE MYSTERY OF THE JAMES OSSUARY

1. André Lemaire, "Burial Box of James, the Brother of Jesus: Earliest Archaeological Evidence of Jesus Found in Jerusalem," *Biblical Archaeology Review* 28:6 (2002): 24–33, 70. The geological analysis conducted by Amnon Rosenfeld and Shimon Ilani was also summarized in this issue, p. 29.

2. *James: Brother of Jesus.* It was shown over the course of the next month in more than eighty additional countries.

3. See the observations of Yuval Goren at http://www.bibleinterp.com/articles/Goren_Jerusalem_Syndrome.shtml.

4. The other inscription, the Joash tablet, was a stone artifact with a Hebrew text that was purported to come from the 9th century BCE (see 1 Kings 12). See Uzi Dahari, ed., *Final Report of the Examining Committee for the Yehoash Inscription and James Ossuary* (Jerusalem: Israel Antiquities Authority, 2003) for the results of the IAA investigation. The reports are conveniently posted at http://bibleinterp.com/articles/Final_Reports.shtml. A summary of this report with comments also appears in the revised edition of Shanks and Witherington's *The Brother of Jesus* (San Francisco: HarperSanFrancisco, 2004), pp. 227–37.

5. Correspondent Matthew Kalman serially reported on the entire trial for *Time* magazine and his articles are archived on his website: http://jamesossuarytrial.blogspot.com/. Oded Golan has recently released his own account of the trial proceedings titled "The Authenticity of the James Ossuary and the Jehoash Tablet Inscriptions—Summary of Expert Trial Witness," avail-

able at http://bibleinterp.com/articles/authjam358012.shtml. His summary appears to provide convincing evidence that he was falsely accused and that both artifacts and their inscriptions are authentic.

6. Neil Asher Silberman and Yuval Goren, "Faking Biblical History," *Archaeology* 56:5 (2003): 20–29; David Samuels, "Written in Stone," *New Yorker,* April 12, 2004, pp. 48–59.

7. Nina Burleigh, *Unholy Business: A True Tale of Faith, Greed, and Forgery in the Holy Land* (New York: HarperCollins, 2008), and Ryan Byrne and Bernadette McNary-Zak, eds., *Resurrecting the Brother of Jesus: The James Ossuary Controversy and the Quest for Religious Relics* (Chapel Hill: University of North Carolina Press, 2009).

8. Byron R. McCane, "Archaeological Context and Controversy," in Byrne and McNary-Zak, eds., *Resurrecting the Brother of Jesus,* p. 20; http://www .bibleinterp.com/articles/West_reply.shtml; http://www.bibleinterp.com/ar ticles/Ossuary_Again.shtml.

9. See the comments of Craig Evans at http://www.bibleinterp.com/articles/ Evans_Thoughts.shtml.

10. See Goren's report at http://www.bibleinterp.com/articles/Goren_re port.shtml.

11. See Oded Golan's summary of the trial testimony cited above.

12. Camil Fuchs: "Demograph, Literacy and Names Distribution in Ancient Jerusalem: How Many James/Jacob Son of Joseph, Brother of Jesus Were There?" *Polish Journal of Biblical Research* 4:1 (2005): 3–30.

13. Gath published this short preliminary report in Hebrew in 1981, but before the ossuary inscriptions had been deciphered; *Hadashot Arkheologiyot* 76 (1981): 24–26. Translation is by Noam Kuzar. The Jesus tomb has two ledges or "primary burial shelves" (*arcosolia*) on the northern and eastern walls, upon which corpses were laid out for the first year so they would decompose.

14. See Rahmani, *CJO*, p. 222.

15. It should also be noted that Rahmani's catalogue often gives two differing measurements for individual ossuaries, recording initial measurements as well as subsequent lab measurements that were more precise. It is also possible, since the James ossuary was broken and restored in November 2002 when it was flown to Canada to be put on display, that its measurements today might tend to be slightly less than when it was first measured.

16. See Tabor, *The Jesus Dynasty,* pp. 73–83.

17. The idea of Mary's "perpetual virginity" was affirmed at the Second Council of Constantinople in 553 AD and the Lateran Council in 649 AD. Although it is a firmly established part of Catholic dogma, it has nonetheless never been the subject of an infallible declaration by the Roman Catholic Church.

18. This is called the Helvidian view, named after Helvidius, a 4th century Christian writer whom Jerome seeks to refute. Eusebius, the early 4th century church historian, regularly quotes early sources and refers himself to the brothers of Jesus "after the flesh," surely understanding them as children of Mary and Joseph. (See Eusebius, *Church History* 2.23; 3.19.

19. This is called the Hieronymian view in honor of Jerome, the 5th century Christian theologian, who was its champion.

20. This is called the Epiphanian view in honor of Epiphanius, a 4th century Christian bishop. It occurs as early as the 2nd century in a text we know as the *Protoevangelium of James*.

21. A discussion of all the main sources and their implications is at http://religiousstudies.uncc.edu/people/jtabor/jamesessay.html.

22. Quoted by Eusebius, *Church History* 2.1.3.

23. Quoted by Eusebius, *Church History* 2.1.4.

24. Eusebius, *Church History* 2.1.2. Translations of Eusebius are by Kirsopp Lake in the Loeb Classical Library edition.

25. Eusebius, *Church History* 2.23.4.

26. S. v. "Diadexomai," in *A Greek-English Lexicon of the New Testament and Other Early Christian Literature* (3rd ed.), p. 227.

27. See April D. DeConick, *Thomasine Traditions in Antiquity: The Social and Cultural World of the Gospel of Thomas*, edited with Jon Ma. Asgeirsson and Risto Uro, Nag Hammadi & Manichaean Studies series (Leiden and Boston: Brill, 2005); *Recovering the Original Gospel of Thomas: A History of the Gospel and Its Growth*, Supplements to the *Journal of the Study of the New Testament* 286 (London: T. & T. Clark, 2005); and *The Original Gospel of Thomas in Translation: A Commentary and New English Translation of the Complete Gospel*, Supplements to the *Journal of the Study of the New Testament* (London: T. & T. Clark, 2006).

28. This idea is found often in ancient Jewish sources (e.g., *2 Baruch* 15:7).

29. The text is embedded in a later source but can be extracted. See Robert E. Van Voorst, *The Ascents of James: History and Theology of a Jewish-Christian Community*, SBL Dissertation Series 112 (Atlanta: Scholars Press,

1989). Van Voorst has isolated this source from *Recognitions* 1.33–71 and demonstrated its antiquity.

30. Syriac *Recognitions* 1.43.3.

31. Josephus, *Antiquities* 20.200–1. The parenthetical addition "called Christ" is likely a later Christian interpolation.

32. Eusebius, *Church History* 2.23.4–7.

33. See Oded Golan's summary of the trial testimony cited above.

34. "The Connection of the James Ossuary to the Talpiot (Jesus Family Tomb) Ossuaries," http://www.bibleinterp.com/articles/JOT.shtml. The two other principal investigators were H. R. Feldman, Division of Paleontology, Touro College; and W. E. K. Krumbein, Department of Geomicrobiology at the Carl von Ossietzky Universität, Oldenburg, Germany.

35. Peak elements such as silicon, phosphorous, titanium, iron, aluminum, and potassium are compared according to their ratios.

36. See Rosenfeld et al., and Amnon Rosenfeld and Shimon Ilani, "SEM-EDS Analyses of Patina Samples from an Ossuary of 'Ya'akov Son of Yossef Brother of Yeshua,'" *Biblical Archaeology Review* 28:6 (2002): 29.

37. The full study by Charles Pellegrino, "The Potential Role of Patina History in Discerning the Removal of Specific Artifacts from Specific Tombs," will appear in *The Tomb of Jesus and His Family? Exploring Ancient Jewish Tombs Near Jerusalem's Walls: The Fourth Princeton Symposium on Judaism and Christian Origins*, ed. James H. Charlesworth and Arthur C. Boulet (Grand Rapids: Eerdmans, 2011).

38. Jacobovici and Pellegrino, *The Jesus Family Tomb*, pp. 175–92 and James Tabor, *The Jesus Dynasty*, pbk. ed. (New York: Simon & Schuster, 2007), pp. 319–31.

CHAPTER SEVEN: RESURRECTION, LOST BONES, AND JESUS' DNA

1. See John 13:23; 19:26; 20:2; 21:7; 21:20. He shows up at the Last Supper, then at the cross, then at the empty tomb, and finally in Galilee, where the disciples had retreated after Jesus' death and returned to their fishing. For a discussion see Tabor, *The Jesus Dynasty*, pp. 206–7.

2. They are together at the cross and at the tomb where Jesus' body was first placed (John 19:25–27; Mark 15:47; 16:1).

3. Josephus, *Antiquities* 18. 23.

4. See Plato's *Death of Socrates* or his *Phaedo*.

5. Translation by C. W. Keyes, *Cicero, De Re Publica,* Loeb Classical Library (Cambridge, MA: Harvard University Press, 1928).

6. See Droge and Tabor, *A Noble Death*, chapter 4, "Acquiring Life in a Single Moment," pp. 85–112.

7. Segal, *Life After Death*, pp. 120–45.

8. For a contemporary scholarly analysis of each of the gospels see Bart Ehrman, *The New Testament: A Historical Introduction to the Early Christian Writings*, 5th ed. (Oxford: Oxford University Press, 2003).

9. See James H. Charlesworth and Arthur C. Boulet, eds., *The Tomb of Jesus and His Family? Exploring Ancient Jewish Tombs Near Jerusalem's Walls: The Fourth Princeton Symposium on Judaism and Christian Origins* (Grand Rapids, MI: Eerdmans, 2011).

10. David Michell, Eske Willerslev, and Anders Hansen, "Damage and Repair of Ancient DNA," *Mutation Research* 571 (2005): 265–76.

11. See the complete standard sequence at http://www.phylotree.org/rCRS _annotated.htm.

CONCLUSION: THE FIRST CHRISTIANS AND CHRISTIANITY TODAY

1. The beginning of the modern Jesus Quest is usually dated to around 1835 with the publication of David Strauss's *Life of Jesus*. The full German title of Strauss's work, *Das Leben Jesu kritisch bearbeitet* (Tübingen, 1835–36) was published in English as *The Life of Jesus, Critically Examined* (3 vols., London, 1846), translated by George Eliot, the pen name of British novelist Mary Ann Evans.

2. The quest was given both its history and its name by Albert Schweitzer, whose groundbreaking book, published in 1906 with the nondescript German title *Von Reimarus zu Wrede* [*From Reimarus to Wrede*], was given the more provocative title in English *The Quest of the Historical Jesus*, translated by William Montgomery (London: Adam & Charles Black, 1910).

3. See Tabor, *The Jesus Dynasty*, pp. 243–304, for the history of the successors of Jesus, beginning with James.

4. See Tertullian, *Resurrection of the Flesh* 11.

ACKNOWLEDGMENTS

First and foremost we thank our families for coping with the challenges of everyday living these past ten years when we were so often away from home, on the phone, buried deeply into our research, or secluded away writing or filming. We particularly thank Rami Arav who teamed up with us on the Talpiot tombs investigation and generously allowed us to draw from his thirty years of archaeological experience. Likewise, our colleague James H. Charlesworth of Princeton Theological Seminary has been an invaluable academic adviser and confidant. The team pulled together by Associated Producers, both in Canada and Israel, too many to mention, were an indispensible part of making our impossible venture a dream come true, but particular thanks to: Yosi Abadi, Simon Andreae, Revital Antman-Rav, Asher Ben Artzi, Nicole Austin, Uri Basson, Meyer Shimony Bensimon, Steve Burns, Shuka Dorfman, Felix Golubev, Joan Jenkinson, Walter Klassen, Noam Kuzar, Raam Shaul, Bill Tarant, Eli Zamir, and Moses Znaimer. Their hard work and dedication in meeting any challenges along the way inspired us all.

We also want to thank colleagues James Cameron, Andrey Feuerverger, Shimon Gibson, Israel Hershkovitz, Eldad Keynan,

Jerry Lutgen, Charles Pellegrino, and Aryeh Shimron, who have so generously offered us their expertise in a diverse range of areas relative to our inquiry. We thank our dedicated and hardworking agents Douglas Abrams and Elaine Markson who made this project their passion as well as our editor at Simon & Schuster, Bob Bender, his assistant, Johanna Li, and the whole marvelous Simon & Schuster team.

INDEX

Page numbers in *italics* refer to illustrations. Page numbers beginning with 213 refer to notes.

A groundbreaking history of the life and times of Jesus as revealed by the untold story of the messianic dynasty he attempted to establish—a new perspective on the origins of Christianity, now in paperback with a new epilogue by the author.

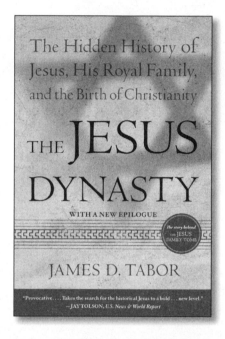

"Many scholars have undertaken studies of Jesus and his legacy; none has dared advance the boldly provocative theses of *The Jesus Dynasty.*"

—**Bart Ehrman, author** of ***Misquoting Jesus:*** ***The Story Behind Who*** ***Changed the Bible and Why***

"Provocative. . . . Takes the search for the historical Jesus to a bold . . . new level."

—**Jay Tolson,** *U.S. News & World Report*

Available wherever books are sold or at
www.simonandschuster.com

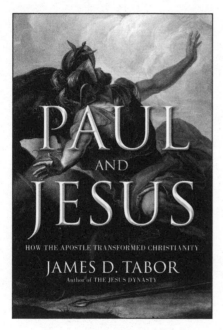